Committed to Justice

The Rise of Judicial Administration
in California

Committed to Justice

The Rise of Judicial Administration in California

Larry L. Sipes

Administrative Office of the California Courts
San Francisco

Published by the Administrative Office of the California Courts
455 Golden Gate Avenue
San Francisco, California 94102-3688

Library of Congress Cataloging-in-Publication Data

Sipes, Larry L.
    Committed to justice : the rise of judicial administration in
California / Larry L. Sipes.
        p. cm.
Includes bibliographical references and index.
    ISBN 0-9721394-1-9
    1. Justice, Administration of—California—History. I. Title.

KFC78 .S58 2002
347.794—dc21

                                        2002151678

*Title page: The Earl Warren Building and the adjoining Hiram W. Johnson
State Office Building, home of the California Supreme Court, the Judicial
Council of California, and the Administrative Office of the California Courts.
Cover and pages 9, 43, 191, and 273: detail of the Earl Warren Building;
photograph by William A. Porter.*

FOREWORD

⁓⦿⁓

*W*e are most fortunate that the vibrant history of judicial branch administration has been laid out for us in the Administrative Office of the California Courts' first formal chronicle, *Committed to Justice: The Rise of Judicial Administration in California.*

Ably rendered by Larry Sipes, this first-ever history of California court administration from statehood to the close of the twentieth century illuminates the debates, challenges, setbacks, and victories of the judges, attorneys, legislators, and others who together built what today is the largest and most successful court system in the world.

Mr. Sipes is uniquely qualified to undertake this project. He is a native Californian who previously served as executive director of the state's Constitution Revision Commission. As the former president of the National Center for State Courts, he is a noted national leader in court administration. Most recently, he served as the inaugural scholar-in-residence for the Administrative Office of the California Courts. His distinguished and varied career has provided him with an in-depth understanding of the most significant events in the 150-year construction of our modern and far-flung court system.

This scholarly presentation first focuses on the most important milestones in our court system's history. In the final chapter, Mr. Sipes applies his background and insight to look ahead at what lies in store for our system during the first fifty years of the new millennium. We anticipate that this publication will be of interest to the legal community, informative for researchers and historians, and useful to policymakers from every branch of government. Without question, it will be a valuable resource for all of us—whether judges, court administrators, staff of the Administrative Office of the California Courts, members of the bar or the public, or officials from the other branches of California government—as we work together to meet the challenges that lie ahead for our branch.

As this book demonstrates, our judicial branch has a long tradition of working cooperatively with others in our state and our nation to ensure that California's courts provide fair and accessible justice for all. This fine contribution adds enormously to our understanding of how best to administer our courts and will greatly assist us in remaining "committed to justice."

Ronald M. George
Chief Justice of California

William C. Vickrey
Administrative Director of the California Courts

DEDICATION

❧

This chronicle honors the 150th anniversary of the California Supreme Court (1850–2000), the 75th anniversary of the Judicial Council of California (1926–2001), and the 40th anniversary of the Administrative Office of the Courts (1961–2001).

IN APPRECIATION

To Chief Justice Ronald M. George and Administrative Director of the Courts William C. Vickrey for sponsoring this undertaking.

To Michael Fischer, Justice Judith McConnell, Dale Anne Sipes, and Judge Roy Wonder for peer review of the manuscript.

To Tina Carroll, Administrative Office of the Courts (AOC), for oversight and troubleshooting.

To the staff of the AOC Library, particularly librarian Gary Kitajo and Tom Kitzmann, for extensive assistance.

To the staff of the California Judicial Center Library, particularly librarian Frances Jones, Linda Sharp, and Steve Feller, for assistance and a place to work.

To Theresa Sudo, AOC, for transcribing the first complete manuscript.

To Lura Dymond and Judy Weiss for editing contributions.

CONTENTS

❧

Chapter 4: The Dynamics of Governing the Judicial System

Chapter 5: Reorganization and Unification of the Trial Courts

Chapter 6: Stable Funding of the Trial Courts

MILESTONES IN CALIFORNIA'S COMMITMENT TO JUSTICE

1849
The first California Constitution is adopted, creating a new judicial system.

1850
California becomes the thirty-first state of the United States of America.

1862
The Supreme Court is expanded from three to five justices.

1879
A new constitution is adopted, with more detailed provisions governing the judicial branch.

1904
The appellate system is expanded by creation of district courts of appeal for intermediate review between the trial courts and Supreme Court.

1924
The establishment of municipal courts is authorized.

1926
The Judicial Council is created.

1934
Contested elections of appellate judges are replaced by retention elections with approval of nominees for appointment by a new Commission on Qualifications.

1950
Courts of limited jurisdiction are reorganized into justice and municipal courts.

1957
The position of trial court executive officer is created in the Los Angeles Superior Court.

1956
Pretrial conferences are mandated in most civil cases but subsequently repealed.

1960
The position of Administrative Director of the Courts is created.

1960
The Commission on Judicial Qualifications is created to administer a new system of judicial discipline. The preexisting Commission on Qualifications is renamed the Commission on Judicial Appointments.

1961
The first Administrative Director of the Courts is appointed, and the Administrative Office of the Courts (AOC) is established.

1967
The first session of the California College of Trial Judges convenes.

1971
Court-sponsored arbitration of small personal injury cases begins in the superior courts for Los Angeles and San Francisco Counties.

1973
The Center for Judicial Education and Research is created.

1973
The Supreme Court for the first time removes a judge on recommendation of the Commission on Judicial Qualifications.

1974
Persons unable to understand English are granted the right to an interpreter if accused of a crime.

1975
Arbitration is extended to smaller civil cases in larger superior courts.

1976
The Commission on Judicial Qualifications is renamed the Commission on Judicial Performance, and its powers are expanded.

1978
Arbitration of smaller civil cases becomes mandatory.

1985
The AOC establishes the Statewide Office of Family Court Services.

1986
The Trial Court Delay Reduction Act directs the Judicial Council to adopt case processing time standards and pilot programs for delay reduction.

1987
The Judicial Council adopts its first annual plan.

1988
The California Legislature directs the Judicial Council to promote Court Appointed Special Advocate (CASA) programs to assist children in court proceedings.

1988
Family law filings exceed total filings for injury, death, or property damage and do so for the balance of the century.

1991
The Commission on the Future of the California Courts is created.

1991
The Judicial Council inaugurates a comprehensive delay reduction program.

1992
The first strategic plan is adopted by the Judicial Council.

1993
A pilot project for mandatory mediation in civil cases begins.

1993
The Court Interpreters Advisory Panel is created to assist the Judicial Council and courts with a comprehensive program to improve interpreter services.

1994
The Access and Fairness Advisory Committee is created by the Judicial Council to continue work by previous committees on gender, racial, ethnic, and other biases in the courts.

1996
Child support commissioners and family law facilitators are provided in each county.

1997
Strategic planning is extended to the trial courts by the Judicial Council.

1997
Responsibility for funding of the trial courts is consolidated at the state level, establishing full state funding for the judicial branch with allocation of funds by the Judicial Council.

1997
Family court programs are consolidated by the Administrative Office of the Courts under the new Center for Children and the Courts (now the Center for Families, Children & the Courts).

1998
Consolidation of the trial courts into a single superior court in each county commences.

1998
A strategic plan for technology is adopted by the Judicial Council.

1999
The Judicial Council adopts a mission statement for itself and the judiciary with supporting goals and principles.

2000
A tactical plan for technology is adopted by the Judicial Council.

2000
The Administrative Office of the Courts adopts a mission statement.

2001
Kings County unifies its courts into a single superior court, the last county to do so.

2001
Responsibility for court employees is transferred from the counties to the courts.

2002
The state assumes ownership and maintenance of court facilities.

INTRODUCTION

❧

*A*dministration of justice, as a concept and in practice, has existed in California at least since statehood in 1850. Judge R. A. Wilson, one of the original superior court trial judges, referred in 1850 to the "administration of justice" when describing the Spanish alcalde system in California.[1] The Committee on the Judiciary, in the same year, reported to the first California Legislature that "the administration of the [justice] system is of more consequence than the system itself."[2] From its inception in 1926, the Judicial Council of California has been constitutionally mandated "to improve the administration of justice."[3]

Administration of justice, however, is hardly self-defining and means different things to different persons. In fact, there is no agreed definition of the term or the several variations that convey approximately the same meaning: "judicial administration,"[4] "court management,"[5] and "to administer the delivery of court system services."[6]

The absence of an agreed definition is matched by the absence of agreed boundaries. Roscoe Pound, for example, in his seminal 1906 speech, "The Causes of Popular Dissatisfaction with the Administration of Justice," addressed, among other topics, procedure, adversarial systems, uncertainty, delay, expense, multiplicity of courts, concurrent jurisdiction, geographic jurisdiction, jury systems, political influence on and in courts, and public ignorance regarding the courts.[7]

Chief Justice Arthur T. Vanderbilt of New Jersey, in his 1949 *Minimum Standards of Judicial Administration,* addressed a rather different list of topics: the selection, conduct, and tenure of judges; managing the business of the courts; rulemaking and the judicial regulation of procedure; the selection and service of juries; pretrial conferences; trial practice; courts of limited jurisdiction; the law of evidence; appellate practice; and state administrative agencies and tribunals.[8]

More contemporary expositions expand the boundaries. Standards of Judicial Administration, the series published by the American Bar Association (ABA), seeks to encompass every tangible aspect of the courts. Volume 1, *Standards Relating to Court Organization,* includes structure, rulemaking, policymaking, administration, finance, budgets, and information systems. With respect to judges, these standards address qualifications, selection, discipline, removal, compensation, retirement, continuing education, and evaluation.[9] In Volume 2, *Standards Relating to Trial Courts,* the ABA addresses a multitude of specific topics ranging from effective procedure to assistance of counsel to cases involving litigants who have AIDS.[10]

The latest generation of standards for administering justice moves from the quantitative aspects of courts to the qualitative by espousing and attempting to measure access to justice; expedition and timeliness; equality, fairness, and integrity; independence and accountability; and public trust and confidence.[11]

The goal of this discussion is neither an attempted definition nor proposed boundaries. Rather, the purpose is to establish that all matters relating to courts, including the substance of judicial decisions, at one time or another have been addressed under "administration of justice" or its kin. The additional purpose is to set the stage for an admittedly selective chronicle of the administration of justice during California's 150 years of statehood and a look forward into the first 50 years of the new millennium.

While the concept of administering justice has traces of antiquity, implementing the concept began in earnest only a few decades ago. The pace has since accelerated dramatically, and speed has either precluded or eclipsed maintaining a daily diary of judicial administration's evolution. Each passing day erodes our ability to reconstruct that evolution in California and elsewhere.

In addition to documenting historical events, this chronicle is important for several further reasons. First, the courts are one-third of our tripartite system of independent and interdependent branches of government, but the past of the judicial branch is history's stepchild.

A recent experience illustrates. The renowned Bancroft Library at the University of California at Berkeley has created and maintains a living history collection containing transcribed interviews with California leaders. During the planning of this book, the expectation was that the Bancroft collection would be a rich source of insights from California's Chief Justices and other leaders of the judicial branch, such as the several Administrative Directors of the Courts. However, Chief Justice Phil S. Gibson is the only Chief Justice in the collection, and the interview with him is directed more to his experiences with Governor Culbert Levy Olson, who appointed him to the Supreme Court, than as the leader of the judicial branch of government. Lost forever are the perspectives of subsequent, but now deceased, Chief Justices Roger J. Traynor, Donald R. Wright, and Rose Elizabeth Bird. We have suffered the same loss in the cases of Ralph N. Kleps, the inaugural Administrative Director of the Courts, and his successor Ralph J. Gampell.

The second reason for this chronicle is that administration of the judicial branch, compared to the executive and legislative, is still maturing here and elsewhere and therefore is possible to capture at an important evolutionary stage. According to Robert W. Tobin in 1999, "What passed for a state judicial branch, until very recently, was a group of appellate judges who performed the adjudicative functions of their office but had a very tenuous control over the trial courts, which remained local institutions immersed in local political culture, local government operations, and the local legal culture. The judicial branch of state government was, in large part, a legal fiction, rather than an operational reality."[12]

Finally, throughout California, and in many parts of America, courts as institutions are undergoing metamorphoses. In the process they are probing new areas of accountability, community relations, and justice. These efforts deserve to be memorialized.

Even so, the balance between inclusion and exclusion is delicate. Some will decry the amount of detail that follows. Others will complain of omissions or emphasis and join Cervantes' ancient indictment of "those grave chroniclers who give us such brief and succinct accounts that we barely taste, the gist of matter being left in their inkwells out of carelessness, malice or ignorance."[13]

Hopefully, the balance struck here will satisfy most readers. The choices in no way reflect anything other than a desire to capture as accurately as possible an important part of California's past and future.

California has the largest court system among the states, has one of the largest in the world, and has been at or near the cutting edge in the evolution of justice administration. In recent years California has enacted justice system changes on an unprecedented scale.

This is an auspicious time for drawing attention to the historical significance of these momentous changes. The Supreme Court turned 150 in 2000. The Judicial Council celebrated its 75th anniversary in 2001, followed immediately by the 40th anniversary of the Administrative Office of the Courts (AOC) that same year. The longevity and contributions of these vital institutions, both at home and elsewhere, warrant the focus on California's judicial branch.

It is useful to dwell briefly on the tendency to attribute achievements to incumbents at the time the achievement occurs. That tendency must be resisted here and throughout because the most notable improvements in the administration of justice evolved across the tenures of several Chief Justices and Administrative Directors of the Courts and required decades of effort to attain success. Chief Justice Arthur T. Vanderbilt could here find ample support for his statement: "Manifestly judicial reform is no sport for the short-winded or for lawyers who are afraid of temporary defeat."[14]

Consider, as one of many examples, trial court unification, which is later presented in detail. It could be argued that Chief Justice Ronald M. George and Administrative Director of the Courts William C. Vickrey deserve full credit since unification was legislatively, constitutionally, and practically achieved between 1998 and 2001 during their watch. It certainly is a fact that without their leadership, diplomacy, and tenacity, unification would today remain an unfulfilled goal.

But in many ways, their remarkable efforts were a culmination of collective efforts stretching back to midcentury. The foundation for trial court unification, it could reasonably be proposed, was laid in 1950 with lower court reorganization accomplished under Chief Justice Phil S. Gibson prior to creation of the Administrative Office of the Courts. That foundation was expanded and strengthened by efforts in the early 1970s under Chief Justice Wright and Administrative Director of the Courts Ralph N. Kleps that produced Judicial Council and legislative consideration of both further lower court reorganization and a single-level trial court. Although those efforts were unsuccessful at the time, these topics remained on the agenda of the Judicial Council and received continuing legislative consideration. They also made possible in 1994 ultimate establishment of the municipal courts as the sole trial court of limited jurisdiction, which occurred during the overlapping tenures of Chief Justice Malcolm M. Lucas and Administrative Director Vickrey.

The fact is that hands too numerous to credit pulled on the oars of justice administration over the years. The equally important fact is that California was blessed, particularly during the second half of the last century, with several Chief Justices and Administrative Directors of the Courts who contributed remarkable leadership skills. Those skills were invaluable in establishing effective governance and other monuments in the administration of justice.

California was doubly blessed. In addition to several outstanding leaders at the state level, there was a rich supply at both trial court and appellate levels of leadership, courage, creativity, and commitment. Indeed, it is all too easy to imagine either the subversion or collapse of the many initiatives for improvement of the administration of justice during this period in the absence of this cavalry of leaders.

Credit reaches beyond the judicial branch. At key times and on key issues, leaders in the legislature stepped forward to enlist in these efforts. This also was true of several governors, senior executive-branch staff members, and county officials.

At various times and in various ways important progress in the administration of justice was achieved thanks to contributions from entities such as the State Bar of California, local or specialty bar associations, and the California Judges Association, as well as organizations external to California or the court system. Even if it were possible to identify and attribute those contributions (a dubious assumption), it seems no more appropriate than individual recognition in view of the duration and complexity of organizational effort required for the fundamental changes that occurred in these many decades.

Finally, the matters recorded here obviously did not occur in a vacuum. There has been continuous interaction between justice administration in California and significant national movements or experiments in other states. Indeed, these interactions spanned a spectrum—from the campaign early in the 1900s to create judicial councils as vehicles for reform to the consortium of entities in the latter part of the century dedicated to eradicating gender, racial, and other biases in our judicial systems. These synergies are noted when they have been especially vivid. To capture and do justice to all these interactions is beyond the capacity of this chronicle, but this in no way depreciates their importance or the importance of California's contributions to national advances.

Notes

1   [R. A. Wilson], "The Alcalde System of California," 1 Cal. 559 (San Francisco: Bancroft-Whitney, 1906).

2   [California] Senate Committee on the Judiciary, February 27, 1850, "Report on Civil and Common Law," 1 Cal. 588 (San Francisco: Bancroft-Whitney, 1906), p. 599.

3   California Constitution, article VI, section 6.

4   Arthur T. Vanderbilt, ed., *Minimum Standards of Judicial Administration: A Survey of the Extent to Which the Standards of the American Bar Association for Improving the Administration of Justice Have Been Accepted throughout the Country*, The Judicial Administration Series ([New York]: Law Center of New York University for the National Conference of Judicial Councils, 1949).

5   Ernest C. Friesen, Edward C. Gallas, and Nesta M. Gallas, *Managing the Courts* (Indianapolis: Bobbs-Merrill, 1971).

6   American Bar Association, Judicial Administration Division, *Standards Relating to Court Organization*, Standards of Judicial Administration, volume 1 ([Chicago]: American Bar Association, 1990), p. vii.

7   Roscoe Pound, address delivered to the American Bar Association's National Conference on the Causes of Popular Dissatisfaction with the Administration of Justice (August 29, 1906, St. Paul, Minnesota); text reported in *The Pound Conference: Perspectives on Justice in the Future* (St. Paul: West Publishing Co., 1979), pp. 337–53.

8   Vanderbilt, ed., *Minimum Standards of Judicial Administration*.

9   American Bar Association, *Standards Relating to Court Organization*.

10   American Bar Association, Judicial Administration Division, *Standards Relating to Trial Courts*, Standards of Judicial Administration, volume 2 ([Chicago]: American Bar Association, 1992).

11   U.S. Department of Justice, Bureau of Justice Assistance, National Center for State Courts, *Trial Court Performance Standards and Measurement System Implementation Manual* (Washington, D.C.: Bureau of Justice Assistance [1997]).

12   Robert W. Tobin, *Creating the Judicial Branch: The Unfinished Reform* (Williamsburg, Va.: National Center for State Courts, 1999), p. 3.

13 Miguel de Cervantes, *Don Quixote de la Mancha*, Modern Library Edition (New York: Random House, 1998), p. 136.

14 Vanderbilt, ed., *Minimum Standards of Judicial Administration*, introduction, p. xix.

Part 1
The First 100 Years

The Act for the Admission of the State of California into the Union, enacted by Congress on September 9, 1850, reads:

Whereas the people of California have presented a constitution and asked admission into the Union, which constitution was submitted to Congress by the President of the United States, by message dated February thirteenth, eighteen hundred and fifty, and which, on due examination, is found to be republican in its form of government:

Be it enacted by the Senate and House of Representatives of the United States of America in Congress assembled, That the State of California shall be one, and is hereby declared to be one, of the United States of America, and admitted into the Union on an equal footing with the original States in all respects whatever.

With the adoption of the first California Constitution in 1849 and admission into the United States, the stage was set for a new system of justice to be established.

Chapter 1
The Century from 1850 to 1950

Overview

he Constitution of 1849, under which California became a state in 1850, was drafted in convention by delegates who were mostly recent immigrants. The constitutions of the United States, New York, and Iowa greatly influenced its content.

The new court system, superseding the Mexican alcaldes, consisted of a Supreme Court with three justices, district courts of general jurisdiction, county courts, and justices of the peace. The California Legislature was authorized to establish additional courts of limited jurisdiction.

The Supreme Court was expanded to five members in 1862.

The Constitutional Convention of 1879 produced a far more detailed constitution, approved by the voters, but effected few major changes in the judicial system. A significant exception was increasing the size of the Supreme Court from five to seven justices.

The district courts of appeal were created in 1904 to ease delay and congestion in appellate litigation.

In 1924, the legislature was authorized to establish municipal courts in larger counties.

The Judicial Council was created by constitutional amendment in 1926 to, among other things, survey the condition of court business, simplify and improve "the administration of justice," and make suggestions to courts regarding "uniformity and expedition of business."

Contested elections of appellate justices were abolished in 1934. In their place a system was established, by constitutional amendment, whereby governors would appoint to fill vacancies and appointees would be subject to approval by a new Commission on Qualifications. All appellate justices would, under the new system, be subject to retention elections at the end of their terms at which voters would vote whether or not to approve an incumbent for a new term.

*C*o appreciate the tremendous changes that occurred during this century, we can compare the state of society in 1850 and in 1950 and then compare the California court systems in those same years.

The Beginning and End of the Era: Comparisons

The United States in 1850

The year is 1850, and the 23 million residents of our nation are:

♦ Living in an agrarian society in which agriculture accounts for 59 percent of the national economy

♦ Living in a rural society with only 15 percent of the population residing in urban areas

♦ Living in a segregated society in which more than 2 million of the population are slaves and 1 million are freed slaves

♦ Recovering from the recent war with Mexico

♦ Assessing the impact of admitting California as a free state, which changes the preexisting balance of fifteen slave states and fifteen free states

♦ Anticipating the publication in 1851 of *Uncle Tom's Cabin* by Harriet Beecher Stowe

♦ Puzzling over Levi Strauss's new bibless overalls

California has an estimated population of 93,000 in 1850, inflated by the Gold Rush from a population of 10,000 in 1846. Four out of every 100 persons in the United States reside here.

The United States in 1950

The year is 1950, and the 151 million residents of our nation are:

♦ Recovering from World War II

♦ Grappling with the implications of using atomic bombs in Japan

♦ Confronting Communism, the Cold War, the Iron Curtain, and the reality that China has fallen to Communists led by Mao Tse-tung

♦ Engaging in a new war in Korea on behalf of the United Nations after North Korea invaded South Korea

- Adapting to the Soviet Union's successful development and explosion of its first atomic bomb

- Marveling at new technology such as television

- Soon to be reading the bestseller *From Here to Eternity* by James Jones

- Hoping for the success of a young scientist named Jonas Salk, who is on the brink of developing a vaccine for polio

California has an approximate population of 10 million in 1950 with one out of fifteen Americans residing here.

Comparing California Courts: 1850 and 1950

1850	1950
NUMBER OF COURT LOCATIONS	
Unknown; but district courts were organized into nine judicial districts; a special district court existed for San Francisco; county courts were provided for in each county; and justice courts were organized for each township	830
TRIAL COURT STRUCTURE	
District courts County courts Justice courts	Superior courts City courts Municipal courts Police courts Township courts City justice courts
FILINGS	
Unknown	2,473,282 (appellate, superior, and municipal)
JUDGES/JUDICIAL OFFICERS	
Unknown	1,056
FUNDING	
Presumed township, county, and state	City, county, and state
STATE-LEVEL ADMINISTRATION	
Supreme Court	Judicial Council

1850   1950

TRIAL COURT ADMINISTRATION	
Judges	Presiding judges
County and court clerks	County clerks and officials
	Court clerks

JUDICIAL DISCIPLINE	
Legislative impeachment, failure to achieve election or reelection	Legislative impeachment, voter recall, defeat at a regular election, or retirement for disability by the governor with consent of the Commission on Qualifications

JUDICIAL SELECTION	
Contested elections, gubernatorial appointments to fill vacancies	Retention elections for appellate courts; contested elections for trial courts; gubernatorial appointments to fill vacancies

ALTERNATIVE DISPUTE RESOLUTION	
Legislature authorized to create tribunals for conciliation, but they were never enacted	No court-annexed programs

JUDICIAL EDUCATION	
No program	No program

PLANNING	
Not a part of judicial administration	Not a part of judicial administration

The California Constitution referred to by Congress in the Act for the Admission of California into the Union was adopted in 1849. The first constitution and the context in which it was adopted furnish important ingredients for understanding the administration of justice during the following 100 years.[1]

The Population of California

Congressional and other references to "the people of California" on the eve of statehood should be considered with care. The frequently cited statistics are that California had an estimated population of 10,000 in 1846, which had grown to more than 90,000 by 1850. These numbers refer primarily to persons of European or American descent.

Far less frequently mentioned, however, are the indigenous natives of California. When the Spaniards arrived in the late 1700s, there were an estimated 300,000 such persons living in tribes with dozens of different cultures and languages. In fact, the area that is now California is thought to have been the most densely populated area in North America.

By 1850, diseases introduced by foreigners, war, and deprivation had wiped out two-thirds of the native population. Spanish missionary and military initiatives had shattered native multiculturalism. The declines in both numbers and cultures continued following statehood.[2]

The Eve of Statehood

California in the 1840s was destined to be wrested from Mexico in one way or another. Even Californians of Spanish and Mexican descent resisted the "feeble yet despotic Mexican rule," rejecting governors appointed by Mexico and laying plans for an independent republic.[3]

The United States was so eager to acquire California that in 1842 an overenthusiastic commodore of the U.S. Navy, acting on an incorrect belief that Mexico had declared war on the United States, sailed to Monterey, demanded immediate surrender by the Mexican commandant, and issued a proclamation to Californians announcing his conquest. Upon being reliably informed of his error, he was compelled to restore Monterey to its lawful officials and withdraw.[4]

When war between the United States and Mexico did in fact begin in 1846, Commodore John Drake Sloat entered Monterey Bay with a squadron of vessels and raised the American flag over the customhouse. Within the next several days the American flag was raised in San Francisco, Sonoma, Sacramento, San Diego, and Los Angeles.[5]

The war ended in 1848 with the signing of the Treaty of Guadalupe Hidalgo, which became effective on May 30. "The most important provision of this treaty was the cession of California to the United States."[6]

Just ten days prior to the signing of the treaty, James Marshall discovered gold at Coloma on the American River in the vicinity of Sutter's Mill.

"Notwithstanding the distance to the Atlantic seaboard and the lack of telegraphic communication, news of the discovery traveled rapidly and within a few months the famous Gold Rush was underway."[7]

The expectation was that Congress would provide a territorial government for California and with it the much-needed structure for a civil government. This was not to be, however, because of the slavery issue. When California was acquired, the number of slave and nonslave states in the United States was equally divided at fifteen per side, and the question of whether any new states or territories, such as California, were to be slave or nonslave created an unbreakable impasse in Congress.

In the absence of congressional action to provide a government in California, such government as there was flowed from proclamations by the succession of military governors, several of whose names are still memorialized in the street names of San Francisco: Sloat, Stockton, Kearny, Mason, and Riley. Notwithstanding these proclamations and various references in them to a civil government for California, conditions suggest a void in actual governing. To cite just three indicators from among many:

1. There was a conceptual muddle over whether the laws of Mexico still applied until legislatively superseded.

2. There was a practical muddle since few of the Americans or other non-Hispanic immigrants knew anything of Mexican law or the preexisting system of government established by Mexico in California.

3. Thanks to the Gold Rush, the nonnative population of California, perhaps setting a pattern for California in the future, burst from 10,000 in the summer of 1846 to 50,000 by August 1849 to 93,000 during 1850.[8]

In the words of one historian, "No effectual measures were employed to perpetuate even the Mexican civil law, itself entirely inadequate under the new conditions; hence California had no suitable, properly constituted system of government from the conquest to the adoption of the Constitution."[9]

While martial law was in effect for the rudimentary purpose of maintaining order, among Californians old and new, the "greatest grievance was the very want of law adequate to the protection of life and property, and to the complete administration of justice."[10]

Justice Nathaniel Bennett, an inaugural member of the California Supreme Court, described the dire legal predicament immediately prior to statehood:

> Before the organization of the state government, society was in a disorganized state. It can scarcely be said that any laws were in existence further than such as were upheld by custom and tradition. This was the case more particularly in Northern California and in the mineral region—in Southern California, perhaps, to a less extent. Commercial transactions to an immense amount had been entered into, and large transactions in real estate had taken place between Americans, with reference to the Common Law as modified and administered in the United States, and without regard to the unknown laws of the republic of Mexico, and the equally unknown customs and traditions of the Californians; and the application of the strict letter of Mexican law in all cases, would have invalidated contracts of incalculable amount, which had been entered into without any of the parties having had the means of knowing that such laws ever existed.[11]

It appears that Colonel Richard Barnes Mason, during his tenure as the military governor of California, had the power to establish a temporary civil government but instead deferred, first, to the imminent conclusion of the war with Mexico and then to Congress for provision of a civil government.[12] Civil government, to the extent it existed at all, was handcrafted locally on an ad hoc basis. In rural areas and the rough-and-tumble world of the gold miners, rules and tribunals were created as circumstances demanded, often accompanied by swift penalties for infractions.

Dissatisfaction with these conditions precipitated a series of meetings in 1848 held in San Jose, Sacramento, San Francisco, and Sonoma that were the beginning of a movement, at least in the northern part of the state, to organize some type of civil government.[13] The most refined was in San Francisco, where the citizens created a temporary government in the form of a Legislative Assembly of fifteen members.[14]

In the spring of 1849, General Bennet Riley became the military governor of California. Upon learning that Congress for the third time had adjourned without addressing a government for California, Riley called for a Constitutional Convention, with the election of delegates to occur on August 1 and a convention to commence on September 1 in Monterey.[15]

The Constitution of 1849

The Constitutional Convention convened as scheduled. Although seventy-three delegates were authorized, only forty-eight attended the convention.

> Most of the members were young men, more than thirty of them were less than 40 years of age, nine were less than 30 years of age, and the oldest was 53. The occupations were varied. There were 14 lawyers, 11 farmers, and 7 merchants. It is probable that a large number of the members were, temporarily at least, miners. Fifteen of the members may be considered as from the southern states and there were 23 members from the northern states. The northern members had also on the average been in California for a greater number of years. There were seven native Californians, and five foreign-born members, one from France, one from Scotland, one from Switzerland, one from Ireland and one from Spain.[16]

Not surprisingly, the federal constitution and the constitutions of other states were influential as the delegates proceeded with their substantive work. It appears that at least one copy of the constitution from each of the other thirty states was available for reference.[17] "The influence of the Constitutions of New York and Iowa is easily apparent in almost every article of California's [1849] Constitution: other States, as Michigan, Virginia, Louisiana, and Mississippi, while leaving an influence, are not at all to be compared to the two great models."[18]

The threshold issue was whether the convention should provide for a territorial or a state government. This was emphatically resolved in favor of creation of a constitution for the state of California. While important issues touching on capital punishment, slavery, education, corporations, and banks were addressed, the most vexatious issue was the boundary of the proposed state. Some argued for a boundary coterminous with the territory ceded by Mexico in the Treaty of Guadalupe Hidalgo, which embraced not only present-day California but Nevada, Arizona, New Mexico, Utah, and part of Colorado.[19] Others who were not prepared to embrace such a vast territory argued for what is now California and Nevada.

The northern and southern boundaries were not so difficult. The northern boundary was rather easily fixed at the forty-second parallel and the southern at the Mexican border. The debated eastern border ultimately was fixed somewhat east of the Sierra Nevada mountains but not including any area in Nevada or any part of Arizona east of the Colorado River.[20]

After six weeks of work, the convention completed and approved a proposed constitution, which subsequently was approved on November 13 by the men of California (since there were no female voters), with an overwhelming majority of 12,061 to 811.[21] This was the constitution embraced by Congress the following year when granting statehood to California.

> The achievement illustrates the great capacity of the American people for self-government. The Constitution offered to the citizens of California for their consideration and their votes sprang immediately into great favor, and the members of the Convention were warmly praised for having done their work faithfully and "adjourned with unimpaired good will." The document received the highest commendations from all sources, as the "embodiment of the American mind, throwing its convictions, impulses, and aspirations into a tangible, permanent shape."[22]

The Judicial System in the Constitution of 1849

The court structure, officials, and jurisdiction, as provided in article VI of the 1849 constitution, were:

Judicial Tribunals
Supreme Court—to consist of a Chief Justice and two associate justices.
District Courts—to be held by one judge in each district as established by the Legislature.
County Courts—to be held in each county by the county judge.
Courts of Sessions—to be held by the county judge and two justices of the peace.
Municipal Courts—municipal and other inferior courts as may be deemed necessary [by the legislature].
Tribunals for Conciliation—may be established by the Legislature.
Justices' Courts—to be held by justices of the peace; the number in each county, city, town, and incorporated village to be determined by the Legislature.
Judicial Officers
Justices of the Supreme Court—the first justices to be elected by the Legislature; subsequent justices elected by electors of the State; to hold office for 6 years.
District Judges—the first judges to be appointed by the Legislature, to hold office for 2 years; later judges to be elected by electors or respective districts, to hold office for 6 years.

County Judges—to be elected by voters of the county; to hold office for 4 years.

Justices of the Peace—justices to be elected in each county, city, town, and incorporated village . . . .

Subject-Matter Jurisdiction

Supreme Court—to have appellate jurisdiction in all cases when the dispute exceeds $200, when legality of a tax, toll, impost or municipal fine is in question, and questions of law in all criminal cases amounting to felony; court and justices to have power to issue writs of habeas corpus, and all writs necessary to the exercise of appellate jurisdiction.

District Courts—to have original jurisdiction in law and in equity in all civil cases where the amount in dispute exceeds $200, in criminal cases not otherwise provided for, and in all issues of fact joined in the probate courts.

County Courts—to have such jurisdiction in cases arising in justices' courts, and in special cases, as prescribed by the Legislature, but no other original civil jurisdiction; county judge to perform duties of surrogate or probate judge.

Courts of Sessions—to have such criminal jurisdiction as the Legislature may prescribe.

Justices of the Peace—powers, duties, and responsibilities to be fixed by the Legislature.[23]

Anticipating contemporary alternative dispute resolution, the judicial article contained the following provision, which was never implemented by the legislature:

Sec. 13. Tribunals for conciliation may be established, with such powers and duties as may be prescribed by law; but such tribunals shall have no power to render judgment, to be obligatory on the parties, except they voluntarily submit their matters in difference, and agree to abide the judgment, or assent thereto in the presence of such tribunal, in such cases as shall be prescribed by law.[24]

The Next Thirty Years

The period between 1849 and 1879 was marked by numerous complaints, a series of legislative enactments pertaining to courts, and attempts to amend the original constitution. In fact, the legislature proposed the calling of a second constitutional convention in 1859, 1860, and 1873 "but each time the proposal had been voted down at the election."[25]

The legislature made an effort to construct a comprehensive court system during early statehood by passing the Court Act of 1851. A minor but amusing illustration of their swirling efforts is additional legislation that created the judges of the plains *(jueces del campo),* to be appointed by courts of sessions for one-year terms. These judges were charged with attending rodeos and roundups of cattle to decide disputes over "ownership, mark, or brand."[26]

Chief among the alleged defects in the original constitution were the legislature's practically unrestricted powers of taxation; the legislature's unrestricted control over finance; the absence of any control over legislative disposition of state property; the absence of provision for separate senatorial and assembly districts; the tyranny of corporations, especially the railroads; the unrestricted pardoning power of the governor; excessive borrowing of provisions from constitutions of agricultural states; and an unsatisfactory judicial system in which courts were overcrowded and decisions not reported.[27]

These substantive shortcomings were compounded by far more potent conditions in society. By 1879 California's population had increased ninefold to 865,000, almost a third of whom lived in San Francisco. The 1870s were a period of economic recession with "large-scale unemployment, business failures, homelessness, foreclosures, bank panics and failures, and a collapse of the speculative market in mining stocks."[28] Farmers suffered drought conditions that drove them deeper into debt.

Meanwhile, the unemployed gathered and agitated in the largest cities, finding in the Chinese an easy scapegoat. Since Chinese laborers were no longer employed in construction of the transcontinental railway and were willing to work at a lower wage than white laborers, resentment toward the Chinese grew and the newly formed Workingmen's Party, a supporter of a constitutional convention, adopted the slogan "The Chinese Must Go!"

Hostility toward corporations ran equally high. Railroads, for example, during their infancy in the 1860s were supported by generous subsidies and land grants from local jurisdictions and the state government. Control of the railroads became increasingly centralized in the Central Pacific Railroad, which itself was controlled by a few powerful men: Collis Huntington, Leland Stanford, Charles Crocker, Mark Hopkins, and David Coulton. "By the late 1870s, the company . . . controlled over 85 percent of the state's rail lines and was both the largest landowner and largest employer in California. Charging arbitrary freight rates, it favored certain merchants and ruined others and further undermined public opinion. Location of new routes was decided by bribery, not need, with the knowledge that whole towns could be destroyed if the railroad refused to service them."[29]

During the otherwise tumultuous period between 1849 and 1879, the judicial system was tuned but hardly changed in epic dimensions. The following were the more notable developments:

1850: The Supreme Court asserted that "it will exercise a supervisory control over all the inferior courts of this state. . . ."[30]

1851: The legislature enacted the Court Act of 1851, fleshing out constitutional provisions in the areas of judicial officers, jurisdiction, and the creation of several minor courts of limited jurisdiction. This act was replaced by a more concise version with little substantive change by the Court Act of 1853.

1862: Article VI of the constitution was revised. While dealing in minor respects with the structure and staffing of the trial courts, the major changes were to expand the Supreme Court by the addition of two associate justices; to extend Supreme Court terms to ten years rather than six; and to clarify that the Supreme Court had original jurisdiction, in addition to appellate jurisdiction, to issue writs of mandamus and certiorari, as well as habeas corpus. This was an area that had been in dispute since adoption of the 1849 constitution.

1872: The Code of Civil Procedure was adopted by the legislature.[31]

The Constitution of 1879

The sequence of events leading to the Constitution of 1879 began on September 5, 1877, when the voters of California approved calling a convention to revise the state's constitution. Six months later the legislature adopted the enabling act for the convention, providing for the election of 152 delegates on June 19, 1878, to meet in Sacramento on September 28. The convention adjourned on March 3, 1879, and on May 7 the new constitution was approved by a statewide vote of 77,959 to 67,134.[32]

The most significant changes restricted the power of the legislature and its role in the system of government.[33] The sentiment behind this treatment of the legislative branch was captured in the following excerpt from an address to the people of California, adopted by convention delegates, asking for ratification of the proposed constitution and explaining the legislative provisions:

For many years the people of this State have been oppressed by the onerous burdens laid upon them for the support of the government, and by the many acts of special legislation permitted and practiced under the present Constitution. Its provisions have been so construed by the Courts as to shift the great burden of taxation from the wealthy and non-producing class to the labourers and producers.

The only restriction upon a Legislature is the Constitution of the State and of the United States. It, therefore, becomes necessary that State Constitutions should contain many regulations and restrictions, which must necessarily be enlarged and extended from time to time to meet the growing demands of the sovereign people.[34]

The judicial branch certainly received attention but apparently without the rancor that had been directed toward the legislature. Abundant proposals to revise court structure were made just prior to and during the convention but not adopted. For example, while the convention's Judiciary Committee was deliberating, the San Francisco Bar Association adopted and arranged to have presented to the committee a plan to create a single-level trial court, with at least one judge in each county, and to abolish all inferior trial courts.[35]

The Judicial System in the Constitution of 1879

The key provisions are summarized in some detail, not because substantive change was extensive, but because they reflected the objective of convention delegates to place considerable restraints on the legislature and to do so by constitutional specifications that would be beyond legislative reach.

Courts and Officers

- ◆ Supreme Court—to consist of a Chief Justice and six associate justices, with permission to sit in two three-judge departments and en banc and to be always open for business (not just during court sessions or terms). The justices to be elected statewide for twelve-year terms.

- ◆ Superior courts—one for each county or city and county; specified courts to have one judge, others to have two judges, San Francisco to have twelve judges; to be always open (legal holidays and nonjudicial days excepted). Judges to be elected by county, or city and county, for six-year terms. The legislature may also provide for appointment of one or more superior court commissioners by each superior court to perform chamber business of the judges, to take depositions, and to perform such other business as may be prescribed by law.

- ◆ Justices' courts—number and terms to be fixed by the legislature. Justices to be elected by the unit of local government served by the court.

- ◆ Inferior courts—to be established at the discretion of the legislature in any incorporated city or town, or city and county, with powers, terms, and duties fixed by statute.

Other Officers

- ◆ Clerk of the Supreme Court—the legislature to provide for the clerk's election.

- ◆ Supreme Court reporter—the justices to appoint the reporter; the individual to hold office at their pleasure.

- ◆ County clerks—to be ex officio clerks of courts of record in the counties or cities and counties.[36]

Jurisdiction

The scope of jurisdiction for each category of court was not particularly notable. What was striking was the level of detail embedded in the constitution rather than statute. Superior courts, for example, were constitutionally granted

original jurisdiction over all cases in equity, . . . certain cases at law involving title or possession of real property, the legality of any tax, impost, assessment, toll, or municipal fine and demands amounting to $300, . . . criminal cases amounting to felony [or] misdemeanor cases not otherwise provided for, actions of forcible entry and detainer, proceedings in insolvency, actions to prevent or abate a nuisance, all matters of probate, divorce, and for annulment of marriage, and special cases and proceedings not otherwise provided for; . . . power of naturalization; appellate jurisdiction of cases arising in justices' courts and other inferior courts as are prescribed by law; courts and judges to have power to issue writs of mandamus, certiorari, prohibition, quo warranto, and habeas corpus.[37]

A major change, obviously, was the increase in the size of the Supreme Court to seven justices with authorization to sit in three-judge departments. Another significant change also involving the Supreme Court was to require in the determination of causes that all decisions of the court be in writing and the grounds of the decision stated.[38] The reasons were to assure that the law of the state was clear and, in cases of remand to the trial court, to furnish instruction to both the trial judge and attorneys as to the issues resolved by the Supreme Court and the rationale.[39] While there apparently was a fair amount of discussion regarding the methods of selecting Supreme Court justices and the length of their terms, no significant changes were made in this respect.

A change that did not receive majority support was a proposal that all sessions of the Supreme Court be held "at the seat of government," which of course was Sacramento rather than the court's established location in San Francisco.

> In the debate that followed, two principal questions were raised: (1) Which is better, a Supreme Court held at one place (the State capital), or a Supreme Court held at different places in the State, referred to as a "Court on wheels"? (2) If the latter, should the places be fixed by constitutional provision, or left to the Legislature? After extended discussion which included the climate, population, and other features of the three cities mentioned, Byron Waters, a delegate-at-large from the Fourth Congressional District, moved to strike the whole provision, warning, "You had better leave this to the Legislature." His motion was carried by a vote of 64 to 45. This result must have placated those who had suggested that any provision adopted would antagonize many voters, and jeopardize the approval of the constitution.[40]

The remaining notable change was the provision in civil jury cases that eliminated the need for unanimous verdicts and permitted civil verdicts by a three-fourths vote of the jury.[41]

Intermediate Appellate Courts

Apparently the addition of two justices on the Supreme Court and authorization to sit in divisions did not assure prompt appellate justice. By January 1882, approximately three years following adoption of the new constitution, the Supreme Court had a backlog of 790 cases and attorneys were protesting that a system under which a case must remain on the calendar for two years before a decision was heard was a "positive denial of justice."[42]

This dissatisfaction led the legislature in 1885 to direct the Supreme Court to appoint three commissioners to aid the court in performance of its duties and to clear the backlog of pending cases.[43] In 1889 the number of commissioners was increased from three to five.[44]

While the authority of the legislature to impose a system of commissioners on the Supreme Court appears not to have been legally challenged, the court explicitly declared that commissioners "do not usurp the functions of judges of this court, and do not exercise any judicial power whatever."[45]

Dissatisfaction continued to mount, culminating in a 1904 amendment to the constitution creating district courts of appeal. The amendment also divided the state into three appellate districts, specifying the counties encompassed by each district, with further provision for three elected justices in each district, to hold regular sessions in San Francisco, Los Angeles, and Sacramento.[46] Concurrently, the California experiment of utilizing commissioners to aid the Supreme Court came to an end.[47]

During the following half-century there were numerous constitutional amendments to increase the number of appellate districts and the number of divisions within each district. The need to achieve expansion by constitutional amendment was finally eliminated as part of the work of the Constitution Revision Commission when the voters in 1966 approved an amendment authorizing the legislature to determine the number of districts, divisions, and justices within the intermediate appellate courts.[48]

Municipal Courts

The lower court structure that had evolved since 1849 was a matter of continuing concern. That concern produced a constitutional amendment in 1924 authorizing the legislature to establish a municipal court in "any city and county . . . containing a population of more than 40,000 inhabitants. . . ."[49] Acting under authority of this amendment, the legislature adopted enabling legislation permitting the establishment of municipal courts with detailed specifications regarding matters such as jurisdiction, selection and qualification of judges, and court staff.[50] Although only larger charter cities were authorized to act, most of them did so by the 1940s. By establishing municipal courts within city boundaries, they succeeded in displacing the existing justice, police, and small claims courts.[51]

Creation of the Judicial Council of California

The role and evolution of the Judicial Council of California are explored in Chapters Three and Four in connection with governance of the judicial branch during the latter half of the twentieth century. The creation of the Judicial Council in the earlier part of the century was achieved by a constitutional amendment in 1926.[52] The extraordinary expectations underlying creation of the council were stated in the supporting ballot arguments by Senators M. B. Johnson and J. M. Inman. There were no opposing arguments.

> The purpose of this amendment is to organize the courts of the state on a business basis. The "judicial council" which the amendment creates is not a commission, but will be composed of judges in office. The chief justice of the state and ten other judges chosen by him from both the trial and appellate courts will meet from time to time as a sort of board of directors, and will be charged with the duty of seeing that justice is being properly administered. No new office is created; the chief justice will act as chairman of the council and the clerk of the supreme court will act as its secretary.
>
> One of the troubles with our court system is that the work of the various courts is not correlated, and nobody is responsible for seeing that the machinery of the courts is working smoothly. When it is discovered that some rule of procedure is not working well it is nobody's business to see that the evil is corrected. But with a judicial council, whenever anything goes wrong any judge or lawyer or litigant or other citizen will know to whom to make complaint, and it will be the duty of the council to propose a remedy, and if this cannot be done without an amendment to the laws the council will recommend to the legislature any change in the law which it deems necessary.
>
> Similar judicial councils have recently been created in Oregon, Ohio, North Carolina, and Massachusetts. The chief justice will fill the position that a general superintendent fills in any ordinary business. He will be the real as well as the nominal head of the judiciary of the state, and will have the power of transferring judges

from courts that are not busy to those that are. This will make it unnecessary to have judges "pro tempore," or temporary judges, as now provided in the constitution.[53]

A "board of directors . . . charged with the duty of seeing that justice is being properly administered"? A Chief Justice filling "the position that a general superintendent fills in any ordinary business"? A Chief Justice who is "the real as well as the nominal head of the judiciary of the state"? A new institution and new role for the Chief Justice with responsibility for assuring that the work of the courts is "correlated" and further responsibility "for seeing that the machinery of the courts is working smoothly"? These reasonably stated propositions were quietly planted seeds of major, perhaps at the time radical, change that blossomed later in the century. The fruit was self-governance of the judicial branch and major growth of the judicial system toward its rightful place as an equal and independent partner in our tripartite form of government.

As originally enacted, the Judicial Council consisted of the Chief Justice or Acting Chief Justice and an additional ten members appointed by the Chief Justice. These consisted of one associate justice of the Supreme Court, three justices of courts of appeal, four judges of superior courts, one judge of a police or a municipal court, and one judge of an inferior court. The council was directed to:

(1) Meet at the call of the chairman or as otherwise provided by it.

(2) Survey the condition of business in the several courts with a view to simplifying and improving the administration of justice.

(3) Submit such suggestions to the several courts as may seem in the interest of uniformity and the expedition of business.

(4) Report to the Governor and legislature at the commencement of each regular session with such recommendations as it may deem proper.

(5) Adopt or amend rules of practice and procedure for the several courts not inconsistent with laws that are now or that may hereafter be in force; and the council shall submit to the legislature, at each regular session thereof, its recommendations with reference to amendments of, or changes in, existing laws relating to practice and procedure.

(6) Exercise such other functions as may be provided by law.[54]

The Chief Justice as chair was also directed to seek to "expedite judicial business and to equalize the work of the judges" by assigning judges to assist "a court or judge whose calendar is congested, to act for a judge who is disqualified or unable to act, or to sit and hold court where a vacancy in the office of judge has occurred."[55] The clerk of the Supreme Court was designated as secretary to the Judicial Council.

The amendment was approved by the voters. In fact, the voters must have been quite favorably disposed toward the judiciary since they also approved measures that increased the state's contribution toward salaries of trial judges (Proposition 16) and provided for judicial pensions (Proposition 19). The proposal to create the Judicial Council passed by a vote of more than two to one.

Early Judicial Council Efforts

The Judicial Council made a fast start under Chief Justice William H. Waste, who had become Chief Justice in January 1926 and served until 1940. Members were appointed on December 3, 1926, approximately one month after the election, and the first meeting was held on December 10 in the chambers of the Supreme Court in San Francisco.[56]

The first report of the Judicial Council was made on February 28, 1927, approximately two and one-half months after the first meeting. The report was as ambitious as the Judicial Council's timetable, covering an array of subjects ranging from court workloads to arbitration to criminal procedure.

However, two aspects of that inaugural report are particularly noteworthy. The first is the importance that the council attached to its own existence. "The members of the council are of the opinion that the adoption of the Judicial Council amendment marks the beginning of the most significant movement in the interests of the administration of justice in California that has been initiated since the inauguration of the state government in 1849. Behind the motive which led the people to approve the amendment was the appreciation of the fact that there should be a coordination of the courts with the resultant speeding up of the judicial business of the state."[57]

Acknowledging that "expectations have been aroused which it will be difficult to satisfy," the Judicial Council nonetheless also acknowledged that "the time has come for a bold advance in the administration of the judicial business of this state. . . ."[58]

The second noteworthy matter was the decision by the Judicial Council at its initial meeting to make its top priority the state of affairs in the superior courts.

> As a result of the deliberations of its initial session, the council reached the conclusion that its first duty was to survey the condition of business in the superior court throughout the various counties of the state—that being the principal trial court, and to ascertain the present condition of the trial calendars in the several courts. It was decided to at once determine in what counties the superior court has a comparatively small amount of business to attend to, and the judge little to do; what courts afford litigants a reasonably speedy hearing; where trials are delayed so long as to virtually amount to a denial of justice; to ascertain where judicial assistance is needed, and to determine from what courts judges can be spared, in order to render such relief. These were matters that seemed to demand urgent attention.[59]

In this endeavor the Judicial Council confronted a reality that was to persist until creation of the Administrative Office of the Courts (AOC) in 1961: the Judicial Council had no supporting staff. This was overcome at the outset by relieving Judge Harry A. Hollzer, a Los Angeles Superior Court judge and council member, from his judicial duties to assume direction of a survey of judicial business throughout the state. He completed a preliminary survey in approximately two months and was able to present his findings to the Judicial Council on February 11–12, 1927. The report was accepted and appended to the first Judicial Council report to the governor and legislature.

With equal measures of pride and criticism, the Judicial Council hailed this achievement: "To appreciate the difficulties involved, it should be borne in mind that, after the lapse of more than three-quarters of a century, the State of California, for the first time, is now engaged in making a scientific study of its judicial system, 'with a view to simplifying and improving the administration of Justice.' No commercial organization could have survived which had delayed for so long a period of time to investigate its methods of transacting business."[60]

Two years later Judge Hollzer submitted to the Judicial Council his "Report of the Condition of Judicial Business in the Courts of the State of California," together with a summary of research studies of judicial systems in other jurisdictions.[61]

Judge Hollzer's efforts constituted the substance of the Judicial Council's second report to the governor and legislature. Before launching into his methodology, statistics, and conclusions, Judge Hollzer struck an energetic note: "Approximately two years ago, California gave notice to the world that this commonwealth no longer would tolerate antiquated, 'go-as-you-please,' methods in the operation of its courts, but, instead, would insist upon establishing business efficiency and economy in its judicial system, to the end that the disposition of litigation might be expedited and the administration of justice improved."[62]

This report, embraced by the Judicial Council, furnished for the first time a respectable snapshot of the volume of litigation in California, particularly in the superior courts. The conclusions drawn from these data were not timid. The Judicial Council concluded that there was a gross inequality in the amount of work imposed upon various superior courts around the state, in both civil and criminal litigation. This also was true with respect to the number of contested cases around the state. The report stressed that businesslike methods were essential to the efficient and economical administration of the courts. Use of the master calendar in Los Angeles County was cited as a commendable example.[63]

During ensuing years, the Judicial Council institutionalized the gathering and publication of information regarding the volume and disposition of business in the courts of California.[64]

The Judicial Council also on occasion ventured into substantial matters of public policy. For example, the Judicial Council officially recommended against a proposal (Senate Constitutional Amendment 13) presented for voter approval in November 1936 that would have created a separate appellate system for criminal cases and established a court of criminal appeals.[65] The Judicial Council, likewise, in 1946 opposed a proposed constitutional amendment that would have created a separate court of tax appeals.[66]

Judicial Council Projects at Midcentury

As the first half of the twentieth century drew to a close, the Judicial Council launched two major endeavors. The first was a review of procedures in the various administrative agencies of the state. This was undertaken in response to a 1943 request of the legislature. The result was extensive recommendations and proposed legislation in January 1945. In a nutshell, the Judicial Council proposed (1) a uniform procedure for the conduct of formal adjudicatory hearings by forty state agencies engaged in licensing and disciplining of members in various businesses and professions;

(2) maintenance of a staff of qualified hearing officers to preside over such hearings, to be administered by a newly created Division of Administrative Procedures; and (3) detailed procedures for judicial review of adjudicatory decisions by administrative agencies.[67] These recommendations were enacted by the legislature.

In addition to the extent and substance of the measures proposed by the Judicial Council, the research and analysis required to support those measures were truly remarkable. For these purposes the Judicial Council required a special, ad hoc research staff directed by a member of the San Francisco Bar, Ralph N. Kleps, later destined to be the first Administrative Director of the Courts.

The second extraordinary undertaking by the Judicial Council also was at the request of the legislature, which in 1947 adopted a concurrent resolution stating: "The Judicial Council is requested to make a thorough study of the organization, jurisdiction and practice of the courts in California exercising jurisdiction inferior to the superior court, and to make recommendations for the improvement of the administration of justice therein, and to report the result of its studies to the Governor and Legislature. . . ."[68]

The Judicial Council responded in 1948 with a major proposal to reorganize the courts of limited jurisdiction. These recommendations also were supported by an extraordinary research effort conducted with the assistance of special staffing.[69] This culminated in a successful ballot measure to reorganize these courts (addressed in detail in Chapter Five).

Selection of Judges and the Commission on Qualifications

The remaining event of significance in the first century of justice administration in California involved selecting judges. The crucial event occurred in 1934 and is described below, but the story is prolonged and begins much earlier.

The Commonwealth Club played a leading role. Based in San Francisco, the club was and is a membership organization devoted to providing "an impartial forum for the discussion of disputed questions" and aiding in the solution of problems affecting the welfare of the commonwealth.[70]

In December 1912, the club convened a meeting on court delay that evolved into a proposal to the club's board to formulate an appointive system for judges. This request launched a twenty-year effort. The highlight of this effort was the establishment of a Committee on Selection of Judges, which promulgated a plan, approved in 1914 by the club's membership, for appointment of judges by the governor with confirmation by the voters. Legislation was prepared and introduced in 1915 to implement the plan, and thus began more than a decade of legislative defeats for the Commonwealth Club.[71]

Malcolm Smith, in his article "The California Method of Selecting Judges," attributes these defeats "to the subtle pressure of several groups."[72] First were attorneys, who believed the elective system offered better chances for a judicial career. Next were organized labor groups, who remembered earlier injunctions and court orders and feared losing their power over judges in contested elections. Both urban and rural superior court judges were reluctant to change a known system.[73]

In the early 1930s the Commonwealth Club withdrew from the fray. However, the State Bar of California took up where the club left off. Thanks to a well-coordinated effort, the State Bar succeeded in securing legislative approval of a proposed constitutional amendment to be placed on the November 1934 ballot. The thrust of the measure was to provide for appointment by the governor of judges from a list of candidates presented by a nominating commission consisting of the Chief Justice, the presiding justice of the district court of appeal, and the state senator for the county in which the appointment would be made. After a period of service from four to six years, a superior court judge would be required to submit his candidacy for reelection to the voters of the county (Proposed Assembly Constitutional Amendment 98). Although the measure originally was intended to apply statewide, a legislative amendment confined application of the system to counties with a population more than 1,500,000, which in effect made the system applicable only in Los Angeles County.[74]

There was a significant parallel development. The California Committee on Better Administration of Law was formed in 1934 to draft legislation to combat crime in California. The committee had two auxiliary groups: the Committee on Better Administration of Justice, established by the California State Chamber of Commerce, which acted as a coordinating agency; and an advisory committee consisting of prominent members of the State Bar.[75]

The California Committee on Better Administration of Law ultimately proposed a series of constitutional amendments, using the initiative process. One of its measures pertained to selection of judges. After considering numerous proposals and attempting to coordinate plans with the State Bar, the committee ultimately embraced the revived proposal of the Commonwealth

Club and endorsed appointment of appellate judges by the governor, conditioned upon approval by a Commission on Qualifications consisting of the Chief Justice, the district court of appeal presiding justice, and the attorney general; twelve-year terms; and confirmation by the voters at an appropriate time, with a local option at the county level as to whether to use the system for selecting superior court judges.[76]

Although it had a competing proposal on the ballot, the State Bar also endorsed the proposal of the statewide committee.[77]

At the November 1934 election, the voters approved the statewide committee's proposal (Proposition 3) and, at the same time, rejected Proposed Assembly Constitutional Amendment 98, sponsored by the State Bar and approved by the Legislature.[78]

Why the voters should choose to accept appointment of judges in one instance and reject it in another is not wholly explainable. It is difficult to determine to what extent the voters were confused by two judicial selection amendments appearing on the ballot. Inferentially, it would seem that A.C.A. No. 98 received less favorable treatment in the position it received on the ballot. As Proposition No. 14 it followed a very unpopular local option amendment, which was overwhelmingly defeated. Considering the vote, however, it seems quite likely that the committee proposal (Proposition No. 3) would also have been defeated had it appeared separate from the "package" arrangement, that is to say, if it had not appeared as one of the "curb crime" amendments.[79]

During its early years the Commission on Qualifications functioned as intended. The only public eruption occurred when the commission by a two-to-one vote rejected a Supreme Court nominee proposed for appointment by Governor Culbert Levy Olson in 1940.[80]

As the first half of the century drew to a close, this assessment was offered by Malcolm Smith, a scholar who had studied both judicial selection and the commission in commendable detail: "There seems to be a consensus that the Qualifications Commission has worked well, but that it has been unwilling or unable to offer a serious check to the governor. Again, this is only part of the opinion on the subject.

"That changes in the plan are needed, few will deny. But the plan was, and remains, a major step toward providing a means whereby only the best shall be selected to be judges."[81]

End of the First Century

The first 100 years of California's judicial history drew to a close in 1950. Twenty-two men served as Chief Justice of California during this time.[82] Chief Justice Phil S. Gibson spanned the conclusion of the first century and the commencement of the ensuing "golden era."

The most striking feature of this period was the rather modest nature and extent of changes in the judicial system. Court organization or structure remained substantially intact, with recognition of the necessity of easing appellate litigation by creating an intermediate tribunal and a partial attempt to rationalize limited jurisdiction by providing for municipal courts. Likewise, jurisdictional arrangements endured substantially unchanged during this period.

The remarkable developments were the move in the appellate courts away from an egalitarian insistence on popular election of all judges and the provision for governance of the judicial branch. While the Judicial Council remained more embryonic than fully developed during its first quarter-century, its untapped potential began to be exploited at mid-century and was in early maturity by the end of the century.

Notes

1   Numerous sources were consulted in exploring the first 100 years of statehood, but the cited works by the following scholars were invaluable and heavily used in crafting the text: Professor William Wirt Blume, Peter Thomas Conmy, Professor Rockwell Dennis Hunt, Carleton W. Kenyon, Paul Mason, Professor Noel Sargent, and Dr. Malcolm Smith.

2   James J. Rawls, "The Hispanicization of California"; and J. S. Holliday, "The California Gold Rush: Its Impact and Influences" (audiotapes) (Berkeley: The Bancroft Library, University of California at Berkeley).

3   Rockwell Dennis Hunt, *The Genesis of California's First Constitution (1846–49)*, Johns Hopkins University Studies in Historical and Political Science, 13th series, no. 8 (Baltimore: Johns Hopkins Press, 1895) [New York: Johnson Reprint, 1973], p. 10.

4   Ibid.

5   Peter Thomas Conmy, *The Constitutional Beginnings of California* (San Francisco: Native Sons of the Golden West, 1959), p. 5.

6   Ibid.

7   Ibid.

8   Hunt, *The Genesis of California's First Constitution*, p. 30; Conmy, *The Constitutional Beginnings of California*, pp. 9–10; and Paul Mason, "Constitutional History of California," *Constitution of the State of California and of the United States and Other Documents* (California Senate), 1958, pp. 293, 301–3.

9   Hunt, *The Genesis of California's First Constitution*, p. 17.

10   Id., p. 19.

11   1 California Reports (San Francisco: Bancroft-Whitney, 1851), preface, pp. vi–vii.

12   Hunt, *The Genesis of California's First Constitution*, pp. 21–23.

13   Id., p. 26.

14   Hunt, *The Genesis of California's First Constitution*, pp. 26–27; Mason, "Constitutional History of California," pp. 301–3.

15   Hunt, *The Genesis of California's First Constitution*, pp. 29, 34–35.

16   Mason, "Constitutional History of California," p. 306.

17   Id., p. 309.

18   Hunt, *The Genesis of California's First Constitution*, p. 56.

19   Conmy, *The Constitutional Beginnings of California*, p. 16.

20   Id., pp. 16–17.

21   Id., p. 23.

22   Hunt, *The Genesis of California's First Constitution*, p. 57.

23   William Wirt Blume, "*California Courts in Historical Perspective,*" *Hastings Law Journal* 22 (1970–1971): pp. 127–28.

24   California Constitution of 1849, article VI, section 13.

25   Mason, "Constitutional History of California," p. 318.

26   Blume, "California Courts in Historical Perspective," pp. 140–41. These judges apparently rode into the sunset upon enactment of the Court Act of 1853.

27   Noel Sargent, "The California Constitutional Convention of 1878–9," *California Law Review* 6 (1917–1918).

28   Joseph R. Grodin, Calvin R. Massey, and Richard B. Cunningham, *The California State Constitution: A Reference Guide*, Reference Guides to the State Constitutions of the United States, no. 11 (Westport, Conn.: Greenwood Press, 1993), p. 9.

29   Id., p. 10.

30   *People ex rel. The Attorney General, ex parte*, 1 Cal 85, 89 (dictum).

31   Blume, "California Courts in Historical Perspective," pp. 133–51.

32   Id., pp. 153–55.

33   Sargent, "The California Constitutional Convention of 1878–9," pp. 8–12.

34   Quoted in Sargent, "The California Constitutional Convention of 1878–9," p. 8.

35   Blume, "California Courts in Historical Perspective," p. 158.

36   Id., pp. 158–60.

37 Blume, "California Courts in Historical Perspective," p. 160.

38 California Constitution of 1879, article VI, section 2, as originally adopted.

39 Sargent, "The California Constitutional Convention of 1878–9," pp. 13–14.

40 Blume, "California Courts in Historical Perspective," p. 163.

41 California Constitution, article I, section 7.

42 Quoted in Blume, "California Courts in Historical Perspective," p. 169.

43 California Statutes 1885, chapter 120, section 1, p. 101.

44 California Statutes 1889, chapter 16, section 1, p. 13.

45 *People ex rel. Morgan v. Hayne* (1890), 83 Cal. 111, p. 121.

46 California Constitution (1904), article VI, section 4.

47 Id., section 25.

48 California Constitution (1966), article VI, section 3.

49 California Constitution (1924), article VI, section 11.

50 California Statutes 1925, chapter 358, p. 648.

51 Alden Ames, "The Origin and Jurisdiction of the Municipal Courts in California," *California Law Review* 21 (1933), p. 117.

52 California Constitution (1926), article VI, section 1a.

53 Senators M. B. Johnson and J. M. Inman, Argument in Favor of Proposition 27, Senate Constitutional Amendment No. 15 (1925 Regular Session), submitted to voters on November 2, 1926.

54 California Constitution (1926), article VI, section 1a.

55 Ibid.

56 Judicial Council of California, *First Report of the Judicial Council of California to the Governor and the Legislature* (1927), p. 11.

57 Id., p. 25.

58 Ibid.

59 Id., p. 11.

60 Id., p. 13.

61 Judge Harry A. Hollzer, "Report of the Condition of Judicial Business in the Courts of the State of California, together with a Summary of Research Studies of Judicial Systems in other Jurisdictions," in Judicial Council of California, *Second Report of the Judicial Council of California to the Governor and the Legislature* (1929), part 2, p. 11.

62 Ibid.

63 Id., pp. 15–23.

64 See, for example, Judicial Council of California, *Fifth Report of the Judicial Council of California* (covering Period July 1, 1932, to June 30, 1934).

65 Judicial Council of California, "Special Report on Proposed Court of Criminal Appeals," *Sixth Report of the Judicial Council of California* (June 30, 1936), part 1.

66 California Statutes 1945, p. 3165; Judicial Council of California, *Eleventh Biennial Report to the Governor and the Legislature* (1946), pp. 11–12.

67 Judicial Council of California, "Report on the Administrative Agencies Survey," *Tenth Biennial Report to the Governor and Legislature* (December 31, 1944), part 2, pp. 8–46.

68 California Statutes 1947, chapter 47, p. 3448.

69 Judicial Council of California, *Twelfth Biennial Report to the Governor and the Legislature* (1948).

70 Commonwealth Club bylaws quoted in Malcolm Smith, "The California Method of Selecting Judges," *Stanford Law Review* 3 (1951), p. 573.

71 Id., pp. 573–6.

72 Id., p. 576.

73 Ibid.

74 Id., pp. 576–8.

75 Id., pp. 579–80.

76 Id., pp. 582–4.

77 Id., p. 585.

[78] Based on [California Secretary of State], "Statement of Vote at General Election 31 (November 6, 1934)," cited in Smith, p. 586, n. 93.

[79] Smith, p. 586.

[80] Id., pp. 591–3.

[81] Id., p. 600.

[82] Supreme Court of California, *Supreme Court of California Practices and Procedures* (1997 revision; June 2000 reprint). Appendix I lists all Chief Justices from 1850 to 2000.

Part 2

The Golden Era

etween 1950 and 2000 the momentum of improvement accelerated. By century's end the administration of justice had both matured and achieved new plateaus. The most prominent milestones in this era marked achievements that spanned the half-century and impacted the entire system: creation of governance institutions, dynamic governance, trial court reorganization and unification, stable trial court funding, a system of judicial discipline, and delay reductions.

Chapter 2
The Golden Era: 1950 to 2000

Overview

he tenure of Chief Justice Donald R. Wright (1970–1977) was once described as a "golden era of court administration in California."[1] The phrase aptly can be applied to the entire half-century commencing in 1950 and concluding with the end of the millennium. While progress was neither continuous nor consistently monumental, the cumulative achievements during these fifty years are remarkable. A catalog of achievements large and small, even if feasible, would be voluminous. The focus here and in the following chapters is on the more notable improvements in the administration of justice. Those achievements include:

- ◆ The creation of governing institutions
- ◆ The dynamics of governance resulting in planning and policy-making
- ◆ The reorganization and unification of the trial courts
- ◆ State funding of the trial courts
- ◆ A system for judicial discipline
- ◆ The reduction of delay in the trial courts

*T*n Chapter One, we compared the United States in 1850 and in 1950. Now we can take a look at the nation at the millennium, followed by a comparison of California courts in 1950 and in 2000.

The Beginning and End of the Era: Comparisons

The United States at the Millennium

By the year 2000, America had grown from 151 million to approximately 275 million. In the intervening fifty years since midcentury:

♦ The Korean War is fought to a truce.

♦ Racial segregation in public schools is prohibited by judicial decision.

♦ The Union of Soviet Socialist Republics (USSR) successfully launches "Sputnik," the first earth-orbiting satellite in outer space.

♦ The United States fights and loses a prolonged war in Vietnam and adjoining countries.

♦ President Kennedy is assassinated and President Reagan is shot in an attempted assassination.

♦ The era of the flower children and the Beatles arrives and passes.

♦ The United States becomes the first nation to land a man on the moon.

♦ The use of illegal drugs has grown dramatically, prompting a continuing "war on drugs" by the government.

♦ The USSR fractures and along with it the Iron Curtain.

♦ Governmental and private satellites circumnavigate the earth for an array of scientific, commercial, and military purposes.

♦ The use of computers is widespread both at home and at work.

♦ The Internet evolves, accompanied by a revolution in techniques of communication, research, and marketing.

♦ Biotechnology emerges with genetic mapping, cloning, and bioengineering.

♦ Americans are reading the best-selling adventures of young Harry Potter and his life at the Hogwarts School of Witchcraft and Wizardry.

♦ The average life span in the United States increases for women from 71.1 years to approximately 80 and for men from 65.6 years to approximately 74.

♦ California's population grows from 10 million to more than 34 million during these fifty years, with no ethnic majority. One out of every nine Americans now resides here.

California Courts in 1950

It is January 1, 1950, and in the California courts:

♦ The system consists of the Supreme Court, four district courts of appeal, superior courts in each of the fifty-eight counties, and an array of 767 limited jurisdiction courts.

♦ There are 203 superior court judges, 83 municipal court judges, and apparently 736 judges of various "inferior courts."

♦ Total filings in 1950 are 222,207 for the superior courts and 2,249,205 for the municipal courts. Filings in city and township courts are so voluminous that the Judicial Council declines to print them.

♦ Funding is furnished by local government for all aspects of the trial courts except for the salaries of judges in the superior courts.

♦ Appellate court costs are paid by the state.

♦ The Judicial Council exists, but there is no Administrative Office of the Courts (AOC) and the trial courts are administratively autonomous.

California Courts at the Millennium

It is the year 2000, and the following groundbreaking changes have occurred in the intervening fifty years in the California court system:

♦ There is a single-level trial court system consisting exclusively of the superior court as the only court of general jurisdiction.

♦ There are 440 court locations and 1,980 judicial officers consisting of 1,579 judges and 401 commissioners or referees.

♦ During 1999, matters of judicial business filed in the trial and appellate courts total 8,649,552—approximately one filing for every four persons in California and 4,368 matters for every judicial officer.

◆ All operating expenses of the court system are the responsibility of the state with fixed contributions by larger counties to a state-wide trust fund for court support.

◆ During this past half-century, the state is served by six different Chief Justices.

◆ The first trial court administrator position in the nation is created in 1957 for the Los Angeles Superior Court.

◆ The position of Administrative Director of the Courts is created in 1960, and four incumbents serve between 1961 and 2000.

◆ The AOC is created in 1961 by the Judicial Council.

◆ Every trial court jurisdiction in California has an administrator and administrative staff by the year 2000.

◆ The Commission on Judicial Performance is independently established in 1976 after evolving from the Commission on Judicial Qualifications.

◆ The Center for Judicial Education and Research is created in 1973 to train and educate judges and court staff and ultimately becomes the Education Division of the AOC.

◆ Alternative dispute resolution programs emerge.

◆ Special court divisions are formally established in trial courts with responsibility for litigated matters involving probate, families, juveniles, and drugs.

◆ Planning becomes an integral part of administering justice.

Comparing California Courts: 1950 and 2000

1950	2000
NUMBER OF COURT LOCATIONS	
830	440
TRIAL COURT STRUCTURE	
Superior courts City courts Municipal courts Police courts Township courts City justice courts	Superior courts
FILINGS	
2,473,282 (appellate, superior, and municipal)	8,649,552 (superior and appellate)
JUDGES/JUDICIAL OFFICERS	
1,056	1,980
FUNDING	
City, county, and state	State
STATE-LEVEL ADMINISTRATION	
Judicial Council	Judicial Council Administrative Office of the Courts
TRIAL COURT ADMINISTRATION	
Presiding judges County clerks and officials Court clerks	Presiding judges Executive officers Administrative staff County officials
JUDICIAL DISCIPLINE	

Legislative impeachment, voter recall, defeat at a regular election, or retirement for disability by the governor with consent of the Commission on Qualifications	Legislative impeachment, voter recall
	Code of Judicial Ethics by the Supreme Court
	By the Commission on Judicial Performance:
	    disqualification
	    suspension
	    retirement (for disability)
	    censure
	    admonishment

1950   2000

	1950	2000
JUDICIAL EDUCATION	No program	AOC's Center for Judicial Education and Research California Judges Association Private organizations
JUDICIAL SELECTION	Retention elections for appellate courts; contested elections for trial courts; gubernatorial appointments to fill vacancies with unexpired terms	No change except the governor fills vacancies by appointment for periods linked to general elections
ALTERNATIVE DISPUTE RESOLUTION	No court-annexed programs	Court-sponsored programs at both the trial and appellate levels including arbitration, mediation, conciliation, and evaluation
PLANNING	Not a part of judicial administration	Strategic and other types of planning are integral to judicial administration and drive budget, rules, and legislative priorities

Note

1   Ralph N. Kleps, "Tribute to Chief Justice Donald R. Wright," *Hastings Constitutional Law Quarterly* 4 (1977), p. 683.

Chapter 3
The Creation of Governing Institutions

Overview

The Judicial Council matured and began to fulfill its potential as the policymaking institution for the judicial branch of government.

Membership expanded repeatedly over the years, growing to almost double the original eleven members, who were all judges. By century's end membership included representatives of the legislature, State Bar, and court administrators.

The organization of the council also expanded, from nine committees consisting primarily of council members to four standing committees for internal administration and twenty-eight advisory bodies with more than 300 members.

Creation of the position of Administrative Director of the Courts in 1960 was indispensable to the Judicial Council and the courts. Establishment of the Administrative Office of the Courts (AOC) shortly thereafter completed a structure of governance institutions at the state level.

The AOC furnished a new ability for the Judicial Council to delegate, obtain information, and implement policy. By the end of the century the AOC's more than 400 staff members were supporting the needs of the Judicial Council as well as responding to needs in the trial courts ranging from human resources to technology.

Governance at the trial court level is opaque—not because it didn't exist, but because it has not been documented. Suffice to say that the presiding judge system, often supplemented by executive or other governing committees, prevailed.

The major development was establishment of court executive officer positions to administer nonjudicial aspects of the trial courts. The first such position was in the Los Angeles Superior Court in 1957. Court executive officers were universal by 2000.

*G*overnance ranks high among the significant changes in the judicial branch during this half-century. While there are explicit provisions for governance of the judicial branch in California, much must be inferred from constitutional provisions pertaining to the Judicial Council.

The Judicial Council: A Fifty-Year Snapshot

Constitutional Provisions

The duties and powers of the Judicial Council, as originally adopted in 1926, were constitutionally intact as of 1950. At the core were surveying business in the courts to improve the administration of justice, reporting to the governor and legislature with recommendations, and adopting rules of practice and procedure consistent with statutes.[1]

The formally prescribed role of the Judicial Council was substantially the same throughout the period 1950 to 2000, although rephrased more concisely on recommendation of the Constitution Revision Commission in 1966 and refined by a specific amendment in 1996 regarding the relationship between rules and statutes:

> To improve the administration of justice the council shall survey judicial business and make recommendations to the courts, make recommendations annually to the Governor and Legislature, adopt rules for court administration, practice and procedure, and perform other functions prescribed by statute. The rules adopted shall not be inconsistent with statute.[2]

Leaders

Chief Justice Phil S. Gibson served as chair of the Judicial Council from 1940 until his retirement in 1964. He brought an interesting background to these responsibilities. He was a successful attorney in Los Angeles but was persuaded in 1938 to serve as director of finance in the new administration of Governor Culbert Levy Olson. Within less than two years he was appointed an associate justice of the California Supreme Court and shortly thereafter elevated by Governor Olson to the position of Chief Justice.

Chief Justice Roger J. Traynor followed and served as chair of the Judicial Council from 1964 to 1970. Chief Justice Traynor brought to the position a span of distinguished experience in academia and government. For most of his career, he had served as a faculty member of the Boalt Hall School of Law at the University of California at Berkeley. In 1940 he was appointed to the Supreme Court by Governor Olson, assuming the associate justice position left vacant when Justice Gibson became Chief Justice. In 1964, Traynor became Chief Justice by appointment of Governor Edmund G. "Pat" Brown, and he retired in 1970.

In 1970, Chief Justice Donald R. Wright assumed office and became chair of the Judicial Council following his appointment by Governor Ronald Reagan. He was the first Chief Justice in this era with experience as a trial judge. Indeed, Chief Justice Wright had served at all levels of the California court system: municipal court (1953–1961), superior court in Los Angeles County (1961–1968), and Court of Appeal, Second Appellate District (1968–1970). He retired in 1977.

Chief Justice Rose Elizabeth Bird was appointed in 1977 by Governor Edmund G. "Jerry" Brown, Jr., and chaired the Judicial Council for almost a decade. Prior to becoming Chief Justice, she had served in the cabinet of Governor Jerry Brown as secretary of the Agriculture and Services Agency. Prior to that, she had held a series of positions in the Public Defender's Office of Santa Clara County. After almost ten years of service, Chief Justice Bird failed to receive a majority of affirmative votes in the retention election of 1986 and left the Supreme Court at the conclusion of her term in January 1987.

Chief Justice Malcolm M. Lucas was appointed by Governor George Deukmejian and was sworn in on February 5, 1987. Like Chief Justice Wright, Chief Justice Lucas brought extensive judicial experience to his new position. He had served for four years on the Los Angeles Superior Court, which he left in 1971 to accept a lifetime appointment as a judge on the U.S. District Court for the Central District of California in Los Angeles. After thirteen years of service in that position, he was appointed in 1984 to the California Supreme Court by Governor Deukmejian and served for three years as an associate justice prior to being appointed Chief Justice. He retired in 1996 after chairing the Judicial Council for almost a decade.

Chief Justice Ronald M. George was appointed by Governor Pete Wilson in 1996. For the second time in this half-century, California acquired a Chief Justice who had served at every level of the court system, with the added distinction of service on the Supreme Court prior to becoming Chief Justice. From 1972 to 1977, he served on the Los Angeles Municipal Court, followed by ten years of service on the Los Angeles Superior Court. In 1987, he was elevated to the court of appeal, where he served until 1991 when he was appointed to the Supreme Court as an associate justice by

Governor Wilson. Chief Justice George continued to preside over the Judicial Council as the century concluded and a new millennium began.

Membership

Just as the original duties of the Judicial Council were unchanged as of 1950, so was the membership. As originally composed, the Judicial Council consisted of eleven members: the Chief Justice, one associate justice from the Supreme Court, three justices of the district courts of appeal, four judges of the superior courts, one judge of a police or municipal court, and one judge of "an inferior court." All were "assigned" by the Chief Justice for two-year terms. From the beginning and continuing through the 1950s, the clerk of the Supreme Court was secretary to the Judicial Council.[3]

Revision of the judicial article of the California Constitution was proposed by the Judicial Council in 1959 and enacted in 1960. Among the specific proposals was a broadening of the Judicial Council's membership from eleven to eighteen in order "to include representatives of all groups directly concerned with improvement of the administration of justice."[4] The courts of limited jurisdiction gained additional representation by provision for two judges of municipal courts rather than one. The major expansion, however, occurred in new areas. Provision was made for four members of the State Bar, appointed by its board of governors, and for one member from each house of the legislature, designated by the Assembly and Senate.[5]

Thanks to further amendments in 1966 and 1994, membership was expanded again to equalize trial court participation at five members each from superior and municipal courts.

The next expansion occurred by constitutional amendment in 1996, which provided for "2 nonvoting court administrators, and such other nonvoting members as determined by the voting membership of the council."[6] The 1996 amendment also expanded the term of membership on the Judicial Council from two years to three years. With the prospect of trial court unification, a 1998 amendment provided: "Vacancies in the memberships on the Judicial Council otherwise designated for municipal court judges shall be filled by judges of the superior court in the case of appointments made when fewer than 10 counties have municipal courts."[7]

Throughout this fifty-year era all Judicial Council members were appointed by the Chief Justice except for legislators and State Bar representatives. But in 1992 the process was strengthened and enriched by formal processes of application and nomination.

Organization

The story of Judicial Council organization is one of expansion that parallels that of Judicial Council membership.

The minutes of the Judicial Council from the early 1950s indicate the existence of the following committees, each created by motion and approval of the council, with members appointed by Chief Justice Gibson as chair:

- ◆ Committee on Rules on Appeal
- ◆ Committee on Superior Court Rules
- ◆ Committee on Municipal Court Rules
- ◆ Pretrial Committee (with North and South Subcommittees)
- ◆ Extraordinary Legal Remedies Committee
- ◆ Committee on Legal Forms
- ◆ Committee on Extraordinary Writs
- ◆ Committee on Traffic
- ◆ Juvenile Committee (also referred to at different times as the Juvenile Court Committee, Juvenile Justice Committee, and Committee on Juvenile Courts and Procedure)

By the 1960s, the organization of the Judicial Council had become more complex as reflected by the committee structure. In 1962, the above committees were supplemented by new committees to address judicial statistics, administrative procedure, automobile accident litigation, opinion writing and publication, and cooperation with the State Bar and the Conference of California Judges. While there was significant representation on each of these committees by members of the Judicial Council, the occasional practice of utilizing nonmembers to serve on committees had become a trend.[8]

By 1970, the core committees had been reduced to an Executive Committee, chaired by the Chief Justice, and committees on appellate courts, superior courts, court management, and municipal and justice courts. The number and breadth of special committees, however, accelerated. For example, there were now special committees on fair trial and free press, juvenile courts and family law, and Public Utilities Commission decisions. There were also advisory committees for the courts of appeal workshop, domestic relations institute, sentencing institute, and municipal and justice courts institute.

By 2000, the Judicial Council's standing committees had been rigorously streamlined into four important bodies for internal governance of the council. The Executive and Planning Committee directs and oversees the conduct of business and operating procedures of the Judicial Council and the AOC, oversees the implementation of the council's long-range strategic plan, develops and conducts the council's annual planning sessions, ensures that the judicial branch budget is tied to the long-range plan, and serves as the nominating committee for vacancies on the Judicial Council and advisory bodies.

The Rules and Projects Committee oversees the advisory bodies and development of proposed rules of court, standards of judicial administration, and statewide forms for use in court proceedings.

The Policy Coordination and Liaison Committee represents the Judicial Council with other branches of government and the State Bar, oversees the progress of legislation sponsored by the Judicial Council, and formulates and advocates policy positions on proposed legislation.

The Litigation Committee monitors lawsuits involving the courts, judges, or court personnel.

Advisory Committees and Task Forces

Although the standing committee structure was simplified, the universe of advisory entities expanded. At the close of the century, the relationship between the advisory committees and task forces and the Judicial Council was described as follows: "To provide leadership for advancing the consistent, impartial, independent, and accessible administration of justice, the Judicial Council must be aware of the issues and concerns confronting the judiciary, as well as appropriate solutions and responses. The council carries out this mission primarily through the work of its advisory committees and task forces."[9]

As the 1900s ended, there were twenty-eight of these advisory bodies with more than 300 persons serving on them. Membership is by application or nomination, review and recommendation of the Executive and Planning Committee, and appointment by the Chief Justice. In 1999 alone, more than 600 persons were considered for such appointments. In addition to subject matter expertise, Chief Justice George, with assistance from the Executive and Planning Committee, considers gender, racial, geographic, and professional diversity in selecting advisory body members. (While this statement of procedure and the following list of entities were current at the time of writing, it is anticipated that both will be regularly reviewed and revised by the committee, Chief Justice, or council.)

These twenty-eight entities are divided into two categories. Advisory committees are responsible for monitoring specified areas of continuing significance and making advisory recommendations to the Judicial Council. Task forces are responsible for particular projects or proposals.

The Administrative Office of the Courts: A Forty-Year Snapshot

Birth of an Institution

From its creation in 1926 until 1960, the Judicial Council enjoyed few resources beyond the knowledge and prestige of its members. By 1950, several attorneys and a statistical staff were available for routine assistance, but that was the extent of support. The council lacked the capacity to conduct large-scale research on a regular basis, oversee ongoing programs, or be extensively involved in external relationships with such organizations as bar associations, the legislature, and executive branch departments such as the Department of Finance.

Two notable exceptions, previously described, occurred when the legislature in the 1940s requested the Judicial Council to study and present recommendations regarding judicial review of decisions by administrative agencies and to do the same regarding lower court reorganization. These were substantial endeavors for which special, temporary staffing was arranged. These were, however, ad hoc exceptions rather than the rule.

The Judicial Council's restricted capacity was not lost on Chief Justice Gibson nor was he willing to accept this and various other aspects of the status quo. In an effort closely orchestrated with the legislature, Chief Justice Gibson led the way in promulgation of a revision of the judicial article of the California Constitution, an effort that began with Judicial Council discussions in 1953 and culminated in 1960.[10]

Six amendments were proposed by the council in 1959 as part of the revision of article VI of the constitution. The major parts of the revision as proposed by the Judicial Council expanded council membership and added representatives from the State Bar and legislature; granted to the council control over rules of practice and procedure; created the position of Administrative Director of the Courts; provided for assignment of retired judges, with their consent, to any level of court; expanded the already-existing Commission on Qualifications and renamed it the Commission on Judicial

continued on page 62

Advisory Committees

ADMINISTRATIVE PRESIDING JUSTICES ADVISORY COMMITTEE, TRIAL COURT PRESIDING JUDGES ADVISORY COMMITTEE, AND COURT EXECUTIVES ADVISORY COMMITTEE

Membership in these committees is determined by the positions of the members: administrative presiding justices of the courts of appeal, presiding judges of the superior courts, and executive officers of the superior courts, respectively. These committees strengthen access to and participation in the Judicial Council decision-making process by reviewing rules, forms, standards, studies, and recommendations relating to court administration that are proposed to the council by advisory committees or task forces; identifying issues of concern to the courts, including legislative issues, that might be addressed by the council or its advisory committees or task forces; and improving communication with the council. Membership in these committees is determined by the positions of the members: administrative presiding justices of the courts of appeal, presiding judges of the superior courts, and executive officers of the superior courts, respectively. These committees strengthen access to and participation in the Judicial Council decision-making process by reviewing rules, forms, standards, studies, and recommendations relating to court administration that are proposed to the council by advisory committees or task forces; identifying issues of concern to the courts, including legislative issues, that might be addressed by the council or its advisory committees or task forces; and improving communication with the council.

ACCESS AND FAIRNESS ADVISORY COMMITTEE

This committee monitors issues and proposes policy direction related to access to the judicial system and fairness. The committee's five subcommittees address racial and ethnic fairness, sexual orientation fairness, gender fairness, and access for persons with disabilities, as well as education and implementation.

APPELLATE ADVISORY COMMITTEE

Representing the appellate courts, this committee advises the Judicial Council on matters relating to procedures, forms, standards, practices, and operations.

CIVIL AND SMALL CLAIMS ADVISORY COMMITTEE

This committee identifies issues and suggests solutions regarding civil procedure, practice, and case management, including small claims.

COURT INTERPRETERS ADVISORY PANEL

This panel works to improve the number and quality of interpreters in the courts and advises the Judicial Council on standards, training, and legislation.

Appointments; provided for approval of gubernatorial appointees to municipal and superior courts by the renamed Commission on Judicial Appointments; created a new mechanism for removal of judges by the Supreme Court on recommendation of a new entity to be called the Commission on Judicial Qualifications; created a new path for review of inferior court decisions; and made the State Bar a constitutional entity.[11]

The specific proposal regarding governance and resources for the Judicial Council added a new constitutional provision: "The Council may appoint an administrative director of the courts, who shall hold office at its pleasure and shall perform such of the duties of the council and of its chairman, other than to adopt or amend rules of practice and procedure, as may be delegated to him."[12]

In support, the Judicial Council cited the fact that the federal government and at least ten other states had created administrative director positions for courts.[13] The council argued its position to the legislature and governor.

> The need for an Administrative Director of a court system as large as that of California is self-evident. Working under the direction of the Judicial Council and its committees, he would be of great assistance in maintaining an efficiently operating judicial system and in freeing the Council Chairman from a mass of administrative detail. He would be in a position to direct research, statistical, and assignment functions for the Council and the Chairman, assist the committees of the Council, and represent the Council in cooperative work with the State Bar and other organizations.[14]

This and several other components of the Judicial Council proposal were approved by the legislature and appeared as Proposition 10 on the ballot of the general election held on November 8, 1960. There was no opposing argument in the voter pamphlet, and the supporting argument by Senators Edwin J. Regan and Joseph A. Rattigan asserted that the amendment strengthened the Judicial Council by authorizing "it to appoint a Court Administrator to supervise the administrative work of the courts. Some 18 other States and the Federal Government have learned that such a Court Administrator performs an important function in increasing the efficiency of the courts and equalizing the workload of the judges."[15] Proposition 10 was approved by the voters.

Following creation of the position of Administrative Director of the Courts in 1960, Judicial Council funding was supplemented in 1961 by the legislature to provide resources for the establishment of the Administrative Office of the Courts.

continued on page 64

Advisory Committees

COURT TECHNOLOGY ADVISORY COMMITTEE

This committee promotes, coordinates, and facilitates the application of technology to the work of the courts, including standards for technological compatibility; proposed rules, standards, or legislation to ensure privacy, access, and security; and assistance for the courts in acquiring and developing useful technology systems.

CRIMINAL LAW ADVISORY COMMITTEE

The charge of this committee is to identify issues and suggest solutions regarding criminal procedure, practice, and case management.

FAMILY AND JUVENILE LAW ADVISORY COMMITTEE

In a similar fashion, this committee identifies issues and suggests solutions regarding procedure, practice, and case management for cases involving marriage, family, or children.

GOVERNING COMMITTEE OF THE CENTER FOR JUDICIAL EDUCATION AND RESEARCH (CJER)

The governing committee determines and administers the operating policies, funding, staffing, and programs of the Center for Judicial Education and Research and makes recommendations to the Judicial Council or California Judges Association for action.

TRAFFIC ADVISORY COMMITTEE

This committee works toward improving adjudication of traffic and bail-forfeitable offenses and recommends rules or model procedures to promote statewide consistency in processing.

TRIAL COURT BUDGET COMMISSION

In the all-important area of budgeting, the commission develops annual trial court budget requests to the governor and the legislature and allocates and reallocates state funds appropriated for the operation of the trial courts.

TRIAL COURT COORDINATION ADVISORY COMMITTEE

This committee reviews and makes policy recommendations regarding trial court coordination issues, including reviewing for the Judicial Council the progress of coordination implementation and coordination plans for the trial courts.

At the December 8, 1961, meeting of the Judicial Council, the following resolution was adopted:

> *Be It Resolved* that, pursuant to the authority vested in it by the Constitution of the State of California, the Judicial Council does hereby delegate authority to the Administrative Director of the California Courts, under the supervision of the chairman, to employ, organize, and direct a staff which shall be known as the Administrative Office of the California Courts and which shall be operated as the staff agency to assist the Council and its chairman in carrying out their duties under the Constitution and laws of the State.[16]

Leaders

From creation of the position in 1960 until 2000, four persons served as Administrative Director of the Courts. Similar to the varied backgrounds of the incumbent Chief Justices during this period, each Administrative Director brought to the position a unique background and assets.

Ralph N. Kleps was appointed by the Judicial Council as the first Administrative Director in November 1961. Mr. Kleps was no stranger either to government service or to the Judicial Council. He had interrupted his law practice in 1943, at the request of Chief Justice Gibson, to temporarily serve as the Judicial Council's research director overseeing the survey of administrative procedure requested by the legislature—one of the exceptional occasions when Judicial Council resources were enhanced. That survey led to the creation of the state Office of Administrative Procedure and Mr. Kleps was selected to serve as the first director, which he did for five years, until in 1950 he was appointed legislative counsel. He served for eleven years until he became the first Administrative Director of the Courts. A small but interesting facet of Mr. Kleps's selection is the fact that, as legislative counsel, he was one of the officials responsible for preparation of voter pamphlets. The last voter pamphlet to bear his name is the one for November 1960 containing Proposition 10, which created his new position. During his sixteen-year tenure as Administrative Director, he served with Chief Justices Gibson, Traynor, Wright, and Bird, retiring in 1977 shortly after Chief Justice Bird assumed office.

Chief Justice Bird appointed Ralph J. Gampell as the second Administrative Director. Mr. Gampell, a native of Great Britain and a physician, also was a member of the California Bar, practicing in San Jose. He was serving as president of the State Bar when appointed Administrative Director in 1977. Mr. Gampell retired following the election in 1986 at which Chief Justice Bird was not retained in office.

continued on page 66

Task Forces

APPELLATE INDIGENT DEFENSE OVERSIGHT ADVISORY COMMITTEE

This is really a task force though it is named an advisory committee. It develops recommendations and administers programs to ensure adequate assistance of counsel to indigent defendants in criminal cases.

APPELLATE MEDIATION TASK FORCE

This task force oversees an experimental mediation program in the Court of Appeal, First Appellate District.

APPELLATE PROCESS TASK FORCE

Also concerned with the appellate courts, this task force recommends ways to enhance the efficiency of the appellate process with emphasis on court organizational structures, workflow, and technological innovations.

BENCH-BAR PRO BONO PROJECT

The project works to increase pro bono activity by attorneys by educating the bar and the judiciary about the crisis in legal services funding, developing proposals to deal with the growing numbers of pro per litigants, identifying ways the judiciary can encourage pro bono work, and studying other models for system changes to streamline processing of legal services cases.

COMMUNITY-FOCUSED COURT PLANNING IMPLEMENTATION COMMITTEE

This task force links planning and budget development, provides a clearinghouse of planning resources, oversees compliance with grant requirements, and supports efforts to institutionalize community outreach programs in the courts.

COMPLEX CIVIL LITIGATION TASK FORCE

The responsibility of this task force is to work to improve management of complex cases by defining complex litigation, helping to identify complex cases, preparing a resource manual to help state judges, and recommending appropriate amendments to statutes and the California Rules of Court to permit flexible management of complex cases.

EXECUTIVE LEGISLATIVE ACTION NETWORK

The network solicits and forwards the views of judges and court administrators about legislative or policy issues, communicates the Judicial Council's position on legislative and policy issues, and establishes and maintains a local network of judges and court staff who are responsible for ongoing relationships with legislators and their staffs to ensure the ability of the judiciary to communicate council positions in a coordinated, timely manner.

Shortly following the oath of office by Chief Justice Lucas in February 1987, William E. Davis was appointed Administrative Director by the Judicial Council. Mr. Davis also was a member of the California Bar and, like Ralph Kleps, was no stranger to the Judicial Council, having served under Mr. Kleps as a staff attorney at the AOC from 1973 to 1975. During the time between his initial employment with the AOC and his return, Mr. Davis served as the director of the Administrative Office of the Courts in his home state of Kentucky (1975–1979). In addition, between his service in Kentucky and his appointment as Administrative Director in California, Mr. Davis served as circuit executive of the U.S. Court of Appeals for the Ninth Circuit in San Francisco (1981–1986). With his return to the AOC, he became one of the pioneers in judicial administration with experience as the administrative head of court systems in more than one state. He resigned in 1991.

Following a nationwide search, the Judicial Council announced in 1992 the appointment of William C. Vickrey as the fourth Administrative Director of the Courts and the first non-attorney to be appointed. Previously, Mr. Vickrey's career had been in the Utah justice system. When appointed by the Judicial Council of California, he was serving as the state court administrator of Utah, so Mr. Vickrey also brought to bear the rare qualification of having served as the chief executive of another state court system. While in Utah and prior to becoming the state court administrator, Mr. Vickrey had worked extensively in youth and adult corrections and was serving as director of the Department of Adult Corrections when he accepted his appointment with the Utah court system.

Mr. Vickrey served during the remaining tenure of Chief Justice Lucas, continued following the appointment of Chief Justice George, and was the incumbent Administrative Director as the century closed.

Organization

Prior to establishment of the AOC, the Judicial Council, as described above, had maintained a statistical staff to collect, analyze, and report statewide court data. For approximately twenty years, the council also had a legal research staff dealing primarily with changes in rules and proposed constitutional or statutory amendments. When the AOC was established, this staff consisted of eighteen persons divided about equally among legal, statistical, and clerical functions.

At the threshold, Administrative Director Kleps reorganized this staff "in accordance with principles which have proved themselves in other areas of government, and its structure will resemble other major departments of

continued on page 68

Task Forces

TASK FORCE ON JURY INSTRUCTIONS

This task force concentrates on drafting jury instructions that accurately state the law and are understandable by jurors.

TASK FORCE ON JURY SYSTEM IMPROVEMENTS

Also concerned with the jury system, this task force encourages excellence by conducting a pilot project to screen jurors before their arrival and studying improved one-day or one-trial implementation, one-step summons processes, a statewide jury list, and a jury orientation video.

OVERSIGHT COMMITTEE FOR THE CALIFORNIA DRUG COURT PROJECT

This committee oversees the California Drug Court Project, which encourages the development of drug courts in the state.

PROBATE AND MENTAL HEALTH TASK FORCE

The duty of this task force is to assist with probate and mental health issues in the courts, including developing proposed uniform statewide probate rules and revising the *Handbook for Conservators.*

TASK FORCE ON THE QUALITY OF JUSTICE: SUBCOMMITTEE ON ALTERNATIVE DISPUTE RESOLUTION AND THE JUDICIAL SYSTEM

This task force was made up of two subcommittees. This subcommittee studies and makes recommendations on the effect of the increasing use of private alternative dispute resolution procedures; ethical standards governing retired judges, attorneys, and nonattorneys acting as arbitrators and mediators; and standards governing the referral of disputes by courts to private judges or attorneys.

TASK FORCE ON THE QUALITY OF JUSTICE: SUBCOMMITTEE ON THE QUALITY OF JUDICIAL SERVICE

This subcommittee addresses and makes recommendations to ensure that judges remain on the bench for full careers, older judges who are healthy and fit have the option to remain on the bench, judges who are no longer fully able to serve retire at an appropriate time, and highly qualified attorneys from all areas of legal practice are attracted to judicial service.

state government."[17] Characterizing the Judicial Council as a policymaking board of directors, Mr. Kleps characterized himself as equivalent to the director of a department of state government with a deputy director to supervise the legal staff, an assistant director to supervise research and statistics, and an assistant director for management.[18]

Approximately fifteen years later, the staff had grown to forty persons with more interdisciplinary diversity: lawyers, statisticians, management analysts, business officers, and researchers. This expanded staff continued to operate under a deputy director and two assistant directors. The major management change in the intervening years was the addition of a third assistant director for legislation. The budget was $12 million per year with an additional infusion of $2 million in federal funds used for court-related projects.[19]

The AOC maintained communications with the Chief Justice that were "daily, if not hourly, occurrences."[20] The AOC also furnished all staffing for Judicial Council committees, which at the time consisted of Executive, Appellate Court, Superior Court, Court Management, and Municipal and Justice Courts Committees. In addition, there was a growing number of advisory committees.[21]

Although the size of the AOC staff had grown from eighteen to forty members during the years since establishment of the AOC in 1961, it is interesting to note that the dozen or so professional positions as of 1961 had increased to only fifteen by 1974.[22]

By the end of the century, major growth had occurred, leading the AOC to note that its "staff of 408 provides varying levels of services to approximately 20,000 judges and judicial branch employees of the trial and appellate courts in more than 75 courts at over 390 locations. . . . AOC staff work with 15 Judicial Council advisory committees and 13 task forces, with more than 600 representatives from the courts and bar helping the council to shape policies and create programs to address the many challenges facing the California court system in the 21st century."[23]

At the close of the century there were, in addition to the Administrative Director, a deputy director and four major departments with external focuses: the Trial Court Services Division, the Education Division, the Council and Legal Services Division, and the Office of Governmental Affairs. Internally, the support services for the AOC, appellate courts, and increasingly the trial courts included the Human Resources Bureau, the Information Systems Bureau, the Finance Bureau, the Administrative Support Unit, the Office of Court Security, and Appellate Court Services.[24]

Trial Court Governance

If the judicial branch of government is history's stepchild, the trial courts are history's orphans. This is not to say that governance of the trial courts is unimportant. Indeed, it arguably comes closer than state-level governance to the public served by the judicial system. Nonetheless, two facts are inescapable. First, reliable information regarding administration at the trial court level is scattered, anecdotal, episodic, or nonexistent. Second, for much of the era from 1950 to 2000 the trial courts of California operated autonomously with relative freedom from interference or direction by the Judicial Council. Little of trial court stewardship during this period has been documented. Of course it is known that the presiding judge, often assisted by an executive or other governing committee, was the centerpiece of governance, but beyond that the picture is rather opaque.

Having said that, it is equally important to acknowledge that administration of the trial courts exploded during the latter part of the century in both quality and quantity. There was not a single trial court administrator in California until the year 1957 when the Los Angeles Superior Court created the position of administrator, beating the Judicial Council to the proverbial punch three years prior to creation of the position of Administrative Director of the Courts at the state level. Between that time and the end of the century, every superior court and most courts of limited jurisdiction with multiple judgeships acquired administrators or executive officers. By the end of the century, every trial court jurisdiction had such a position.

Generalizations are risky in a state as diverse as California, particularly with a long and strong tradition of local variations. Nonetheless, it seems safe to observe that the trial court judges, acting collectively or by committee, have firmly retained control over local policy and procedure. The permissible and accepted nonjudicial administrative functions performed in trial courts by the executive officers may be generalized:

> In courts having an executive officer or court administrator selected by the judges of the court and under the direction of the presiding judge, the officer or administrator shall. . . .
> (1) supervise the court's staff and . . . draft for court approval and administer a court approved personnel plan or merit system for court-appointed employees, which may be the same as the county personnel plan, that provides for wage and job classification, recruitment, selection, training, promotion, discipline, and removal of employees of the court;
> (2) prepare and implement court budgets, including accounting, payroll, and financial controls;

(3) negotiate contracts;

(4) supervise and employ efficient calendar and caseflow management, including analyzing and evaluating pending caseloads and recommending effective calendar management techniques;

(5) analyze, evaluate, and implement automated systems to assist the court;

(6) manage the jury system in the most cost effective way;

(7) support and encourage court participation in community outreach activities to increase public understanding of and involvement with the justice system and to obtain appropriate community input regarding the administration of justice . . . ;

(8) plan physical space needs, and purchase and manage equipment and supplies;

(9) act as a clearing house for news releases and other publications for the media and public;

(10) create and manage uniform recordkeeping systems, collecting data on pending and completed judicial business and the internal operation of the court, as required by the court and the Judicial Council;

(11) identify problems, recommending procedural and administrative changes to the court;

(12) act as a liaison to other governmental agencies;

(13) act as staff for judicial committees; and

(14) perform other duties as the court directs.[25]

Notes

1   California Constitution (1950), article VI, section 1a.

2   California Constitution, article VI, section 6.

3   California Constitution (1959), article VI, section 1a.

4   Judicial Council of California, *Seventeenth Biennial Report [of the] Judicial Council of California to the Governor and the Legislature* (1959), p. 15.

5   Id., pp. 15–16.

6   California Constitution, article VI, section 6.

7   Ibid.

8   Judicial Council of California, *Nineteenth Biennial Report to the Governor and the Legislature* (1963), p. 6.

9   Judicial Council of California, California Courts Web site, *www.courtinfo.ca.gov /courtadmin/jc/advisorycommittees.htm.*

10   See, for example, Judicial Council of California, minutes (October 6, 1953), pp. 1–2.

11   Judicial Council of California, *Seventeenth Biennial Report* (1959), pp. 15–26.

12   California Constitution (1960), article VI, section 1a.

13   Judicial Council of California, *Seventeenth Biennial Report* (1959), p. 18, n. 17.

14   Id., pp. 18–19.

15   Senators Edwin J. Regan and Joseph A. Rattigan, Argument in Favor of Proposition 10, Senate Constitutional Amendment No. 14, submitted to California voters on November 8, 1960.

16   Judicial Council of California, minutes (December 8, 1961).

17   Ralph N. Kleps, "The Judicial Council and the Administrative Office of the California Courts," *Journal of the State Bar of California* 37 (1962), p. 333.

18   Id., pp. 333–35.

19   Ralph N. Kleps, "Courts, State Court Management and Lawyers," *California State Bar Journal* 50 (1975), p. 47.

20 Id., p. 48.

21 Id., p. 49. Advisory committees in 1974 included Selective Publication of Appellate Court Opinions, Superior Court Judges Sentencing Institute, Fair Trial and Free Press, Comparative Study of ABA Standards of Criminal Justice, Superior Court Calendar Management Workshop, Institute for Juvenile Court Judges and Referees, Municipal Court Calendar Management Workshop, Judicial Reporting of Criminal Statistics, Judicial Weighted Caseload Study, National Center for State Courts' Court of Appeal Study, Master-Individual Calendar Study, Branch Court/Nonjudicial Staffing Study, and Governing Committee of the Center for Judicial Education and Research; Judicial Council of California, *Annual Report to the Governor and Legislature* (1974), pp. 6–7.

22 Judicial Council of California, *Annual Report of the Administrative Office of the California Courts* (1974), p. 70.

23 Administrative Office of the Courts, *People and Programs* (July 2000), section 3-1.

24 Administrative Office of the Courts, *A Guide to AOC People and Programs* (1999), section 4-3.

25 California Rules of Court, rule 207.

Chapter 4
The Dynamics of Governing the Judicial System

Overview

 uring the 1940s the Judicial Council began to establish itself as a problem solver. This budding reputation was enhanced by sweeping reform of the courts of limited jurisdiction in 1950 as proposed by the Judicial Council, passed by the California Legislature, advocated by the Chief Justice, and approved by the voters.

The Administrative Office of the Courts (AOC), founded in 1961, promptly established itself as the administrative arm of the Judicial Council, responsible for implementing policies adopted by the Judicial Council and assisting with the council's constitutional duties including simplifying and improving the administration of justice.

In addition to crafting solutions to specific problems, the council and AOC were drawn into planning in the governance process. A major instigator was the federal government through the Law Enforcement Assistance Administration (LEAA), created in the late 1960s and endowed with substantial funds for grants to state and local government.

This external introduction of planning among California's courts was followed by voluntary Judicial Council and AOC use of contingency planning in the 1970s, annual planning in the 1980s, and futures planning in the early 1990s. All of these strengthened and deepened the dynamics of governance.

Strategic planning by both the Judicial Council and the AOC moved governance to a new level by the late 1990s. Forging, revising, and committing to missions for the council, courts, and AOC were the heart of this undertaking. The missions were reinforced by major goals, guiding principles, and steps toward implementation.

The role, size, and organization of the AOC have been transformed to fulfill its original responsibility for implementation of council policy, as well as new responsibilities flowing from unification of the trial courts and state funding of the courts.

*T*he institutions of governance tell an important story. The creation of the AOC and the expansion and refinement of the Judicial Council's superstructure are vital pieces of justice administration from 1950 to 2000.

Equally impressive are the dynamics of governance during this period. The judicial branch evolved from a passive and reactive entity to a responsive and proactive entity. By century's end the Judicial Council, in tandem with the AOC, had crafted a vision for the judicial branch and reinforced it with articulated missions, strategic goals, and plans for implementation. Initial links were forged to tie allocation of resources to mission fulfillment and goal achievement. In effect, the foundation was laid for self-governance within our system of separate but interdependent branches of government. The judicial branch, for the first time really, was charting its own course rather than following an itinerary and map thrust upon it.

The 1950s: The Judicial Council Emerges as a Problem Solver

For the first quarter-century following its creation in 1926, the Judicial Council was diligent in its efforts. Judge Harry A. Hollzer's 1929 report to the Judicial Council on the business of California courts is a good example, but it also is a good example of the reactive posture of the judiciary.[1] The effort probably never would have been undertaken at the time but for the constitutional mandate directing the newly created Judicial Council to "survey the condition of business in the several courts" coupled with the requirement to "report to the Governor and Legislature at the commencement of each regular session."[2]

Although still reactive, the role of the Judicial Council began to change subtly in the 1940s, culminating in the 1950 reorganization of the courts of limited jurisdiction. This event is explored in detail in Chapter Five, but it is important here because it illustrates the emerging role of the Judicial Council as a problem solver. While it is true that the Judicial Council undertook examination of the so-called lower courts at the direct request of the legislature and thus was in a reactive posture, the greater truth is that the Judicial Council with very meager resources rose to the occasion with a solution that was bold for the time. This established credibility as a problem-solving resource, which was reinforced by the active part played by Chief Justice Phil S. Gibson in developing public support for approval of the constitutional amendment needed to implement the solution.

During the latter part of the 1950s, the Judicial Council enlarged its role as a repository for problems and a source of solutions by preparing for consideration by the legislature and governor a proposed revision of the judicial article of the state constitution. This was still a reactive endeavor since it was undertaken in large part at the legislature's request, but it established an important precedent for favorable consideration of major institutional change initiated by the Judicial Council.

From a governance perspective, the most important of these changes, by far, was creation of the position of the Administrative Director of the Courts, which in turn led to establishment of the Administrative Office of the Courts. The addition of that vital resource to the policymaking capacity of the Judicial Council is the story of the decade, beginning in 1960.

This achievement was consistent with the observation that "when Chief Justice Phil Gibson began his term in 1940, the Judicial Council was essentially an untapped resource for purposes of both central administration of the courts and reform of the judicial system. . . . Under Gibson, the Council began a methodical overhaul of the judicial system, using powers that had been at its disposal since 1926."[3]

The 1960s: The Administrative Office of the Courts Is Created as a Resource

The story of the Administrative Office of the Courts begins with the creation of the position of Administrative Director of the Courts, who, at the outset in 1960, had only such "duties . . . as may be delegated to him" by the Judicial Council or chairman.[4] That was significantly clarified a year later when the Judicial Council appointed Ralph N. Kleps to the position and shortly thereafter delegated to him authority to establish the AOC "to assist the Council and its chairman in carrying out their duties. . . ."[5]

The initial scope of AOC activity was expressed as follows by Administrative Director Kleps: "[T]he range of activity and interest for the new Administrative Office of the Courts is as broad as the authority vested in the Judicial Council itself."[6] Within that range, this was the governing operational principle articulated at the time:

> The major point which should be made in connection with the creation of an Administrative Office is that, for the first time, the Judicial Council and its chairman have available to them the vital *power to delegate*. In the absence of such a power to delegate duties it is apparent that only general decisions, involving primarily

broad policy questions, could result from the Council's deliberations. The use of a qualified staff as agents to carry out the details of Council policy is the important new factor in the establishment of an Administrative Office of the Courts.[7]

The importance of this new power to delegate was poignantly underscored in 1951 when all members of the Judicial Council, prior to having an Administrative Director, concurred in "the view that the Chairman [Chief Justice] had done an amazing job in connection with the preparation, passage and effectuation of Proposition 3" (relating to lower court reorganization) and suggested "that the Chairman, in the interests of his health, should cut down on the amount of work he has been doing."[8]

Administrative Director Kleps further answered the rhetorical question "How is the administrative office related to the Judicial Council itself?" by stating that "[c]reation of an Administrative Office of the Courts means that there is now an administrative arm for the Council, through which continuous and effective action can be taken to carry out the policies adopted by the Council. Its work in the field of legal and statistical research will continue, and at an increased tempo, but those efforts will be followed by staff action to implement both the rules and policies adopted by the Council for the improvement of judicial administration and statutes adopted by the Legislature in that field."[9]

This meant, from the outset, that the mission as envisioned by the first Administrative Director of the Courts, presumably with concurrence by Chief Justice Gibson, was for the AOC to engage, on behalf of the Judicial Council, in surveying "the condition of business in the several courts with a view to simplifying and improving the administration of justice . . ."; submitting "suggestions to the several courts as may seem in the interest of uniformity and the expedition of business . . ."; reporting "to the Governor and Legislature . . . such recommendations as it may deem proper . . ."; submitting to the legislature the Judicial Council's "recommendations with reference to amendments of, or changes in, existing laws relating to practice and procedures . . ."; and supporting the Judicial Council's adoption of "rules of practice and procedure for the several courts. . . ."[10]

It is clear that the major focus of the AOC during the 1960s was direct support of and reporting to the Chief Justice and Judicial Council. Administrative Director Kleps noted with pride in the mid-1970s that "[a]ll staff work, except routine correspondence, is approved by one or more of these [Council] committees before it sees the light of day. 'Not for release' is stamped on every piece of staff work and on most committee reports until after Council approval is obtained. Even then, the Judicial Council's standard practice is to give tentative approval to committee work, leaving a six-month period for distribution and comment prior to final action."[11]

All of this began to expand as the phenomenon of planning was thrust upon the courts, beginning late in the 1960s and continuing throughout the 1970s.

Another interesting development pertaining to both the Judicial Council and governance occurred during the 1960s. The mandate to adopt rules for "court administration" was inferred during the Judicial Council's formative years but made explicit by the Constitution Revision Commission recommendations in 1966.[12] Another noteworthy change effected by the 1966 revision involved the "administration of justice." As originally enacted, this phrase appeared in connection only with the Judicial Council's obligation to "survey the condition of business in the several courts with a view to simplifying and improving the administration of justice."[13] However, the Constitution Revision Commission made this the guiding imperative by providing that the Judicial Council in performing all its mandated duties should do so "to improve the administration of justice."[14]

The 1970s: Planning Comes to the Courts

The governance story of this decade revolves around planning. During the latter part of the last century, various planning mechanisms that had existed for some time in the private and other governmental sectors migrated to the courts: annual plans, strategic plans, planning by objectives, contingency planning, crisis planning, master plans, and future planning with multiple variations of each one. They in turn spawned galaxies of goals, objectives, tasks, scenarios, preferred futures, and action plans, to name but a few.

By the year 2000, examples of most, and perhaps all, variations of planning existed in court contexts throughout the nation.[15] Nonetheless, planning within individual courts or court systems is a recent phenomenon. Moreover, the stimulus to engage in planning was primarily external to the courts, and it all began around 1970.

The most explicit external nudge began in the late 1960s and came from the federal government. The vehicle generally was the federal war on crime, and the specific vehicle was the Omnibus Crime Control and Safe Streets Act of 1968.[16] Before delving into this legislation and its consequences, it will be useful to consider conditions in California and other state courts at the time of enactment.

The Judicial Council's posture of reactive problem solver was very much in the mainstream of other state courts systems and certainly was in tune with that of local courts in California, which also tended to focus on specific problems.[17]

Following establishment of the Administrative Office of the Courts in 1961, the scope and pace of problem solving accelerated, but planning was not an explicit part of AOC activities, either on its own or in support of the Judicial Council. This fact brings us, the California court system, and the state courts of the nation to the federal response to crime. War was declared by Congress and President Lyndon B. Johnson in 1968 through the Safe Streets Act.

It is necessary to tell the story of this federal program in fair detail because it lays the foundation for the story of court planning and its impact on governance in California and elsewhere. The concerns, objectives, and strategies were disclosed with surprising clarity in the "Declarations and Purpose" section of Title I of the Safe Streets Act.

Congress finds that the high incidence of crime in the United States threatens the peace, security, and general welfare of the Nation and its citizens. To prevent crime and to insure the greater safety of the people, law enforcement efforts must be better coordinated, intensified, and made more effective at all levels of government.

Congress finds further that crime is essentially a local problem that must be dealt with by State and local governments if it is to be controlled effectively.

It is therefore the declared policy of the Congress to assist State and local governments in strengthening and improving law enforcement at every level by national assistance. It is the purpose of this title to (1) encourage States and units of general local government *to prepare and adopt comprehensive plans based upon their evaluation of State and local problems of law enforcement;* (2) authorize grants to States and units of local government in order to improve and strengthen law enforcement; and (3) encourage research and development directed toward the improvement of law enforcement and the development of new methods for the prevention and reduction of crime and the detection and apprehension of criminals. [Emphasis added.][18]

The mechanism was federal money to be distributed through and by a new agency, the Law Enforcement Assistance Administration, established in the U.S. Department of Justice. At the core of the program were annual block grants to be made by the LEAA to each state with the statutory requirement that a substantial percentage of the funds be passed through to local units of government.[19] To receive and administer these block grants, each state was called upon to create a state planning agency (SPA) within the executive branch of government.

In practice, each state created a criminal justice council served by its SPA. Together they were responsible for developing and approving comprehensive, statewide criminal justice plans and distributing the federal funds by grants to other entities within state and local government.

California was ahead of the curve. In 1967, in anticipation of the federal funding legislation, the legislature created the California Council on Criminal Justice (CCCJ). As originally enacted, there were twenty-five members.[20] The composition of the CCCJ set or at least shared the national pattern of heavily weighting the compositions of the criminal justice councils in favor of law enforcement and corrections agencies with nominal, if any, representation from the courts.

The legislature empowered the CCCJ to develop crime-related plans and encouraged coordination among law enforcement and criminal justice agencies, but its true mission as a receptacle for federal funds was clearly revealed: "[T]he council may develop plans to fulfill the requirements of any federal act providing for the adoption of comprehensive plans to facilitate the receipt and allocation of federal funds for planning, research, demonstration and special project grants."[21]

Subsequent to the creation of the CCCJ, the legislature established the California version of the SPA, titled the Office of Criminal Justice Planning (OCJP). The executive director was appointed by, responsible to, and served at the pleasure of the governor. The director's primary duty was developing, with the advice and approval of the CCCJ, "the comprehensive statewide plan for the improvement of criminal justice throughout the state."[22]

Over the life of the LEAA the federal government distributed hundreds of millions of dollars. When the federal funds began to flow from the LEAA to California and the CCCJ, they rapidly grew from $2.4 million in 1968 to $46.5 million in 1972.

Planning clearly was an explicit theme in both the Safe Streets Act and the California statutes creating the CCCJ and the OCJP. Indeed, without an approved statewide criminal justice plan, neither California nor any other state would have secured LEAA funds. As stated at the time by a recent official of the U.S. Department of Justice, federal "funds must be wisely and effectively used. . . . One way to ensure this proper utilization of funds is to insist on thorough planning."[23]

Reactions among state court officials in the early days of the LEAA ranged from indifference at one end of the spectrum to the Chief Justice of one state at the other end, who this author remembers hearing crusade against permitting "the federal eagle to scream above state courthouses."

Several realities emerged that changed the dynamics. State courts, with rare exceptions, were receiving little or none of the LEAA money. Even in states where the judicial system at the state level or individual courts were willing to compete for and accept federal money, they were not permitted to share significantly in the financial bonanza. The first reason was they were dealing with an executive branch agency. The second reason was the voting membership of the criminal justice councils, which, for the most part, heavily favored police and related law enforcement agencies. The final reason was that the LEAA had unilaterally and arbitrarily defined "courts" to include prosecutor and defense functions with the result that a grant, for example, to expand the number of prosecutors was classified as benefiting courts. California was no exception in any of these realities.

Another reality soon caught up with both the LEAA and the state criminal justice councils and state planning agencies. State plans were required to be "comprehensive" in order to achieve LEAA approval and release of funds. This meant that state plans had to include courts. Judicial institutions, however, had little incentive to participate in the development of plans since in their view they were not being given a place at the banquet table or a fair share of the federal block grants.

Reality was reinforced by principles that were well summarized by the resolution of the Conference of State Chief Justices in 1973:

1. It is incompatible with, and injurious to, the traditional common-law role of the state judiciary for it to compete before an agency of the executive branch for its "rightful" share of federal block grant funds.

2. For different courts or levels of courts in a state judicial system to be in competition for federal block grant funds, with such competition to be decided by an agency of the executive branch, is destructive of the dignity of the judiciary and inimical to its improve-ment and to the public interest.

3. Present and proposed programs of federal assistance to state courts should require that some appropriate percentage of a state's block grant funds be allocated directly to the judiciary, as distinct from law enforcement, prosecution, defense, corrections, or other criminal justice components; and that funds so allocated be expended in accordance with a plan developed and programs approved by the Supreme Court or other judicial entity of the state with rulemaking powers or administrative responsibility for the state's judicial system.

4. Provisions in present and proposed programs for federal financial assistance to state courts which restrict or limit the amount of a state's block grant funds which can be spent for personnel or which require a percentage of such funds to be spent by local units of government, unnecessarily impede and are inimical to the improvement of the judicial system of a state. . . . [24]

An additional reality was that the LEAA could not restrain itself to oversight. The impulse to direct and control proved irresistible.

In the early days, LEAA officials recognized there were "almost no validated models of good comprehensive planning in crime control."[25] In addition, the federal role was described as "advisory," and it was stated that "a dominant purpose of comprehensive criminal-justice planning is to permit jurisdictions to select, adapt, and apply general measures and con-cepts of improvement to the context and needs of a particular state, city, or metropolitan area."[26] That was in 1968 and near the dawn of the LEAA.

It took only three years for the LEAA to abandon self-restraint and local discretion. On October 20, 1971, the administrator of the LEAA created the National Advisory Commission on Criminal Justice Standards and Goals with the mandate "to formulate . . . national criminal justice standards and goals for crime reduction and prevention at state and local levels."[27] In other words, federal strings were being woven and would soon be affixed to state block grants and pulled.

This commission produced six reports on various components of the criminal justice system, including a volume on courts, which was released in January 1973. In considerable detail, the commission set standards for how criminal cases should flow, including screening, diversion, and negotiated pleas. Other aspects of criminal justice also were addressed in similar detail, such as the size and composition of the jury, sentencing, and appellate review. The scope and depth of the commission's prescriptions for state courts in the section "Personnel and Institutions" ranged from calling for unification of state court systems to insisting on a chief court administrator in each state.[28]

Should one mistakenly think that these standards were generalizations or nonprescriptive, consider the segment of Standard 8.1 regarding unification:

> State courts should be organized into a unified judicial system financed by the State and administered through a statewide court administrator or administrative judge under the supervision of the chief justice of the State supreme court.
> All trial courts should be unified into a single trial court with general criminal as well as civil jurisdiction.[29]

Many knowledgeable and distinguished people participated in the promulgation of the standards. The substance of the standards, including the foregoing standard on court organization, was attractive. Those facts did not overcome the greater fact that the federal government through the LEAA was promulgating standards prescribing state court structure, staffing, and methods of operation.

Not surprisingly, the next step was creation by the LEAA of another commission to assess the extent to which each state court system was in conformity with the LEAA's standards. Predictably, state comprehensive criminal justice plans, including the court sections, were increasingly expected to promote and conform to the LEAA's standards.

It is tempting to suggest that the LEAA's standards and goals were the straw that broke the camel's back for California's court system. We will never know, but 1973 was apocalyptic. As the LEAA standards and goals for courts were being finalized and published early in 1973, the Judicial Council and AOC directly denounced the California arrangement, and by implication denounced the LEAA, on multiple counts: "In California, the judicial system has a statewide structure created under the Constitution and implemented by state statutes and rules of court, with the Judicial Council as the constitutionally established state agency having rulemaking powers and administrative responsibility for the operation of that structure. . . ." In creating the CCCJ and the OCJP, the legislature failed to recognize "the primary role to be played by the judiciary as an independent branch of government in criminal justice planning for California's courts."[30]

". . . The several judges who have served on the CCCJ by appointment of the speaker [of the Assembly] or the senate rules committee, however, did not have any direct relationship to the Judicial Council." Until 1971, the designated representative of the Judicial Council was merely one of the legislators serving on the Council and those legislators "could not effectively represent the Council or its Chairman as a spokesman for the judiciary."[31]

The Judicial Council calculated that of the 139.3 million federal dollars given to California during the initial five years of the LEAA, only 5 percent went to the judicial system, and that included grants made to prosecution and defense services, since LEAA definitionally lumped courts, prosecution, and defense into a single category.[32] The Judicial Council reported that "[d]uring the 1969–1973 period not only have the funds for the judiciary been low, but the statewide nature of the California judicial system has not been adequately recognized in the operational procedures of the CCCJ structure. . . . The court system has, as a result, been treated by the CCCJ in much the same way as is the police function or the correctional function. Under these circumstances, California's statewide system of 355 trial courts tends to be treated as are its 400-plus local police agencies. The difference between the two groups, of course, is that the court system is a statewide system, regulated by state law and state policy decisions, with an independence that is guaranteed by the constitutional separation of powers clause."[33]

These grievances led the Judicial Council, supported by the AOC, to strike back in 1973. Exercising its constitutional prerogative to make recommendations to the governor and the legislature, the Judicial Council proposed and successfully obtained legislation restructuring the CCCJ and creating a separate role for the judicial system in criminal justice planning. At the council's request, the legislature created a seven-member Judicial Criminal Justice Planning Committee whose members were appointed by and held office at the pleasure of the Judicial Council. The statute further required that "any grant of federal funds made or approved by the office [OCJP] which is to be implemented in the California court system shall be submitted to the Judicial Criminal Justice Planning Committee for its review and recommendations. . . ."[34] The OCJP was further required to consult with and seek the advice of the new committee before carrying out any functions that affected the courts. The new committee was also directed to report independently to the governor and legislature on the status of LEAA-funded projects affecting the judicial system.[35]

To drive home the point that the courts now had an independent voice, the legislature also directed that the expenses of the new judicial review committee should be paid by the OCJP from federal funds.[36]

It is interesting to note that the first chair of the Judicial Criminal Justice Planning Committee was Justice Winslow Christian from the court of appeal, who recently had completed a two-year tour as the first full-time director of the fledgling National Center for State Courts. Also, the chief staff person assisting the committee was an attorney assigned from the AOC by the name of William E. Davis, later to become Administrative Director of the Courts.

The Judicial Criminal Justice Planning Committee worked diligently and cooperatively for more than seven years, terminating its activities in March 1982 with the demise of the LEAA and the termination of federal funding for the committee's activities. During those years, the committee reviewed and evaluated hundreds of court projects proposed for funding, stimulated and strengthened planning among courts at both the local and state levels, and facilitated a collaborative but independent role for the court system in the midst of California's response to the LEAA and federally imposed criminal justice planning.

The legacy of the LEAA in many respects is murky, debatable, lamentable, and laudable. However, it seems indisputable that planning within the courts, both in California and throughout the nation, is a part of that legacy. Numerous national efforts support this conclusion. A prominent and good example is *State Courts: A Blueprint for the Future*, which was formulated by the second National Conference on the Judiciary in 1978, conducted by the National Center for State Courts and funded in large measure by the LEAA.[37]

Within California, it seems fair to conclude that the Judicial Criminal Justice Planning Committee appointed by the Judicial Council and operating de facto as an adjunct entity of the Judicial Council, both for itself and for the courts of the state, paved the way for planning within the judicial branch of government.

Perhaps the most compelling tribute to the planning impact of the LEAA came from Ralph N. Kleps, the first Administrative Director of the Courts. He acknowledged in 1975 that "[t]he idea of mandated comprehensive planning for state judicial systems has attained wide acceptance recently under the stimulus of federal criminal justice funding."[38] He also observed at the same time that "[c]omprehensive criminal justice planning . . . has also become overstated, oversold and underachieved."[39]

While taking swipes at the LEAA and mandated criminal justice planning, Kleps also broke new ground by explicitly acknowledging the role of planning in a court context independent from the LEAA and criminal justice planning. The context was the impact of the 1974 decision in *Gordon v. Justice Court*,[40] which is explained in Chapter Five. Suffice to say here that the decision invalidated procedures that had long been in use in the justice courts.

Kleps's theme was that the California court system was dependent on annual budgets at both the state and local levels and concurrently at the mercy of unanticipated crises. This led him to conclude that "[i]n such an environment, it may be that the most needed resource of a state judicial system is the capacity for contingency planning."[41] In his view, the response of the Judicial Council and the AOC to the decision in *Gordon* and the resulting solution of creating a new cadre of law-trained judges in the justice courts was an exemplary act of contingency planning.

One could quibble about whether the Judicial Council or the AOC response to the *Gordon* crisis was planning or merely a continuation of the tradition of reactive problem solving. One cannot argue, however, with the importance of the fact that the solution was perceived and described by the Administrative Director of the Courts as the fruit of planning.

Acknowledgment and use of planning terminology and, perhaps, techniques by Administrative Director Kleps did not, however, appear at the time to lead to systemic planning by the Judicial Council or the AOC. Indeed, the formal process of planning within California's judicial branch is not discernable during the balance of the tenures of Administrative Director Kleps and Chief Justice Donald R. Wright, or those of their successors, Chief Justice Rose Elizabeth Bird and Administrative Director of the Courts Ralph J. Gampell.

The 1980s: Planning and Policymaking Merge

That all changed in 1987 when Malcolm M. Lucas became Chief Justice and William E. Davis became Administrative Director of the Courts.

It was clear from the outset that this new leadership would chart a new course. The Judicial Council made the following bold announcement in its 1988 *Annual Report*: "In 1987, the Judicial Council of California reasserted its leadership role as a policy-making agency for the state's court system."[42]

The statement was based on several factors:

◆   The annual "flood of new bills designed to solve perceived problems in the courts" and the increasing tendency of the legislature "to regard the Judicial Council as just another state agency whose primary role is to carry out its directions."

◆   The imbalance between using the council's limited resources to implement legislative mandates at the expense of "planning and policy-making functions for which the council was originally created."

◆   Review of recent council agendas indicating the danger "that the council was becoming almost entirely reactive."[43]

In an explicit assertion of its leadership role, the Judicial Council for the first time developed an annual plan for its activities. At the heart of this plan was identification of major issues confronting the court system, followed by assigning priorities for addressing these problems.

The process was twofold. First, the council enunciated five general principles: reducing delay, improving funding, encouraging uniformity, improving public access to and understanding of courts, and ensuring fair and equal treatment for all participants. The second step was to direct each of the Judicial Council's standing committees to develop a list of priorities to be addressed during 1987 and 1988. As an example of the responses from standing committees, the Court Management Committee in 1987 established the following four key planning priorities: seek to reduce delay in the trial courts, implement state funding of the trial courts, improve the method used to prepare weighted caseload studies and judgeship needs reports, and increase the use of automation in the trial courts.[44]

From no planning at midcentury, the Judicial Council and the AOC thus moved to annual plans by the latter part of the 1980s. It seems reasonable to suggest that this new commitment to planning was made easier by several years of experience in the LEAA context as well as the experience brought to bear by Administrative Director William E. Davis as the first staff director of the California Judicial Criminal Justice Planning Committee.

The 1990s: Strategic Governance

In a very short time, annual plans became an integral part of endeavors by the Judicial Council and the AOC. Citing one of many examples, the action plan for 1991 included as an approved priority a "plan for the future of the California court system" consisting in large part of developing and integrating "the planning process in the judicial branch" and appointing a committee "to develop future-related issues and options for courts."[45]

This was a natural evolution from Chief Justice Lucas's statement in 1990 in an address to the State Bar board of governors: "We need to anticipate change and plan for action. We need to lead and not wait to be led into the next millennium."[46]

The Judicial Council implemented one of these planning priorities in 1991 by creating the Commission on the Future of the California Courts, whose forty-five members were appointed by Chief Justice Lucas. The chair was Dr. Robert R. Dockson, founder and former dean of the graduate school of business at the University of Southern California and the chairman-emeritus of CalFed, Inc., a financial institution.

What the Chief Justice and the Judicial Council contemplated was a planning process fairly novel in the nation's courts at that time, one known as "alternative futures planning." Embracing conventional forecasting, trend analysis, and scenario construction, alternative futures planning allows policy and decision makers better to anticipate what the future *might* be, in order to propose what it *should* be. That "preferred future" then becomes the target at which subsequent planning efforts are aimed.[47]

Two years later the Commission on the Future of the California Courts concluded its labors. During the intervening twenty-four months, a prodigious effort had been successfully carried out that included securing federal and private grants for supplemental funding; a broad survey of public opinion regarding courts in California; a "Delphi study" involving hundreds of interviews, surveys, and meetings; a comprehensive forecast of California's demographic, economic, sociological, and technological futures; extensive outreach efforts including a statewide symposium and public hearings; and finally production of massive documentation with the final report *Justice in the Balance, 2020* as the flagship. Based upon radically different future demographics and economics in California, the commission addressed the major subjects of multidimensional justice, access to justice, equal justice, public trust and understanding, information technology and justice, children and families, civil justice, criminal justice, the appellate courts, governing the judicial branch, and financing of future justice.[48]

Although Hawaii, Virginia, and Arizona had previously undertaken programs regarding the future of courts, the California effort was at the time the most ambitious of its kind. It also was able to draw upon the information and momentum created by the National Conference on the Future of Courts, held in May 1990 in San Antonio, Texas.

While the futures commission was laboring, the Judicial Council and AOC stepped up to a new level of governance. Annual planning gave way to strategic planning.

This was far more than a mere evolutionary step in planning sophistication. It involved reexamination of the Judicial Council's responsibilities as well as those of the AOC. Responsibilities were reexamined internally in relationship to the entire judicial system and externally in relation to the other branches of government, participants in the judicial process, and the public served by that system.

The original justifications for creation of the Judicial Council in 1926 were revisited to determine whether and to what extent those early promises were being fulfilled. Was the Judicial Council performing as a "board of directors" for the system? Were the Judicial Council and AOC discharging the "duty of seeing that justice is being properly administered"? Was the Chief Justice performing the duties that "a general superintendent fills in any ordinary business"? Was the Chief Justice serving as "the real as well as the nominal head of the judiciary of the state"? Were the Judicial Council and the AOC assuring that the work of the courts is "correlated" and that "the machinery of the courts is working smoothly"? Apparently the answers to these and many other questions on penetrating issues of governance were less than affirmative.[49]

The council responded by engaging in an unprecedented endeavor of self-governance, which resulted in an equally unprecedented "Strategic and Reorganization Plan," adopted on November 9, 1992. The plan included adoption of mission statements and principles regarding the roles of both the Judicial Council and the judiciary as well as approved goals, objectives, and strategies to pursue during the following five years.[50]

The reorganization portion of the plan involved a new system of internal committees with a new group of standing advisory committees. Close to the heart of the reorganization was a fundamental change in the manner by which the Chief Justice exercised the power of appointment to the council and to its advisory bodies. While the constitution confers upon the Chief Justice the unrestricted power to make such appointments, Chief Justice Lucas agreed to a new nominating procedure designed to broadly solicit applicants and nominees. From these the executive committee would offer candidates to the Chief Justice after screening applicants and nominations, and then the Chief Justice would make appointments with consideration given to experience as well as gender, ethnic, and geographic diversity.[51]

What accounted for this sea change? Had the process of annual plans become moribund or routine? Was a new and bolder drive needed to reassert the Judicial Council's "role as a policy-making agency for the state's court system"[52] as promised in the late 1980s? The likely answer is "all of the above." But most compelling was the determination of the Judicial Council to function as a board of directors by "steering not rowing."[53] And the likely catalyst for confronting these issues and reaching these conclusions was the arrival in 1992 of William C. Vickrey as the new Administrative Director of the Courts.

Prompt steps were taken to institutionalize and disseminate the fruit of the Judicial Council's efforts. In February 1993 a two-stage meeting was convened in Sacramento. The first phase was attended by members of the Judicial Council and chairs of the various advisory bodies to the council as well as key staff of the AOC and the Center for Judicial Education and Research. Led by Chief Justice Lucas and Administrative Director Vickrey, this assembly, through plenary and small group sessions, delved into the new structure, direction, and responsibilities generated by the strategic plan as well as the role of the Judicial Council in policy development.

During the second phase, the assembly was increased to include members of the Judicial Council's advisory bodies, including the advisory committees made up of presiding judges of the trial courts and court administrators. The program also was expanded to address trends affecting policymaking for the judiciary, enhancing relations with the executive and legislative branches, and governing the affairs of the judiciary.[54]

This was the first gathering of the leaders in California's court system devoted to self-governance, and it was propelled by the Judicial Council's mission statements, principles, goals, objectives, and strategies.

Appropriately, the first strategic plan in 1992 was a beginning and not an end. The strategic planning process has continued to be dynamic and the contents of strategic plans continuously refined and modified. In 1997, the council renamed its strategic plan *Leading Justice Into the Future.* Following further review and evaluation, the Judicial Council in April 1999 embraced the following mission of the judiciary: "The judiciary shall, in a fair, accessible, effective, and efficient manner, resolve disputes arising under the law; and shall interpret and apply the law consistently, impartially, and independently to protect the rights and liberties guaranteed by the Constitutions of California and the United States."[55]

This was supplemented by the mission of the Judicial Council: "Under the leadership of the Chief Justice and in accordance with the California Constitution, the law, and the mission of the judiciary, the Judicial Council shall be responsible for setting the direction and providing the leadership for improving the quality and advancing the consistent, independent, impartial, and accessible administration of justice."[56]

In addition, the council adopted a set of guiding principles and six major goals.

Goal I. Access, Fairness, and Diversity All Californians will have equal access to the courts and equal ability to participate in court proceedings, and will be treated in a fair and just manner. Members of the judicial branch community will reflect the rich diversity of the state's residents.

Goal II. Independence and Accountability The judiciary will be an institutionally independent, separate branch of government that responsibly seeks, uses, and accounts for public resources necessary for its support. The independence of judicial decision making will be protected.

Goal III. Modernization of Management and Administration Justice will be administered in a timely, efficient, and effective manner that utilizes contemporary management practices; innovative ideas; highly competent judges, other judicial officers, and staff; and adequate facilities.

Goal IV. Quality of Justice and Service to the Public Judicial branch services will be responsive to the needs of the public and will enhance the public's understanding and use of and its confidence in the judiciary.

Goal V. Education The effectiveness of judges, court personnel, and other judicial branch staff will be enhanced through high-quality continuing education and professional development.

Goal VI. Technology Technology will enhance the quality of justice by improving the ability of the judicial branch to collect, process, analyze, and share information and by increasing the public's access to information about the judicial branch.[57]

The AOC has engaged in its own process of strategic planning, resulting in commitment to a set of values designed to "earn and maintain the trust of the public, bar, judicial community, and court staff" as well as commitment to the following mission: "The Administrative Office of the Courts (AOC) shall serve the Chief Justice, the Judicial Council, and the courts for the benefit of all Californians by advancing leadership and excellence in the administration of justice that continuously improves access to a fair and impartial judicial system."[58]

Strategic planning as part of the process of governing was not confined to state-level institutions. In 1997, the Judicial Council initiated a statewide program to introduce and support strategic planning in the trial courts of California. By December 1999, most of the state's trial courts had submitted their first strategic plans. Clearly this aspect of strategic planning is well on its way to becoming embedded in both governance and administration of the judicial branch. This is illustrated by the Judicial Council's adoption in 2000 of a framework and guidelines "to institutionalize and integrate state and local planning activities."[59]

Before leaving the 1990s and the dynamics of governance, the transformation of the AOC compels acknowledgment. As noted previously, staff numbered more than 400 individuals by century's end, with important internal and external responsibilities. But numbers and recitation of duties do not capture the vital role of the AOC in the new dynamics of governance.

The flavor of that multifaceted role is suggested when the AOC in its mission statement, after renewing the pledge of service to the Chief Justice and Judicial Council, continues by committing to (1) serving the courts, (2) "advancing leadership and excellence in the administration of justice," and (3) improving "access to a fair and impartial judicial system."[60] This is well beyond merely carrying out the "details of Council policy" as articulated by Ralph N. Kleps at the birth of the AOC.[61]

Manifestations of this broadened mission can be found throughout the AOC but can be illustrated by several examples. The AOC, of course, had no formal representation in the Capitol in 1961; by the year 2000 it had an Office of Governmental Affairs based in Sacramento with a staff of fourteen. In addition to active involvement in the legislative process, this staff maintains ongoing relations with pertinent agencies within state government and with representatives of city and county government while supporting the efforts of the Administrative Director and other AOC staff in dealings with the legislature, the governor's office, and key executive branch agencies such as the Department of Finance.

In the early years of the AOC, support services to trial courts were implicitly beyond the AOC's role. By century's end the AOC was a significant and growing resource for trial courts, with services ranging from legal opinions to budget preparation, technology acquisition and utilization, and labor relations and other areas of human resources. With the advent of trial court unification, presented in the next chapter, this service dimension of the AOC undoubtedly will grow.

While advancing improved administration of justice can be detected throughout the AOC, the effort is nicely captured in the creation and works of the unit for research and planning. With a staff of thirteen, this unit strives to enrich efforts throughout the AOC by systemic information gathering, analysis, and proposal development. By the year 2000 it had made contributions in several important areas such as the adequacy of judicial and nonjudicial staffing.

Judicial and staff education furnishes an insight into AOC efforts to improve access and fairness. As discussed more specifically in Chapter Ten, there was no judicial or nonjudicial education at midcentury. That was corrected as the century progressed, and by 2000 the bulk of education within the courts resided with the AOC, aside from private commercial vendors. In addition to staples such as courses on substantive and procedural law, the AOC's Education Division offered such training programs for judges or staff as "Fairness in the Courts" and "Beyond Bias: Assuring Fairness in the Workplace."

Notes

1   Judge Harry A. Hollzer, "Report of the Condition of Judicial Business in the Courts of the State of California Together with a Summary of Research Studies of Judicial Systems in Other Jurisdictions," in Judicial Council of California, *Second Report of the Judicial Council of California to the Governor and the Legislature* [1929], part 2, pp. 11–69.

2   California Constitution (1926), article VI, section 1a.

3   Preble Stolz and Kathleen Gunn, "The California Judicial Council: The Beginnings of an Institutional History," *Pacific Law Journal* 11 (1979–1980), pp. 884–85.

4   California Constitution (1961), article VI, section 1a.

5   Judicial Council of California, *Nineteenth Biennial Report* (1963), part 2, Annual Report of the Administrative Office of the Courts (1961–62), p. 115.

6   Ralph N. Kleps, "The Judicial Council and the Administrative Office of the California Courts," *Journal of the State Bar of California* 37 (1962), p. 332.

7   Id., p. 331.

8   Judicial Council of California, minutes (April 10, 1951), p. 5.

9   Kleps, "Judicial Council and the AOC," pp. 330–31.

10   California Constitution (1960), article VI, section 1a.

11   Ralph N. Kleps, "Courts, State Court Management and Lawyers," *California State Bar Journal* 50 (1975), p. 48.

12   California Constitution Revision Commission, Proposed Revision of the California Constitution (February 1966), pp. 87–88; California Constitution (1966), article VI, section 6.

13   California Constitution (1960), article VI, section 1a.

14   California Constitution Revision Commission, Proposed Revision (February 1966), pp. 87–88.

15   See, for example, Donald C. Dahlin, "Long-Range Planning in State Courts: Process, Product, and Impact," *Justice System Journal* 17 (1994), pp. 171–92.

16 Omnibus Crime Control and Safe Streets Act of 1968, Public Law 90-351 (June 19, 1968), 82 Statutes 197, 1998 U.S. Code Congressional and Administrative News, pp. 237–85.

17 See, for example, Dorothy W. Nelson, "Should Los Angeles County Adopt a Single Trial Court Plan?," *Southern California Law Review* 33 (1959–60), p. 117.

18 Safe Streets Act of 1968, p. 237.

19 Charles Rogovin, "The Genesis of the Law Enforcement Assistance Administration: A Personal Account," *Columbia Human Rights Law Review* 5 (1973), p. 12.

20 California Statutes 1967, chapter 1661, pp. 4042–43; former section 13800 of the California Penal Code. The attorney general was automatically a member. Twelve members were appointed by the governor, and among those the following three were specified in the statute as mandatory appointees: commissioner of the highway patrol, director of corrections, and director of the youth authority. The governor was further directed to include among his appointments a police chief, district attorney, sheriff, public defender, representative of the Commission on Police Officers Standards, an academician with pertinent qualifications in the field, and an expert in systems technology. Six members were appointed by the Senate Rules Committee with the requirement that two appointees were senators. Six members were appointed by the speaker of the Assembly, to include two Assembly members. The remaining eight legislative appointees had to include a representative of the Judicial Council, a judge, a representative of cities, and a representative of counties.

21 California Statutes 1967, chapter 1661, p. 4044.

22 California Statutes 1973, chapter 1047, section 13823(a)(1), p. 2073.

23 Richard L. Braun, "Federal Government Enters War on Crime," *American Bar Association Journal* 54 (1968), p. 1164.

24 Resolution of the Conference of Chief Justices (August 1973, Columbus, Ohio), quoted in Judicial Council of California, *Annual Report to the Governor and the Legislature* (1974), p. 13.

25 Daniel L. Skoler, "Comprehensive Criminal Justice Planning—A New Challenge," *Crime and Delinquency* 12 (1968), p. 200.

26 Id., pp. 202–3.

27 National Advisory Commission on Criminal Justice Standards and Goals, *Report on Courts* (Washington, D.C.: Government Printing Office, 1973), p. v.

28 Id., pp. 145–286.

29 Id., p. 164.

30 Judicial Council of California, *Annual Report to the Governor and the Legislature* (1974), p. 14.

31 Ibid.

32 Ibid.

33 Id., p. 15.

34 California Statutes 1973, chapter 1047, section 13832, p. 2074.

35 Ibid.

36 Id., section 13834, p. 2074.

37 National Conference on the Judiciary, *State Courts: A Blueprint for the Future: Proceedings of the Second Annual Conference on the Judiciary* ([Denver]: National Center for State Courts, 1978).

38 Ralph N. Kleps, "Contingency Planning for State Court Systems," *Judicature* 59 (1975), p. 63.

39 Ibid.

40 *Gordon v. Justice Court* (1974) 12 Cal.3d 323 [115 Cal.Rptr. 632, 525 P.2d 72].

41 Kleps, "Contingency Planning," p. 64.

42 Judicial Council of California, *Annual Report to the Governor and the Legislature* (1988), part 1, p. 1.

43 Id., p. 2.

44 Id., pp. 2–4.

45 Judicial Council of California, *Annual Report to the Governor and the Legislature* (1991), volume 1, p. x.

46 Quoted in [Judicial Council of California], Commission on the Future of the

California Courts, *Justice in the Balance, 2020: Report of the Commission on the Future of the California Courts* (1993), p. 2.

47 Judicial Council, *Justice in the Balance*, p. 2.

48 Id., p. vii.

49 Quotations from Senators M. B. Johnson and J. M. Inman, Argument in Favor of Proposition 27, Senate Constitutional Amendment No. 15 (1925 Regular Session), submitted to voters on November 2, 1926.

50 Judicial Council of California, *Annual Report to the Governor and the Legislature* (1993), volume 1, p. 2–3.

51 Id., p. 3.

52 Judicial Council, *Annual Report* (1988), part 1, p. 1.

53 Judicial Council of California, Strategic Plan Dinner Meeting (November 12, 1992), presentation outline, p. 8.

54 Judicial Council of California, Administrative Office of the Courts, "Judicial Council Orientation" [conference materials] (February 25–26, 1993), [San Francisco].

55 Judicial Council of California, *Leading Justice Into the Future: Long-Range Strategic Plan* (updated April 29, 1999), p. 2.

56 Ibid.

57 Id., pp. 4–11.

58 Administrative Office of the Courts, *People and Programs* (July 2000), section 1-1-2.

59 Judicial Council of California, *Leading Justice Into the Future: Strategic Plan* (March 2000), appendix A, p. 17.

60 Administrative Office of the Courts, *People and Programs* (July 2000), section 1-1.

61 Kleps, "Judicial Council and the AOC," p. 331.

Chapter 5
Reorganization and Unification of the Trial Courts

Overview

his half-century began and concluded with major trial court reorganizations. Important evolutionary steps occurred in between.

The 1950 reorganization established municipal courts for more populous areas and justice courts for less populous areas as the only courts of limited jurisdiction. This swept away hundreds of preexisting courts that had crept into existence along an array of different constitutional, statutory, and charter routes.

The Judicial Council and the Administrative Office of the Courts (AOC) launched serious efforts in the 1970s to further improve structure—first by examining lower court consolidation and next by examining unification of all trial courts. The several proposals that emerged died in the California Legislature.

Ferment continued, however. The decision in the *Gordon v. Justice Court* case in 1974 disqualified non-attorney justice court judges from presiding over most criminal matters, sowing the seeds for the advent of a completely law-trained judiciary. In 1977 the superior court in San Diego County and the El Cajon Municipal Court launched the successful "El Cajon experiment" by arranging for municipal court judges to hear matters within superior court jurisdiction.

The success was not enough to gain voter approval of a constitutional amendment in 1982 that would have permitted consolidation of a county's superior and municipal courts with legislative and voter approval.

A step forward was achieved, however, in 1988 when the significant differences between municipal and justice courts were eliminated.

Shortly thereafter, the legislature in 1991 imposed "coordination" upon the judicial branch. All trial courts in each county were compelled to submit for Judicial Council approval a plan to achieve maximum utilization of judicial and other trial court resources within the county and to reduce statewide costs. Many regarded coordination as an essential prelude to unification.

The legislature next passed a Judicial Council proposal to create a single category of limited jurisdiction court—municipal courts—by eliminating justice courts. The voters approved in 1994.

Following a substantial but unsuccessful legislative effort from 1992 through 1994, a new push for trial court unification began in 1995 with Senate Constitutional Amendment (SCA) 3 and culminated in ballot Proposition 220 in 1998. Voters approved by a margin of almost two to one.

The decision whether to unify was at the option of each county and became effective only upon a majority vote of the municipal court judges and a majority vote of the superior court judges in the county. Within two months of passage of Proposition 220, fifty counties had created a single trial court. The remaining eight counties did so over the following twenty-five months.

*C*ourt structure and court funding often are inseparable. Certainly they intertwined in California. Both were transformed between 1950 and 2000. They are discussed in this chapter and the next as monuments of major significance in the improved administration of justice. With respect to structure, it is interesting to note that this fifty-year era began and concluded with major reorganizations in the trial courts.

Courts of Limited Jurisdiction: The 1950 Reorganization

A constitutional amendment was approved by California voters in 1950, dramatically reorganizing the "inferior courts" or courts of limited jurisdiction. The story of that amendment, of course, preceded its culmination in 1950. For much of the 1940s, there was agitation from several quarters for improvements in California's lower courts. The State Bar, the Commonwealth Club, and the Justices' and Constables' Association all proposed changes at various times.[1]

These pressures produced a concurrent resolution of the California Legislature in 1947 requesting that the Judicial Council "make a thorough study of the organization, jurisdiction and practice of the courts in California exercising jurisdiction inferior to the superior court, and to make recommendations for the improvement of the administration of justice therein."[2]

The Judicial Council responded in 1948 that:

[T]he principal defect in our present inferior court system is the multiplicity of tribunals and their duplication of functions, a defect inherent in the court structure. There are six separate and distinct types of inferior courts, totaling 767 in number, created and governed under varied constitutional, statutory and charter provisions. The jurisdiction of those courts overlaps, since in almost every instance each court serves a locality which is also served by at least one other court. Conflict and uncertainty in jurisdiction is one result of such multiplicity and duplication. Another result is that many courts are operated on a part-time basis and are presided over by laymen engaged in outside businesses or by lawyers engaged in private practice.[3]

This structure was so complex that Chief Justice Phil S. Gibson remarked: "The average layman would, I am sure, assume that all lawyers are thoroughly familiar with the organization and jurisdiction of all of our courts. I have found, however, that there are very few lawyers who can correctly name all the types of trial courts in the state, much less give the sources and extent of their jurisdiction. This, in itself, is some evidence of the complicated and confusing nature of our inferior court structure."[4]

It is no surprise that Chief Justice Gibson and the Judicial Council further concluded that these structural problems were compounded by operational problems, resulting in a system that was inefficient, confusing, and wasteful. Major contributors were the overlapping geographic and subject matter jurisdiction, part-time operations, widely varying methods of selecting judicial officers, and widely varying qualifications of those officers.[5]

The solution proposed by the Judicial Council was to create only two limited jurisdiction courts below the superior court: municipal courts and justice courts.[6] Each county would be divided into judicial districts by the board of supervisors, and each of those districts would have a single court of limited jurisdiction. Any district with more than 40,000 in population would have a municipal court. Justice courts would be established in each district of lesser population. The municipal courts would have civil jurisdiction in cases involving $2,000 or less and countywide jurisdiction for misdemeanors. Justice court jurisdiction would be limited to $500 or less in civil cases and include "low grade misdemeanors."[7] All municipal and justice court judges would be elected. Elaborate provision was made for grandfathering incumbents of the assorted existing courts of limited jurisdiction.

The Judicial Council's proposal required amending the constitution. It was adopted by the legislature and became Proposition 3 in the statewide general election on November 7, 1950. In anticipation of the proposed amendments, the legislature adopted the Court Act of 1949 enacting implementing statutes recommended by the Judicial Council.[8] These implementing statutes were to take effect only upon voter ratification of the proposed constitutional amendment. The Court Act of 1949 and companion amendments to the Penal Code and Code of Civil Procedure effectively prescribed jurisdiction for the new municipal and justice courts and divided between them jurisdiction over the galaxy of matters previously handled by the preexisting courts of limited jurisdiction.[9]

Chief Justice Gibson referred to this reorganization as "the most significant reform that has taken place in the judicial department of our state government since it began to function nearly 100 years ago."[10] Knowledgeable commentators subsequently endorsed this view.[11]

Proposition 3 was passed by the voters, sweeping into history the patchwork of limited jurisdiction courts that had grown by increment during the first hundred years of statehood.

Gordon v. Justice Court

A quarter-century passed before the next major change in the courts of limited jurisdiction. It was precipitated by the decision of the California Supreme Court in the 1974 *Gordon v. Justice Court* case.[12] At issue was whether it was constitutionally permissible under the due process clause of the federal constitution to allow justice court judges who were not attorneys to preside over criminal trials if the offense was punishable by a jail sentence.

The court, in a unanimous opinion, held: "We have decided that this practice does violate the due process clause of the Fourteenth Amendment of the United States Constitution, and that henceforth defendants in such courts are entitled to have an attorney judge preside over all criminal proceedings involving charges which carry the possibility of a jail sentence, unless such right is waived by the defendant or his counsel."[13]

The *Gordon* decision had a "bombshell effect."[14] At the time of the decision, California's justice courts had jurisdiction over approximately 13,000 preliminary felony proceedings and 130,000 misdemeanors each year. Since non-attorney judges presided over 127 of these justice courts, the decision in *Gordon* created a true crisis in judicial administration. The AOC concluded that the caseload within the scope of *Gordon* and the justice courts presided over by non-lawyer judges required twenty-two new full-time, law-trained judges.

The author of the unanimous opinion in *Gordon* was Justice Louis Burke, a fact that furnishes a noteworthy facet of the decision. Justice Burke at the time was a national leader in judicial administration, having served as a founding member of the National Center for State Courts (NCSC) and as president of its board of directors, chair of the Section on Judicial Administration of the American Bar Association (ABA), and chair of the ABA Commission on Standards of Judicial Administration. It is inconceivable that he or the other justices of the Supreme Court were unaware of the bombshell dropped by the *Gordon* decision on judicial administration in California.

The response to *Gordon*, orchestrated by the Judicial Council and adopted by the legislature, was to create a new class of temporary circuit justice court judges, all of whom would be lawyers and serve full time. These positions were filled by elevating incumbent lawyer judges of the justice courts to full-time judicial office and adding lawyers as full-time judges to several existing lay judge districts. These positions were temporary because the California Attorney General had petitioned the U.S. Supreme Court to review and reverse the *Gordon* decision. Such a reversal would eliminate the need for change in the justice court system.

Early in 1975, the U.S. Supreme Court declined to review the decision of the California Supreme Court in Gordon, and the twenty-two new circuit justice court judges began work.[15]

Steps subsequently were taken to require that all new justice court judges be attorneys. Aside from this, there were no further significant changes in the courts of limited jurisdiction until justice courts were eliminated entirely in 1994.

Early Efforts to Unify the Trial Courts

The 1950 reorganization of limited jurisdiction courts may have been, as Chief Justice Gibson said, the most significant reform in the judicial branch since statehood, but even before the *Gordon* decision efforts were under way to achieve another significant reform: unification of all trial courts into a single-level court of original jurisdiction in each county.

The concept was endorsed by the State Bar as early as 1946, but it was not until 1970 that unification received serious attention. Interestingly, it began as a new effort to further improve the courts of limited jurisdiction.

In 1970, the Judicial Council retained the consulting firm of Booz, Allen & Hamilton to study and prepare recommendations for improvements in the lower courts of California.[16] Following an extensive effort, Booz Allen recommended in 1971 that California "[e]stablish a single type of lower court, with a uniform countywide jurisdiction, to be called the county court, to replace present municipal and justice courts."[17]

While the lower court study was in progress, Chief Justice Donald R. Wright and Administrative Director of the Courts Ralph N. Kleps established the Select Committee on Trial Court Delay with nine members: three appointed by the Chief Justice, three appointed by the governor, and three appointed by the State Bar board of governors. The Select

Committee had a one-year charter, a mandate to investigate the causes of and recommend solutions for delay, and a full-time legal staff. At approximately the same time, Booz Allen's assignment was expanded to examine the possibility of unifying all trial courts.

The work on trial court structure of the Select Committee, Booz Allen, and the Judicial Council became closely interwoven.[18]

The ultimate conclusion and recommendations of Booz Allen were supported by extensive empirical research in the form of field visits, organizational and statistical analyses, questionnaires, and interviews. In addition, the scope of research was substantial, including, probably for the first time, a respectable attempt to document the total cost of operating California's trial courts. With barely concealed astonishment, the consultants identified the major organizational or managerial differences among the three types of trial courts:

> The financial burden of the Superior Court judges' salaries has been largely assumed by the state, while the salaries of Municipal and Justice Court judges are financed entirely by the counties in which these courts are located.
>
> The state financially supports and administers the retirement system for Superior and Municipal Court judges, while Justice Court judges, if members of any retirement system, are members of a county system.
>
> The sheriff supplies bailiffing to the Superior Court and, sometimes, to the lower courts, although the lower courts are more commonly served by marshals or constables.
>
> The county clerk is ex officio clerk of the Superior Court in most counties. The lower courts generally have their own court-appointed clerks. . . .
>
> The Legislature determines the salary levels of Superior and Municipal Court judges, while the compensation of Justice Court judges has been left to the decision of county Boards of Supervisors.
>
> The Governor appoints judges to fill Superior and Municipal Court vacancies, while Justice Court vacancies are filled by the Boards of Supervisors.[19]

After assessing alternative forms of organization, Booz Allen concluded and recommended to the Judicial Council that "a single-level trial court with one type of judge is ultimately the most desirable form for a unified trial court organization."[20] To implement this recommendation, the consultants proposed a three-stage approach commencing with creation of an area administrative structure and unification of the justice and municipal courts. This was to be followed by establishment of the unified trial court system and conclude with the final stage, which would involve phasing counties in to a system of a single-level trial court with one level of trial judge assisted by subordinate judicial officers as needed.[21]

Traveling on a parallel track, the Select Committee on Trial Court Delay, drawing upon the information and recommendations generated by Booz Allen and its own research, "concluded that a unified trial court system is necessary in California and so recommends."[22] Key features of the Select Committee's recommendation were:

◆ Creation of a single trial court in each county with provisions for the position of associate superior court judge, to be filled by municipal court judges and justice court judges who have been members of the bar for at least five years

◆ Central administration with appointment by the Chief Justice of a chief judge in each county

◆ Regional administration with appointment by the Chief Justice of an administrative judge to supervise and assist the courts within the region, assisted by an area court administrator appointed by the Administrative Director of the Courts

◆ Provision for assignment of matters currently within the jurisdiction of municipal courts to associate superior court judges subject to the power of the chief judge to assign any matter to an associate superior court judge and the power of the area administrative judge to assign associate judges to serve as acting superior court judges for longer periods of time[23]

In support of these proposals, the Select Committee noted the jurisdictional differences among the three existing levels of trial courts and commented that "each unit in the trial court system generally determines its own managerial and operational policies" and functions independently of the others. It was also noted that "each judge is relatively autonomous in matters of court management" and that "the administrative direction of a presiding judge can be ignored by individual judges who feel that, as elected officials, they are entitled to operate with complete independence on such matters as working hours or work assignments."[24]

In further support, the Select Committee noted the trial court system was fragmented into 58 superior courts, 75 municipal courts, and 244 justice courts, 74 percent of which were single-judge courts. The result of this large number of administratively separate judicial units was unnecessary expense, underutilization of existing judicial and nonjudicial manpower, the difficulties of coordinating over 360 separate units, limited opportunity for achieving economies of scale, fragmentation of financial resources, insufficient uniformity in procedure and practices, and uncoordinated use of the court facilities.[25]

The Judicial Council acknowledged these recommendations. The council also reviewed the 1950 reorganization of the courts of limited jurisdiction, the 1961 proposal of the legislative analyst to completely revise the trial court system by dividing the state into superior court districts, and various recommendations by national bodies to create single-level trial courts.[26]

The Judicial Council then joined in the indictment of the existing system.

Historically, California has had a trial court system consisting of a multiplicity of relatively uncoordinated tribunals, nearly autonomous in administration, with duplicate administrative and judicial support structures. This fragmented system has generally resulted in a serious lack of uniformity in the administration of the various trial courts and in local court procedures and practices. More importantly, it has prevented the maximum utilization of judicial manpower to meet the modern problems of growing judicial workloads and of increasing congestion and delay in many trial courts. Additionally, the present system has fragmented the financial resources available to the courts and, at the same time, it has permitted a needless duplication of judicial functions. It has also resulted in the relatively uncoordinated use of available court personnel and related facilities, thus precluding economies that could be achieved in an integrated judicial system.[27]

The council, however, deferred formulating recommendations pending an opportunity for study and comment and recommended tentatively:

◆ Creation of a "Judicial Code" to contain future statutes regarding reorganized judicial structures

◆ Legislation to establish an area administrative structure for court administration

◆ A constitutional amendment and implementing legislation to create a system of unified county courts that would supersede and encompass the existing municipal and justice courts[28]

These measures proposed by the Judicial Council were rejected by the legislature.[29]

Included in the mandate to the Select Committee on Trial Court Delay was the direction to report to the "Judiciary, Governor, Legislature and people of California."[30] Since its reported recommendations proposed change that was both more extensive and more immediate than that proposed by the Judicial Council, the Select Committee, as part of its mandate, sought legislative action to enact a single-level trial court system but also was unsuccessful.[31]

Why did these several proposals die in the California Legislature? Later history in this area teaches that major change in court structure involves political forces both varied and powerful. However, it is fair to surmise that in the 1970s there were at least two insurmountable forces opposing change.

First, many superior court judges objected for an array of reasons, stated and unstated. In fact, an ad hoc council of presiding judges from the larger superior courts was cobbled together for the sole purpose of defeating the proposals of the Judicial Council and Select Committee. The second source of opposition centered around the governor's office but probably also involved considerable legislative sentiment. The primary source of this opposition was the threat posed to the system of judicial appointments. With two levels of trial courts, the governor could fill a superior court vacancy by appointing a municipal court judge, thus creating a municipal court vacancy and the opportunity for a second gubernatorial appointment. In crude vernacular, every superior court vacancy gave the governor "two pops" of patronage instead of just one, as would be the case with a single level of trial court.

Legislative rejection of the proposals by the Judicial Council and Select Committee, whatever the reason, effectively terminated consideration, although there were subsequent unsuccessful salvage efforts.[32]

Trial court reorganization lay fallow following these efforts. However, this field revived and again began to produce in the late 1970s.

The first sign of revival was the "El Cajon experiment." Legislation proposed in 1977 authorized a five-year experiment in the El Cajon Municipal Court in San Diego County to test the desirability of permitting a municipal court to hear certain matters within the jurisdiction of the superior court.[33] Concerns about the proposal's constitutionality led the presiding judge of the superior court to request that Chief Justice Rose Elizabeth Bird assign the El Cajon Municipal Court to hear superior court matters, which she did, using the Chief Justice's powers of assignment.[34]

Although the proposed legislation passed effective January 1, 1978, it was never central to the experiment, which actually began in 1977 and was expanded in 1978 and 1979 to other municipal courts in San Diego County.

By 1982, the Judicial Council concluded that the experiment had assisted the superior court at a level roughly equivalent to three or four judicial positions without adversely affecting the municipal court calendars. The council noted but did not seem deterred by objections by some attorneys that consent of the parties should be required before a municipal court judge hears a superior court matter. The council concluded by recommending that counties with conditions similar to those in San Diego County should replicate the program.[35]

Close on the heels of the Judicial Council's endorsement of the El Cajon experiment was a legislatively proposed constitutional amendment that had the potential to significantly alter trial court structure,[36] appearing on the November 1982 ballot as Proposition 10. If passed, it would permit the legislature to authorize a county to unify the municipal and superior courts with the approval of a majority of county voters. Justice court judges also could become superior court judges if not prohibited by the legislature.

Supporters argued this would enhance efficiency, improve accessibility, and reduce costs. They relied on the El Cajon experiment for support and claimed endorsements by the County Supervisors Association and California Trial Lawyers Association, among others. Voter control at the county level was emphasized.

Opponents responded that costs would be increased by awarding the salary of a superior court judge to hundreds of lower court judges and that the municipal courts would be destroyed as the "people's court." They claimed they were joined in opposition by the State Bar and California District Attorneys Association.[37]

The voters of California rejected the proposal by a margin of almost two to one.

Thanks to a series of constitutional and statutory changes proposed by the Judicial Council and promulgated a few years later, improvements continued notwithstanding the rather resounding defeat of Proposition 10. Principal among these enactments was Proposition 91 in 1988, which effected the following changes:

♦ Made the jurisdiction of justice courts equal to that of municipal courts

♦ Subjected justice court judges to the same rules of judicial conduct and discipline as municipal court judges

♦ Provided for identical terms of office and elections for justice and municipal court judges

Proposition 91 further declared justice courts to be courts of record, required justice court judges to have the same minimum experience as municipal court judges, and prohibited justice court judges from practicing law. Minimum experience in this context was defined as being a member of the State Bar or having served as a judge in a court of record in California for five years immediately preceding selection.[38]

Following adoption of Proposition 91, judges in part-time justice courts were granted the option of participating in the Judicial Council's Certified Justice Court Judge Program. Participants received full-time salaries in exchange for full-time work. Certified judges were required to be available to serve on assignment whenever their services were not needed in their home courts. Judges appointed or elected after January 1, 1990, were required to be certified and to serve full time.[39]

Coordination

Coordination is a subplot in the unification story but an important one that begins with the Trial Court Realignment and Efficiency Act of 1991 by Assembly Member Phillip Isenberg, chair of the Assembly Judiciary Committee. It has been suggested that coordination was the phoenix risen from the ashes of Proposition 10 in 1982. Whether or not that is accurate, it is difficult to deny that coordination was an important, perhaps vital, prelude to unification.

After a series of findings regarding the financial plight of government and the fiscal aspects of court funding, the legislature declared in the act its intention to "improve the coordination of trial court operations through a variety of administrative efficiencies, including coordination agreements between the trial courts, and thereby achieve substantial savings in trial court operations costs."[40]

Concurrent with a promised increase in state funding for trial courts, the act further provided: "On or before March 1, 1992, each superior, municipal, and justice court in each county, in consultation with the bar, shall prepare and submit to the Judicial Council for review and approval a trial court coordination plan designed to achieve maximum utilization of judicial and other court resources and statewide cost reductions in court operations. . . ."[41]

The act also directed the Judicial Council to adopt standards applicable to coordination, specifying in detail the topics to be covered by these standards, and further directed the trial courts to submit reports to the Judicial Council on progress toward achieving the cost-reduction goals associated with coordination plans.[42]

Enactment of this legislation precipitated a flurry of activity within the judicial branch of government. It started with adoption by the Judicial Council of Standards of Judicial Administration 28 and 29 suggesting, among other things, techniques for implementing coordination in areas such as judicial resources, calendaring and case processing, court support staff and services, and facilities.[43] These standards were developed by the Advisory Committee on Trial Court Coordination Standards, appointed by Chief Justice Malcolm M. Lucas. The Chief Justice also appointed an Advisory Committee on Trial Court Coordination Plan Review to develop criteria for approval as well as a plan to review the more than 200 anticipated court coordination plans required by the act.[44] These efforts, of course, were staffed by the AOC.

By November 1992 the Judicial Council had approved all but one of the initial coordination plans submitted by the trial courts, and that last one was approved early in 1993.[45] But the road to full coordination meandered and was bumpy. Although the Judicial Council repeatedly stated that it "unequivocally supports coordination,"[46] implementation was easier said than done.

Two additional Judicial Council entities subsequently were required because of the varying levels of coordination compliance by trial courts and the resulting frustration of the Judicial Council: the Trial Court Coordination Evaluation Committee and the Select Coordination Implementation Committee. With the benefit of "almost four years of study and assessment by scores of judges, administrators, and outside consultants,"[47] the Select Coordination Implementation Committee, working against a ninety-day deadline imposed by the Judicial Council, recommended for council approval in 1995 a package of proposed rules, standards, and statutes that significantly revised and refined coordination. Among the proposed "minimum levels of coordination in each county" were required creation of a coordination oversight committee responsible for planning and governance in each county, compulsory adoption of a rule in each county "to coordinate judicial activities in order to maximize the efficient use of all judicial resources," integration of "all direct court support services for all courts within a county," uniform local rules, unified budgets for all trial courts in a county, and a single executive officer with countywide responsibility.[48]

The ultimate result was that in 1996 the Judicial Council was able to report that all fifty-eight counties had coordination plans that met council standards and guidelines and that those plans had been approved by the Judicial Council without exception.[49]

Unification Revived

As coordination was introduced, and that story within a story began to unfold, there were contemporaneous efforts to resurrect the subject of trial court structure. The most prominent effort at the time was Senate Constitutional Amendment 3, proposed in 1992 by Senator Bill Lockyer, which would have unified all trial courts. Following introduction of this proposal, Senator Lockyer invited comment by the Judicial Council, which, in turn, referred the matter to its advisory committees composed respectively of trial court presiding judges and court administrators. In addition, the Judicial Council, anticipating development of recommendations on trial court unification, conducted an extensive program of soliciting comment from and promoting consideration by a wide range of stakeholders in the California judicial system. Input was also sought from judges in other states with unified trial courts.

The presiding judges and court administrators warmed to their tasks. They created a joint subcommittee, chaired by Roger Warren, presiding judge of the Sacramento Superior and Municipal Courts and later to become president of the National Center for State Courts, to identify issues regarding unification and to seek consensus on addressing those issues. The subcommittee submitted to the respective bodies and ultimately the Judicial Council a report titled *Trial Court Unification: Proposed Constitutional Amendments and Commentary,* dated September 11, 1993. That report contained recommendations that would, among other things:

◆ Merge superior, municipal, and justice courts into one level of trial court called the district court

◆ Direct the legislature to divide the state into district courts with one or more counties per district

◆ Provide for districtwide election of judges

◆ Confer on the Judicial Council "power to promulgate rules of court administration" whether consistent with statutes or not

◆ Provide for assignment of judges to other courts if the caseload of that judge's court did not support the number of judicial positions[50]

This report subsequently was presented on behalf of the two advisory bodies at the Judicial Council's 1993 Strategic Planning Workshop. Without taking a position on whether to support SCA 3, the council informally adopted the amendments to SCA 3 proposed in the report along with a couple added by the council. It endorsed seeking legislative actions to implement the amendments as well as referring the amended version for review by the California Law Revision Commission, which is a statutory entity that assists the legislature to keep the law up to date and in harmony with modern conditions.[51] The council subsequently deferred action on the merits pending assurances that the requested amendments had been made and until further information could be gathered regarding fiscal and other impacts of unification.[52]

The Judicial Council's request for further assessment of impacts led to an analysis by the National Center for State Courts of the financial and policy consequences of trial court unification.[53] The overall conclusion of the NCSC was that unification offered net savings of at least $16 million and that "[i]t is impossible to systematically consider the financial and operational impact of unification and not come to the conclusion that SCA 3, if adopted, will lead to major improvements in the California court system."[54] In support of this broad conclusion, the NCSC observed that beneficial financial effects would flow from cost avoidance and more coherent management. Dividends from unification predicted by the NCSC included more efficient allocation of judicial officers, more uniformity in rules, improved caseflow management, improved financial management of court resources, one management policymaking structure, melding court personnel in one system, and maximizing the use of existing facilities.

The Law Revision Commission, at the behest of the Judicial Council and the request of the legislature, examined the proposed SCA 3 for the purpose of developing recommendations concerning implementation of trial court unification. The commission found that the structure of SCA 3 was "basically sound to accomplish its objective of trial court unification."[55]

The commission also recommended a series of revisions while disclaiming any opinion regarding "the wisdom or desirability of trial court unification."[56] The tone of the commission's report, however, was positive and at times reinforcing. For example, the commission expressed the belief "that elevating municipal and justice court judges to the unified court bench, as contemplated in SCA 3, would not pose a serious threat to the quality of judicial decisionmaking in California."[57] This rebutted the critics of unification who thought that municipal court judges lacked the experience, and perhaps the skill, to be entrusted with the presumably more important or complex cases in the superior courts.

As the quest for more information and analysis continued, opposition in various forms surfaced in the legislative process. By May 1994 it was reported that an Assembly member had continuing concerns about the effects of countywide elections on candidates for judicial office who were from ethnic minority backgrounds. Appellate judges had an array of objections.[58] The governor's staff opposed SCA 3 due to concerns around the federal Voting Rights Act and possible reduction of the pool of applicants for judicial office. They also favored coordination.[59]

SCA 3 ultimately was approved by the Senate but failed in the Assembly. It is appropriate, however, to acknowledge the contribution of the debate around SCA 3. It laid important groundwork and provided a forum within the court family to air issues and exchange viewpoints. It also took the momentum and success of coordination to the next logical step of unification. SCA 3 performed another important role by proving, yet again, that compulsory unification was not politically feasible.

A Step Toward Unification

In 1994 the California Legislature proposed and voters passed Senate Constitutional Amendment 7, which finally created statewide a single level of limited jurisdiction courts by converting justice courts to municipal courts. Noting that the measure "neither increases nor decreases the current number of judges, courts, or judicial districts," proponents of the measure successfully argued that justice courts had become identical with municipal courts in everything but name.[60] This appeared to be settling for half a loaf but proved to be another important step toward unification.

Unification Achieved

In 1995 Senator Lockyer introduced Senate Constitutional Amendment 4, another measure that would open the door to unification of California's trial courts into a single level. SCA 4 proposed numerous conforming or implementing changes in the California Constitution, but at the heart of the measure was a remarkably simple provision: "[T]he municipal and superior courts shall be unified upon a majority vote of superior court judges and a majority vote of municipal court judges within the county. In those counties, there shall be only a superior court."[61]

This provision for local option reflected the lesson from SCA 3 that compulsory unification was doomed. Placing the destiny of unification on a local, county basis and placing control of that decision in the hands of a majority of the judges in both the municipal and the superior courts served the further important purpose of alleviating the concern of Chief Justice Ronald M. George that immediate and universal unification of all trial courts would be inappropriate and thus enabling him to support the measure. This provision apparently was persuasive with the legislature, which adopted SCA 4 and made it Proposition 220 at the June 1998 general election.

The battle for voter approval or rejection of the measure was interesting. Proponents embraced California's recent three-strikes law in criminal sentencing and argued that unification would make judges available to handle the explosion in criminal litigation under that law. They went on to argue that it would save taxpayer money, citing the NCSC's analysis that unification of the trial courts in California would save a minimum of $16 million by reallocating judicial resources. These arguments were buttressed by assuring voters of increased efficiency and flexibility in utilizing the resources of the trial courts.[62]

Opponents responded that the supporters of Proposition 220 actually had opposed the three-strikes law and that, in any case, "three strikes" had not increased criminal litigation. They further argued that Proposition 220 would increase the cost of the court system by increasing municipal court judges' salaries by $9,320 per year when they were elevated to superior court judgeships, reduce judges' accountability since superior court judges are elected countywide rather than from smaller districts, and destroy the existing two-tier system and with it cause the loss of municipal courts as the "people's court."[63]

It is noteworthy that the Judicial Council formally endorsed Proposition 220 and Chief Justice George and Administrative Director of the Courts William C. Vickrey were in active support.

While traditionally not viewed as a source of advocacy on ballot propositions, the legislative analyst was remarkably supportive in the analysis of Proposition 220:

> The fiscal impact of this measure on the state is unknown and would ultimately depend on the number of superior and municipal courts that choose to consolidate. To the extent that most courts choose to consolidate, however, this measure would likely result in net savings to the state ranging in the millions to the tens of millions of dollars annually in the long term. The state could save money from greater efficiency and flexibility in the assignment of trial court judges, reductions in the need to create new judgeships in the future to handle increasing workload, improved management of court records, and reductions in general court administrative costs. At the same time, however, courts that choose to consolidate would result in additional state costs from increasing the salaries and benefits of municipal court judges and employees to the levels of superior court judges and employees. These additional costs would partially offset the savings.[64]

Apparently, a great many voters were persuaded, and Proposition 220 passed by a margin of almost two to one—the same margin by which Proposition 10 lost in 1982.[65]

The formalities of implementing unification at the county level were provided by the Judicial Council.[66] The legislature prescribed that a properly executed vote to unify constituted an irrevocable choice that could not be rescinded or revoked.[67] This fulfilled one of the stated purposes of SCA 4, which was to "permit the Legislature to provide for the abolition of the municipal courts," and it was constitutionally prescribed that upon a vote to unify "the judgeships in each municipal court in that county are abolished."[68]

The vast majority of California trial judges apparently favored and were ready for unification. Fifty of the fifty-eight counties voted to unify their trial courts into a single countywide superior court by December 31, 1998, less than two months after passage of Proposition 220.[69] By the end of the year 2000, five of the remaining eight counties also had voted to unify. Among the remaining three counties, Monterey and Kings Counties were unable to act until approval could be obtained by the U.S. Department of Justice that unification would comply with the terms of the federal Voting Rights Act of 1965. By June 2000, Kern County also unified, followed by Monterey and Kings Counties before the end of 2001.[70]

Although a bit beyond the year 2000 perimeter of this history, the final step in unification occurred on February 8, 2001, and is worth noting. On that date, Chief Justice George administered the oath of office to the last four municipal court judges in California, who thereby became judges of the Superior Court of California, County of Kings. That court thereby became the fifty-eighth and last to unify.

The high level of acceptance should not camouflage the fact that unification was in many jurisdictions a hard-fought battle. Generally, municipal court judges overwhelmingly favored unification and the issue turned on whether a majority of the superior court judges in each county could be persuaded to vote in favor of unification.

Nowhere was the question of unification more complex or intense than in Los Angeles County. Consider the size of the task. The superior court, already reputed to be the largest trial court in the world, had 238 judges, 62 commissioners, and 15 referees prior to unification. Headquartered in downtown Los Angeles, the court also had eight branch courts scattered around the county with several locations situated many miles from the main court. The farthest branch, in Lancaster, was eighty miles from downtown Los Angeles. Judges ran for office and were elected countywide.

There were twenty-four separate and autonomous municipal courts in the county, staffed by 190 judges and 76 commissioners. Judges ran for office and were elected from the districts served by their respective courts.

The combined superior and municipal courts would have 650 courtrooms situated in more than sixty buildings throughout the county. Of course, unification of the courts would also require merging hundreds of support staff members.

Among the many issues permeating the unification debate in Los Angeles was whether a single court with 428 judges and 153 subordinate judicial officers operating in dozens of locations could function effectively. Resolution of this issue and its extended family of issues stretched over many months, multiple analyses, protocols between the courts, and several ballots before a majority of judges on both levels voted to unify by a vote in the superior court of 153 to 75 and in the municipal court of 165 to 16. This was a result strongly sought and advocated for by the Judicial Council and the Chief Justice.[71]

This cursory description does little justice to the endless details and anecdotes regarding the creation of California's single largest court, but it does provide dramatic evidence of the challenge in merging the trial courts in the fifty-eight counties of California.

Unification, as a result of the often-divisive process of unifying, carries heavy baggage in terms of calamities predicted by opponents and dividends promised by proponents. For example, more than twenty-five years prior to the adoption of SCA 4, it was argued that unification would be "a major step toward combating the existing problems of trial court structure, management, organization, size, caseload, backlog, and distribution of judicial resources."[72] Unification, it was further asserted, would deliver a simplified court structure, comprehensive countywide jurisdiction, improved administration, maximum utilization of judicial resources, and increased uniformity.[73] Later supporters of unification also argued there would be substantial fiscal savings as a result of increased efficiencies achieved through unification.

By the year 2050, whether these aspirations are fulfilled should be clear. In the meantime, it appears likely that proponents of unification will be vindicated. To cite one of several encouraging assessments, Chief Justice George, addressing a joint session of the California Legislature early in 2001, advised that:

> The speed and enthusiasm with which unification was embraced by the trial courts has been more than justified by the benefits that it has brought. The prime anticipated benefit of unification was the flexibility it would afford in using available judicial and administrative resources. Not only has this flexibility turned out to be tremendously useful in expanding existing services, but another benefit has emerged as well: it has permitted a great amount of innovation, allowing the public's needs to be met by new and previously unavailable means.
>
> What often has been striking has been that the apprehension in some quarters that countywide unification would lead to less responsiveness to local concerns not only has proved unfounded, but the opposite has occurred.[74]

An independent assessment of the impacts of unification, commissioned by the AOC, also has reported favorable results:

> Participants in this study overwhelmingly agreed that unification of the trial courts has been a positive development for the California judicial system—one that has benefited the communities the courts serve as well as the judiciary and court staff. The most often cited improvements that have resulted from or been facilitated by trial court unification are:
>
> ◆ Greater cooperation and teamwork between the judiciary, other branches of government, and the community.
> ◆ More uniformity and efficiency in case processing and more timely disposition of cases.
> ◆ Enhanced opportunities for innovation, self-evaluation and re-engineering of court operations.
> ◆ More coherence to the governance of the courts and greater understanding by other branches of government and the public.
> ◆ Courts becoming a unified entity and speaking with one voice in dealings with the public, county agencies, and the justice system partners.
> ◆ Greater public access and an increased focus on accountability and service.[75]

The Distance Traveled

Before leaving the subject of structure and the promise of unification, it is appropriate to pause and reflect on the progress made during the last fifty years of the twentieth century. Thanks to the culminating efforts of Chief Justice George and Administrative Director Vickrey, acting in concert with a large host of contributors, California concluded the era with fifty-eight superior courts vested with authority and responsibility for all matters of general jurisdiction. By contrast, on January 1, 1950, we had fifty-eight superior courts with limited jurisdiction and a collection of other trial courts as described at the time by Chief Justice Gibson:

> There are 768 courts in this state which exercise jurisdiction inferior to that of the superior court. They may be divided into two groups—city courts and township courts, the basis of the classification being the political subdivision for which the court is organized, that is, whether it is organized in a city or in a judicial township. Each of these two groups may in turn be divided into

types of courts. There are six kinds of city courts: municipal courts of the San Francisco type, a second kind of municipal court such as is established in San Jose and Tulare, two kinds of police courts, city justices' courts, and city courts. There are, as you know, two types of township courts: Class A justices' courts and Class B justices' courts. Thus, there are eight different types of courts below the superior court.

Municipal courts of the first type mentioned, established pursuant to section 11, article VI of the Constitution, are found in San Francisco, Sacramento, Los Angeles, Long Beach, Santa Monica, Pasadena, Compton, Inglewood and San Diego. Although the organizational basis of the municipal court is a city, that court exercises exclusive jurisdiction within the county in certain cases and is generally supported by the county.

There are two municipal courts in the state organized pursuant to section 8½ of article XI of the Constitution, which are very different from those named above. One is established in San Jose and the other in Tulare. Neither of these courts, however, is called a municipal court, both being designated in the city charters as police courts. Accordingly, when I mention municipal courts hereafter, I will be referring to the type established in cities such as San Francisco and Los Angeles.

Police courts are established in 45 cities in this state. The source of the jurisdiction of 43 of those courts is generally found in city charters, and the authority to create them is found in section 8½ of article XI of the Constitution. The jurisdiction of the police courts in the various cities therefore differs according to the charter provisions of each particular city. A second kind of police court has been created by the Legislature pursuant to its general authority to establish inferior courts in incorporated cities. Such courts are located in the cities of Alviso and Gilroy, which are incorporated under special legislative acts.

In four cities, Berkeley, Oakland, Alameda and Stockton, there are city justices' court authorized by statute, and they, of course, are not to be confused with township justices' courts.

The most numerous kind of city court is called a "city court." There are 243 of these courts in fifth and sixth class cities, and they are successors of the old recorders' courts.

The township courts, as you know, are called justices' courts. They are divided into Class A and Class B courts. The classification is, of course, dependent upon population, and the difference between the courts is largely one of jurisdiction. There are 42 Class A township justices' courts and 423 Class B township justices' courts. The Class A justice's court may also exercise exclusive county-wide jurisdiction in certain cases, although its organizational basis is a judicial subdivision of the county.[76]

Fifty years later Chief Justice George placed the progress during this half-century into appropriate perspective when, upon completion of unification, he remarked: "Rather than concluding that Kings County's unification primarily signifies an ending, now that this day has arrived, I suggest instead that the proper image is that of a phoenix—of a rebirth of California's court system."[77]

Notes

1 Judicial Council of California, *Twelfth Biennial Report of the Judicial Council of California to the Governor and the Legislature* (1948), p. 14.

2 California Statutes 1947, chapter 47, p. 3448.

3 Judicial Council, *Twelfth Biennial Report* (1948), p. 15.

4 Chief Justice Phil S. Gibson, Reorganization of Our Inferior Courts, speech to the Stanislaus County Bar Association (October 28, 1949), reported in *Journal of the State Bar of California* 24 (1949), p. 384.

5 Judicial Council, *Twelfth Biennial Report* (1948), p. 15.

6 Id., pp. 17–20.

7 Id., p. 18.

8 California Statutes 1949, chapter 1286, pp. 2268–71.

9 William Wirt Blume, "California Courts in Historical Perspective," *Hastings Law Journal* 22 (1970–1971), pp. 181–85.

10 Chief Justice Gibson, Reorganization of Our Inferior Courts, p. 382.

11 For example, Dorothy W. Nelson, "Should Los Angeles County Adopt a Single-Trial-Court Plan?" *Southern California Law Review* 33 (1960), p. 119.

12 *Gordon v. Justice Court* (1974) 12 Cal.3d 323 [115 Cal.Rptr. 632, 525 P.2d 72].

13 Id., p. 326.

14 Ralph N. Kleps, "Contingency Planning for State Court Systems," *Judicature* 59 (1975), p. 64.

15 Id., pp. 64–65.

16 Booz, Allen & Hamilton Inc., *California Lower Court Study: Final Report* (September 15, 1971).

17 Id., p. 50.

18 For example, the Select Committee on Trial Court Delay's Subcommittee on Court Management, including Judge Homer B. Thompson, judge of the Superior Court of Santa Clara County and chair of the Select Committee,

served as the advisory body for the Booz Allen unified court study, along with Ralph N. Kleps, Administrative Director of the Courts, and Larry L. Sipes, the author of this chronicle, who was at the time director of the Select Committee.

[19] Booz, Allen & Hamilton Inc., *Unified Trial Court Feasibility Study: Final Report* (December 3, 1971), pp. 3–4.

[20] Id., p. 60.

[21] Id., pp. 68–111.

[22] [California] Select Committee on Trial Court Delay, *Report 4* (February 1972), p. 9.

[23] Id., pp. 9–25.

[24] Id., pp. 15–16.

[25] Id., pp. 17–18.

[26] Judicial Council of California, *Annual Report to the Governor and the Legislature* (1972), pp. 14–15.

[27] Id., p. 13.

[28] Id., pp. 17–21.

[29] The Judicial Council was instrumental in arranging introduction of proposed legislation to create the countywide courts of limited jurisdiction and administration of the court system (Senate Constitutional Amendment 15 and Senate Bill 296, Senator Grunsky) but these measures also failed in the legislature.

[30] [California] Select Committee on Trial Court Delay, *Report 1* (July 1971), p. 3.

[31] To achieve this goal, Senate Constitutional Amendment 41 and Senate Bill 852 by Senator Holmdahl and companion measures by Assembly Member Hayes were introduced during the 1972 legislative session to implement the Select Committee on Trial Court Delay's recommendations. None of these measures received favorable action by the legislature.

[32] For example, the *Report of the Advisory Commission to the Legislative Committee on Structure of Judiciary* (1974), a report by the Judicial Council's Management Committee recommending a single, unified superior court with two levels.

[33] Senate Bill 1134 (1977, effective January 1, 1978); California Statutes 1997, chapter 1051, pp. 3180–86.

34 California Constitution, article VI, section 6.

35 Judicial Council of California, Reports and Recommendations (May 1, 1982), tab 7; Court Management Committee, *Report and Recommendations Concerning the "El Cajon Experiment"* (April 22, 1982).

36 Assembly Constitutional Amendment 36 (1982).

37 *California Ballot Pamphlet, General Election* (November 2, 1982), pp. 38–41.

38 Limited exemptions extended to incumbent justice court judges who held office on January 1, 1988, but this exemption expired on January 1, 1995. See *California Ballot Pamphlet, General Election* (November 8, 1988), pp. 52–55.

39 Judicial Council of California, *Annual Report to the Governor and the Legislature* (1994), p. 8.

40 California Statutes 1991, chapter 90, section 2(b)(3), p. 406.

41 California Statutes 1991, chapter 90, section 6, p. 407, adding section 68112 to the California Government Code.

42 Id., pp. 407–9.

43 Judicial Council of California, *Annual Report to the Governor and the Legislature* (1992), volume 1, pp. 7–10.

44 Id., p. 8.

45 Judicial Council of California, *Annual Report to the Governor and the Legislature* (1993), volume 1, p. 18.

46 Judicial Council of California, *Annual Report to the Governor and the Legislature* (1996), p. 21.

47 Id., p. 19.

48 Id., pp. 19–20.

49 Judicial Council of California, *Year in Review* (1996), p. 16.

50 Judicial Council of California, Joint Subcommittee of Trial Court Presiding Judges and Court Administrators Advisory Committees, "Trial Court Unification: Proposed Constitutional Amendments and Commentary" (September 11, 1993), pp. 4–6, in *Reports and Recommendations* (September 23, 1993), tab 3.

[51] Judicial Council of California, "Report on Trial Court Unification: Senate Constitutional Amendment No. 3 (Lockyer)" in *Reports and Recommendations* (September 23, 1993), tab 3.

[52] See, for example, Judicial Council of California, minutes (September 23, 1993), pp. 3–5.

[53] Judicial Council, *Annual Report* (1994), p. 6.

[54] Robert W. Tobin et al., *California Unification Study* (Denver: National Center for State Courts, 1994), p. 4.

[55] California Law Revision Commission, "Trial Court Unification: Constitutional Revision (SCA 3)," *California Law Revision Commission Reports, Recommendations, and Studies* 24 (1994), p. 5.

[56] Ibid.

[57] Id., p. 35.

[58] For example, California Legislature, *Joint Hearing on Trial Court Unification Under SCA 3* (October 8, 1993), pp. 31–41.

[59] Judicial Council of California, "Trial Court Unification: Senate Constitutional Amendment No. 3 (SCA 3)" in *Reports and Recommendations (May 17, 1994), tab 5; Annual Report to the Governor and the Legislature* (1995), p. 21.

[60] *California Supplemental Ballot Pamphlet, General Election* (November 8, 1994), p. 16.

[61] California Constitution, article VI, section 5(e).

[62] *California Voter Information Guide and Ballot Pamphlet, Primary Election* (June 2, 1998), pp. 10–11.

[63] Ibid.

[64] Id., p. 9.

[65] California Secretary of State, *Statement of Vote* (June 2, 1998), p. viii.

[66] California Rules of Court, rules 701–709.

[67] California Government Code, section 70201.

[68] California Constitution, article VI, section 23(a) and (b).

[69] Judicial Council of California, Administrative Office of the Courts, *Invested in Justice: 1999 Annual Report,* p. 4.

70 Judicial Council of California, Administrative Office of the Courts, *Special Report—Proposition 220* (June 12, June 29, and July 16, 1998).

71 Judicial Council of California, Resolution of July 15, 1999, urging unification.

72 Select Committee on Trial Court Delay, *Report 4*, p. 20.

73 Ibid.

74 Chief Justice Ronald M. George, State of the Judiciary Address, California Legislature (March 20, 2001), p. 5.

75 American Institutes for Research, *Analysis of Trial Court Unification in California—Final Report* (September 28, 2000), p. vii.

76 Chief Justice Gibson, Reorganization of Our Inferior Courts, pp. 384–85.

77 Administrative Office of the Courts, Public Information Office, "California Courts Make History, as Last County Unifies Trial Courts Today," Press Release Number 14, February 8, 2001.

Chapter 6
Stable Funding of the Trial Courts

Overview

he story of court funding is a story of trial courts. The state traditionally has paid the expenses of the appellate courts, Judicial
Council, and Administrative Office of the Courts (AOC) and
continues to do so.

Court funding also is a story of both revenue and expenses.

As of 1950, the California Legislature controlled both the revenues
and expenses of trial courts. In general, the state paid most of the
compensation of superior court judges and took a relatively small slice of
the revenues. The balance of the expenses for the superior, municipal,
and justice courts fell with minor exceptions upon counties and cities,
which also divided the lion's share of the revenues.

The proposals for unification in the 1970s were accompanied by
proposals for full state funding of the courts. Although these proposals
were unsuccessful, the seeds were planted.

Proposition 13 in 1978 limited property taxation by local government, which quickly began to pinch budgets. The search for ways to reduce local expenses nourished the seeds of state funding for the courts.

Beginning in the mid-1980s, there was a series of measures in the legislature to increase the state's contribution to payment of trial court expenses. In 1988 the legislature took the first serious step in this direction by appropriating $300 million in the form of block grants to counties. The underlying philosophy was that all citizens of the state should enjoy equal access to the courts free from disparities in justice that might flow from local funding.

By this time, counties were paying almost 90 percent of all trial court costs but receiving only 50 percent of the revenues with a shortfall of approximately $250 million of expenses over revenues.

For the next several years, state funding was a dance of one step forward and two back, due for the most part to economic recession in the early 1990s.

The Judicial Council took the initiative by, among other things, creating in 1990 an advisory body on trial court funding. Concurrently, the legislature enacted the Trial Court Realignment and Efficiency Act of 1991, which introduced trial court coordination and a statewide search for reductions in court costs.

The Judicial Council advanced matters by establishing the Trial Court Budget Commission (TCBC) in 1992. This in turn enabled the Judicial Council and AOC in 1994 to present to the governor and legislature the state's first consolidated trial court budget. The process of budget refinement by the judicial branch continued, as did the failure of the legislature and governor to fulfill promises of increased trial court support.

Matters changed course dramatically with passage of the Lockyer-Isenberg Trial Court Funding Act of 1997, which consolidated all court funding at the state level and conferred responsibility on the Judicial Council to allocate state funds to the courts.

Revenues, of course, were not ignored. The legislature increased civil filing fees, commandeered a larger share of all revenues, and compelled the larger counties to continue contributing based on 1994 trial court expenses.

Two issues were unresolved by the shift to state funding, but substantial progress was being made toward resolution by century's end. First was the status of court personnel, who had been employees of local government. Second was responsibility for court facilities, which traditionally had been vested in local government.

The ultimate fruit of state funding appears attributable in fair measure to governance of the judicial branch in the 1990s. The judicial commitment, through strategic planning, to improving access, fairness, and diversity suggests that the other branches of government were reassured that the realignment in funding would modernize judicial administration practices, as promised by the Judicial Council and AOC.

*B*y the close of the last century, state funding of the entire judicial branch was substantially achieved. There are many reasons this is a monument to the improved administration of justice, but the heart of the matter was captured by Chief Justice Ronald M. George in a March 2001 State of the Judiciary address to the California Legislature.

> The pre-existing system, with funding bifurcated between the counties and the state, bred uncertainty for the courts and discouraged a sense of commitment by either funding partner. Disparities in the quality of justice dispensed across the state were common and erratic. Local courts were on the verge of closing, with staff cutbacks and unfunded payrolls, facilities in a state of dangerous disrepair, services to the public drastically curtailed, and, ultimately, the entire administration of justice at risk.
>
> Why does a funding source matter? Quite simply, state funding allows courts to cope in coordinated fashion with change and the public's needs. But stable state funding has done far more than relieve current anxiety and uncertainty: it has given us room to think ahead and to plan, and it has promoted consistency.
>
> Instead of bracing to react to emergencies and shortfalls beyond their control, our courts can look at current circumstances, project future needs, and decide how best to meet them in orderly fashion. And we also are better positioned to deal with the inevitable crises that occasionally confront our court system.[1]

Similar to unification, the struggle with funding revolves around the trial courts since the appellate courts, the Judicial Council, and the Administrative Office of the Courts traditionally have been supported by the state. Also similar to unification, local interests were prominent and nowhere more so than in issues of revenue.

Revenues

Acquiring the funds with which to operate is only one part of the financial picture of the courts. Revenues and the distribution of those revenues are the remainder of the picture. Leaders within the judicial branch of government traditionally have objected to and resisted efforts to treat courts as revenue-generating mechanisms. Nonetheless, policymakers in the legislative and executive branches, at both state and local levels, have kept a keen eye on the moneys collected by the courts and have had a great deal to say about the use of those moneys.

There are three main revenue streams for courts:

◆ *Fines* imposed on persons guilty of violating criminal statutes or committing infractions. Penalties for traffic violations, including parking infractions, are the largest source of fines.

◆ *Fees* charged by the court for initiating legal proceedings or key steps in legal proceedings, such as filing an appeal after an adverse trial court judgment.

◆ *Forfeitures* of funds deposited with the court to secure action by a litigant. Upon failure to perform that act, the litigant's deposit is forfeited to the court. The most common example of forfeiture is failure to appear at a scheduled court event in criminal proceedings with the result that bail, or a bail bond, is forfeited to the court.

There are additional sources of revenues such as charges for photocopying and certifying court records, but these are minor when compared to the three main revenue streams.

Trial Court Funding in 1950

Before plunging into the thicket of court finance at the midpoint of the last century, it is useful to recall that prior to reorganization of the lower courts in 1950 there were more than 700 judicial entities operating under various titles, as vividly described by Chief Justice Phil S. Gibson.[2] At the beginning of 1950, according to the Judicial Council, there was a close correlation between the provisions made for the financial support of these "inferior courts" and for the disposition of fines and forfeitures collected by them. The council reported that "revenue from misdemeanors is distributed to, or divided between, cities and counties largely according to whether the city or county employs the officer making the arrest or drawing the complaint or bears the expense of court maintenance."[3]

While accurate, this summary of conditions obscured the bewildering complexity of lower court financing.

◆ A municipal court was principally supported by the county in which the court was located, subject to partial reimbursement from the city in which it was situated.

◆ A township justice court was maintained by the county alone.

◆ A city justice court was supported by the city in which it was established unless the city charter also established a police court, in which case the cost of the city justice court was borne by the county.

◆ A police court or city court was supported by the city in which it was established.

Provisions for support of this array of judicial entities were relatively simple compared to provisions for distribution of the revenues, which are generally described as follows with the caveat that the detailed provisions contained exceptions or other qualifications that need not be presented here since even a broad description illustrates the complexity.

◆ In a municipal court, fines and forfeitures in criminal cases were paid to the city if the complaint was drawn by a city officer or employee and to the county if drawn by a county or state officer or employee.

◆ In a township justice court, fines and forfeitures were paid to the county if the offense involved a state law or county ordinance and to the city if the offense involved a city ordinance. The city also retained the proceeds from state Vehicle Code violations unless the arrest was made by a state or county officer, in which case the proceeds belonged to the county.

◆ In a city justice court, fines and forfeitures were paid to the city maintaining the court or to the county if the county provided that support.

◆ In a police court or city court, the city maintaining the court retained fines and forfeitures unless the violation was of the Vehicle Code and the arrest was made by a county officer, in which case 50 percent of the fine or forfeiture had to be paid to the county.[4]

In proposing reorganization of the array of lower courts into justice and municipal courts, the Judicial Council apparently tampered little with the existing formulas for distribution of fines and forfeitures. It did, however, clarify that the expenses of the justice and municipal courts under the reorganization plan primarily were to be county expenses.[5]

The superior court financial picture was somewhat simpler but only because the system was simpler. As required by the California Constitution, there was a superior court in each county. The legislature had broad authority over funding for and distribution of revenues from these courts. For either the superior courts or the lower courts, the ratio of expenses to revenues at midcentury is not readily available.

As enacted in 1950, Proposition 3 retained the power of the legislature to prescribe the number, qualifications, and compensation of lower court judges, officers, and attaches, thus preserving legislative control over the most significant items of cost in lower court operations.

Early Efforts to Achieve State Funding

The first significant proposals for state financing of trial court operations were made in the early 1970s by the same two entities that called for a single-level trial court: the consulting firm of Booz, Allen & Hamilton, retained by the Judicial Council to recommend improvements in the lower courts, and the Select Committee on Trial Court Delay. The Select Committee presented the following snapshot of the existing funding system:

> The present methods of financing our trial courts are a patchwork. The counties bear all capital costs. Salaries for Superior Court Judges are primarily state expenses, while Municipal and Justice Court Judges are paid entirely by the counties in which they sit. The Legislature prescribes the salaries of Superior and Municipal Court Judges but each county determines the salaries for its Justice Court Judges. Likewise, the counties finance any retirement benefits for Justice Court Judges but the State financially supports and administers the retirement system for Superior and Municipal Court Judges. And, as noted above, the counties bear the expense of all non-judicial court personnel.[6]

The supporting reasons for adopting state funding were articulated by Booz Allen and endorsed by the Select Committee:

> It provides an opportunity to use the state's broader revenue base to avoid underfunding of courts in counties with marginal financial resources for supporting judicial services or in counties which are unwilling to provide adequate financing.
>
> It provides a vehicle for insuring that court expenditures for such items as salaries, retirement and training are uniform throughout the state. As a result, opportunities are increased for upgrading the caliber of both judicial and non-judicial personnel.
>
> It provides an approach for the state to unify, strengthen and assert its expanded policy-making and management role over California's trial courts. It also fixes financial responsibility with the state to fund the decisions it makes regarding judicial policies and management.
>
> It reinforces the fact that judicial services, although provided locally, are of statewide importance.
>
> It can be used as a financial subvention to county governments, depending on how court revenues are used, at least in avoiding future court cost increases.

Without state financing, it is doubtful if a unified trial court concept will receive the impetus needed to insure its eventual implementation.[7]

The Judicial Council adopted the more cautious approach of recommending only that "the state assume the costs for salaries and fringe benefits of all judges and court-related personnel in the county court system" (which was intended to supersede the justice and municipal courts).[8]

To further place these proposals in context, it is important to note that prior to the Booz Allen reports in 1971 advocates and opponents were sparring without financial data. In fact, the first comprehensive attempt to assess the total statewide cost of operating any level of trial court apparently was made in connection with the 1971 studies by Booz Allen of lower and unified courts. For fiscal year 1969–1970, the estimated total cost for operating the justice and municipal courts was $61,048,847 and superior court operating costs totaled $57,627,500.[9]

The combined expenses of operating all three levels of trial courts at the time approached $119 million, a figure that Booz Allen estimated would increase to $137 million following unification.[10] Even so, these actual and projected costs were both less than the estimated annual revenues of $161 million from the trial courts.[11]

Approximately $122 million, or almost 80 percent, of these revenues flowed from justice and municipal courts and were distributed among cities, the state, and an array of county funds (general, road, fish and game, and law library). Of this amount the state took approximately 15 percent and the remainder was divided equally among counties and cities.[12]

As with the various proposals for trial court reorganization during the early 1970s, the proposals for a major increase in state funding failed for lack of legislative approval.

The Catalyst: Proposition 13

Serious consideration of state funding for trial courts probably would not have occurred for many more years but for Proposition 13, proposed through the initiative process and adopted by the voters in 1978.[13] The effects of Proposition 13 have been documented, debated, litigated, praised, and cursed in a variety of venues during the intervening years and will not be repeated here. The important fact is that Proposition 13 limited the ability of local governments to increase revenues through increases in property taxes, which were their primary source of funding.

Within a relatively short time, limitations on property taxes began severely to pinch the budgets of counties and other agencies of local government. All expenditures and alternative sources of revenue were closely scrutinized. Among those expenses were the costs for operation of the superior, municipal, and justice courts, which, aside from partial judicial compensation paid by the state, were a responsibility of the counties. Among the revenues were the filing fees, fines, forfeitures, penalties, and other charges imposed by the courts and remitted, in part, to the counties. However, as explained a bit further on in this story, the counties' expenses exceeded the counties' share of revenues.

There was and is considerable merit to the policy position asserted at various times by the Judicial Council that court resources should be equalized throughout the state and that access to justice should not vary from county to county due to variations in resources. The subject of trial court funding, however, was a blend of policy and practicality and should not be considered without also acknowledging the financial predicament of local government created by Proposition 13. The efforts of local government, particularly the counties, to escape the burden of funding court operations were a catalyst in the move toward state funding.

A Second Effort

At the midpoint of the 1980s, the state had responsibility for funding most of the salaries and health and retirement benefits of superior court judges. That had been the extent of state fiscal support since 1955. With the minor exceptions of state subsidies for rural trial courts and modest state reimbursement for mandated programs, the counties were responsible for funding the remainder of trial court operations. The state's contribution equaled approximately 5 percent of the total trial court operating costs.[14]

New stirrings on the subject of increased state funding began in 1984 when Senator Barry Keene, who also was one of the legislative members of the Judicial Council, introduced the Trial Court Funding Act of 1984 (Senate Bill 1850; Assembly Bill 3108 [Robinson]), which included a notable list of legislative findings:

◆ The trial of civil and criminal actions is an integral and necessary function of the judicial branch of state government.

◆ All citizens of this state should enjoy equal and ready access to the trial courts.

◆ Local funding of trial courts may create disparities in the availability of the courts for resolution of disputes and dispensation of justice.

◆ Funding of trial courts should not create financial barriers to the fair and proper resolution of actions.

◆ This legislation is enacted to promote the general welfare and protect the public interest in a viable and accessible judicial system.[15]

The proposed legislation introduced the concepts of local option in the context of funding and block grants.

Counties could elect whether or not to participate. In those counties exercising the option, the state would pay a set sum per year, adjusted for inflation, for every superior court and municipal court judgeship and for subordinate judicial positions. These state funds could only be used for court operations. In return, the counties would relinquish to the state the great bulk of the revenues received by the courts from filing fees, fines, and forfeitures. The bills were joined and passed by the legislature but vetoed by Governor George Deukmejian.

SB 1850 and AB 3108 are important for several reasons. They renewed debate on state responsibility for financial support of the trial courts. Introduction of the mechanism of block grants, as well as the concept of local option, also was significant. And the proposed measure embraced several principles important to Chief Justice Rose Elizabeth Bird and by implication to the Judicial Council:

1. The trial courts are part of a single state court system;

2. State funding should pay for trial court operations while retaining local administrative control;

3. A cap should be placed on escalating civil filing fees limited to a cost-of-living type adjustment to avoid restricted access to the courts by middle class litigants, or the development of a user fee funded court system.[16]

Onward Toward State Funding

The efforts of Senator Keene and Assembly Member Richard Robinson bore modest fruit in 1985. The Trial Court Funding Act of 1985 was enacted but without implementing appropriations.

Real fruit was harvested in 1988 with enactment of the Brown-Presley Trial Court Funding Act.[17] Incorporating the earlier, dual concepts of local option and state block grants to counties based upon the number of judicial positions, the 1988 legislation was funded with approximately $300 million. Philosophically, the bill embraced the legislative findings proposed in 1984 with explicit acknowledgment that "[a]ll citizens of this state should enjoy equal and ready access to the trial courts" and that "[l]ocal funding of trial courts may create disparities in the . . . dispensation of justice."[18]

The act also created a Trial Court Improvement Fund for Judicial Council grants to improve trial court efficiency and management, but it was not funded.[19]

It is interesting to compare the level of support enacted in 1988 with the known revenues and expenses of trial courts. As of 1982[20] the total estimated cost of operating all trial courts, excluding capital or physical expenses, was $526,276,851 per year.[21] The total estimated revenues for the same period were $429,839,354.[22] These revenues were distributed among the counties, cities, and state with approximately one-half ($211,748,909) to counties, more than 30 percent ($144,536,607) to cities, and less than 20 percent ($73,553,838) to the state.[23]

A compelling historical fact is pertinent here. A mere decade earlier, the best estimate that Booz Allen could make of the cost of trial court operations was $119 million, accompanied by an estimate that revenues exceeded costs by 25 percent. By 1983, costs were estimated with presumably better accuracy as almost five times greater than $119 million. Revenues were estimated at less than expenses, instead of more than expenses.

Although the counties received the lion's share of revenues, they were bearing 81 percent of superior court costs, 97 percent of municipal court costs, and 100 percent of justice court costs for a total of 88.5 percent of all trial court costs. The state, by contrast, paid for only 11.5 percent. The counties' share of revenues ($211,748,909) fell considerably below the counties' share of trial court expenses ($465,900,000).[24]

The Trial Court Funding Act of 1985 was a breakthrough both in state funding for trial court operations and in relief for counties, but it obviously was not assumption of full responsibility, either in concept or reality. However, the momentum in that direction had begun. By 1989, the first year of full funding under the terms of the Brown-Presley Trial Court Funding Act of 1988,[25] all counties had opted to participate. The state appropriated $527 million to the counties to support trial court operations.[26]

Implementing a Local Option

The 1988 legislation introduced a new ingredient that was destined to play a significant future role. The Brown-Presley Trial Court Funding Act required that a county's election to participate, and its eligibility to receive state block grant funds for trial court operations, had to be documented annually by a resolution signed by the chair of the county board of supervisors, the presiding judge of the superior court, and the presiding judge of the municipal court (or, in the absence of a municipal court, the justice court judge serving in the county seat). This signing of the resolution indicated the concurrence by a majority of the supervisors and the judges of each court.[27]

Obstruction: The Recession of the Early 1990s

If Proposition 13 in 1978 was a catalyst for state funding of trial courts, the national economic recession that began in 1990, with particularly harsh impact in California, was an obstacle.

As noted, the state furnished block grants and other appropriations to each county for trial court expenses in the total amount of $527 million during 1989. However, that defrayed only 44 percent of total trial court costs and, due to fiscal problems created by recession, the amount was reduced to 38 percent the following year.

The Judicial Council succinctly summarized as follows the status of trial court funding by the state in 1990, which was the second full fiscal year of trial court funding under the Brown-Presley Trial Court Funding Act of 1988. The 1990 state budget provided $398.2 million to fund the program into which all counties opted for 1990. Components of the act were:

◆ Counties would receive quarterly block grants averaging $50,562 per judicial position ($202,248 annually). The 1990 state budget included $340.7 million for these block grants.

◆ Counties would receive supplemental block grant amounts equal to municipal and justice court judges' salaries, based on the existing formula of state participation in superior court judges' salaries. The 1990 state budget contained $51.7 million for this purpose.[28]

◆ The state budget again included no money for the Trial Court Improvement Fund.

◆ The state budget did, however, include $109.5 million for assistance to the trial courts for ongoing programs existing prior to the act. This included $69.2 million for the state's share of superior court judges' salaries and $36.4 million for superior, municipal, and justice court judges' retirement.

◆ Finally, about $3.9 million was budgeted for continuing court-related local assistance programs such as payments to counties for costly homicide trials.

To summarize, for 1990 the state budgeted an estimated $507.7 million in assistance to the trial courts, comprising $109.5 million for preexisting programs and $398.2 million provided under the act.[29]

These conditions led the judiciary to reaffirm the view that the quality of justice in the state's courts neither could nor should be dependent on the financial health or discretion of the counties. Instead, it was necessary to move toward adequate state funding of the courts.

The Trial Court Budget Commission

The first step in this new endeavor was to create a Judicial Council Advisory Committee on State Court Funding. Contributing to creation of this committee was continuing friction between county officials and trial judges over the requirement that a majority of the judges in each trial court approve the county decision to participate in the state funding program. In 1990, this friction had reached the point that a committee of county administrative officers requested and were granted a meeting with key officials in the AOC to discuss removing the requirement for judicial approval.

The counties argued that judges were extracting from the counties enhanced fringe benefits as the price of consent to county participation in the state funding program. The judges in response expressed the concern that the removal of judicial concurrence as a condition of opting into the program would negate the courts' ability to receive an equitable share of funds.[30] This was one of the first items referred to the new committee for consideration and recommendation.

At this point Assembly Member Phillip Isenberg joined the cast in a leading role on both state funding and trial court structure. One of his first actions was to introduce the Trial Court Realignment and Efficiency Act of 1991 (Assembly Bill 1297), which was adopted as described in Chapter Five.

It is interesting to note that Assembly Member Isenberg, as of 1990, had become one of the two legislative members of the Judicial Council. Equally significant is the fact that the other legislative member was Senator Bill Lockyer.

In some respects, the legislative findings in the Trial Court Realignment and Efficiency Act are as notable as the substantive provisions. The legislature recited that the state faced an unprecedented fiscal crisis, requiring the participation of every branch of government in the search for a solution. The legislature also reiterated the findings from past legislation that state funding of trial court operations is the most logical approach for a variety of reasons, including achieving "a uniform and equitable court system" and "increased access to justice for the citizens of California."[31] The legislature further conceded that state assumption of trial court funding had diminished, forcing counties to fund a larger share of the growing costs of trial court operations. This led to a renewed legislative declaration of intent to provide one-half of the funding of trial court operations in 1991 and to increase that share by 5 percent per year until the trial courts were 70 percent funded by the state.

The other half of the picture of court funding was not forgotten, by any means. Revenues were increased by the legislature through increased fines. A larger share of such revenues was acquired by the state. However, the heart of the act, from both fiscal and operational perspectives, compelled "each superior, municipal, and justice court in each county" to "prepare and submit to the Judicial Council for review and approval a trial court coordination plan designed to achieve maximum utilization of judicial and other court resources and statewide cost reductions in court operations of at least 3 percent" in 1992–1993 and a further 2 percent in each of the two following years.[32]

Due to the recession of the early 1990s, the legislatively declared commitment of achieving 70 percent state funding of trial court costs by 1995 was not only fading; it was shriveling. State funding provided for 51.4 percent of such costs in 1991 and declined to 50.6 percent in 1992. The governor's proposed budget for 1993 actually decreased the trial court appropriation by another 6.1 percent to cover approximately 44 percent of costs.[33]

Confronted with the gap between legislative promises and the reality of declining state funding, the Judicial Council began seeking new approaches to court funding. The most prominent result was creation of the Trial Court Budget Commission, proposed by the Judicial Council and sanctioned by the legislature—thanks, again, to the efforts of Assembly Member Isenberg.[34] The legislation directed the Judicial Council to provide for the TCBC by rule and in turn directed the TCBC to prepare annual budget submittals for the trial courts with concurrent authority to "allocate and reallocate funds appropriated for the trial courts" to the extent authorized by the annual budget. The TCBC also was empowered to establish deadlines and procedures for submission of material by the trial courts.

In the meantime, the percentage of trial court expenses funded by the state continued to decline.

The Judicial Council announced establishment of the TCBC in November 1992 as an advisory committee to the Judicial Council. Membership consisted of twenty-six trial judges from ten geographic regions. Each region had two commission members—one judge from a superior court and one from a municipal or justice court. Because of its size, the Los Angeles region had eight members. Six advisory members were appointed—four court administrators and two county administrators.[35]

The TCBC hit the ground running. It created eleven functional categories for trial court budget purposes, to replace block grant funding, and utilized the AOC and the accounting firm of Ernst & Young to establish baseline budget requests for each trial court.[36] These processes were embodied in rule 810 of the California Rules of Court.

Based upon this work and for the first time in state history, the judicial branch through the TCBC presented a consolidated trial court budget proposal to the governor and legislature. Trial court needs were projected at $1.75 billion in 1994, although it is not clear that either the courts or the counties could substantiate the actual costs of trial court operations. Governor Pete Wilson and the TCBC differed on estimated trial court expenses, but the governor proposed a $400 million increase in state support for trial courts for a total of $1.017 billion, which represented 58 percent of total statewide trial court expenditures as approved by the TCBC.[37]

Also in 1994, Assembly Member Isenberg successfully sponsored legislation that, among other things, declared the intent of the legislature to create a budgeting system for the judicial branch that protects the independence of the judiciary while preserving financial accountability (Assembly Bill 2544). The act, adopted by the California Legislature and approved by the governor, also implemented the transition from block grant funding to function funding consistent with the recommendations of the TCBC and rule 810 of the California Rules of Court.

The ensuing two years were a period of dichotomy. The judiciary refined budget justification and accountability. The legislative and executive branches failed to deliver promised financial support for trial courts. As part of budget refinement, the TCBC in 1995 submitted its *Final Report on the Initial Statewide Minimum Standards for Trial Court Operations and Staffing*. The Judicial Council subsequently adopted and forwarded these standards to the legislature. Concurrently, the Judicial Council Task Force on Trial Court Funding endorsed the TCBC budgeting approach and urged the Judicial Council to seek the full funding recommended by the TCBC for 1996 even though the governor's proposed budget was $120 million less. The Judicial Council also accepted these recommendations.[38]

Meanwhile, in Sacramento the financial fate of the trial courts continued to deteriorate. The state provided only 34 percent of trial court funding in fiscal year 1994–1995. The legislature was forced to enact emergency legislation, signed by the governor, to provide $25 million in supplemental state funding, matched by the counties, to avoid trial courts in several counties terminating operations prior to the end of the fiscal year for lack of funds.

In 1996 a valiant effort by Assembly Member Isenberg (Assembly Bill 2553) to achieve full state responsibility for court funding achieved approval in both houses of the legislature—only to fail at the last minute due to conflicts between Assembly Member Isenberg and Senator Lockyer and opposition from Governor Wilson and several Assembly members, based upon provisions relating to collective bargaining by employees working in the courts. This collapse of an emerging consensus was particularly painful. The crisis continued into 1997.

State Funding Achieved

Passage of trial court funding by the Assembly and Senate was finally achieved primarily because of a collaborative search for politically and financially acceptable solutions. The key collaborators were the AOC on behalf of the Judicial Council, the council's Trial Court Presiding Judges and Court Administrators Advisory Committees, the California State Association of Counties, the governor's Department of Finance, and key legislative members and staff.[39]

By September 1997, the roller coaster ride was smoothed by passage of Assembly Bill 233, the Lockyer-Isenberg Trial Court Funding Act of 1997, which significantly restructured trial court funding.[40] This was a giant stride toward resolving major problems plaguing the judiciary.[41]

This legislation was signed by Governor Pete Wilson in October with an effective date of January 1, 1998. It effected major changes and broke considerable new ground in the process by:

◆ Consolidating all court funding at the state level, giving the legislature authority to make appropriations and the Judicial Council responsibility to allocate funds to the state's courts

◆ Capping counties' financial responsibility at the 1994 level, to be paid quarterly into a statewide trust fund

◆ Requiring the state to fund all future growth in the cost of court operations

◆ Authorizing the creation of forty new judgeships, contingent on an appropriation made in future legislation

◆ Requiring the state to provide 100 percent funding for court operations in the twenty smallest counties beginning July 1, 1998

◆ Raising a number of civil court fees to generate about $87 million annually for trial court funding[42]

The broad thrust of the legislation was to shift from the counties to the state the primary responsibility for and the burden of funding the trial courts. In effect, counties were relieved from open-ended financial responsibility for "court operations."[43] Since the appellate system already was state-funded, this meant, for all practical purposes, that the Judicial Council's philosophical and practical goal of state-supported courts throughout the state at long last had been achieved.

Financial cords among the state, counties, and trial courts were not totally severed, nor did counties escape the cost of funding court operations without paying a price. Each county was required, for example, to pay to the state annually a sum equal to the amount paid by that county for court operations in 1994.[44] This burden subsequently was eliminated for the smaller thirty-eight counties but preserved for the twenty largest.

Another price paid was the requirement that each county annually remit to the state a sum equal to the amounts of fines and forfeitures shared with the state in 1994 as well as one-half of all future growth in fines and forfeitures.[45] Even at the end of the funding saga, revenues figured as prominently as expenses.

The transition, however, was rocky. There were cashflow shortfalls. Court revenues declined to levels below those projected. Counties attempted to further shift costs from county to court budgets. Both courts and counties appealed for relief at various critical points in the process. Nonetheless, it seems evident that new directions were charted. Fiscal stability began to prevail. Policy and strategic plans began to drive funding. Finally multi-year strategic efforts were possible in critical areas ranging from technology to assisting small courts to jury reform to protecting children in court processes.

Two issues were unresolved by the Lockyer-Isenberg legislation. The most prominent was the status of the county employees working for the trial courts. Would they remain county employees, become employees in a statewide judicial personnel system, or be given a new status crafted for the occasion? The other major issue involved courthouses and related facilities. They remained local responsibilities pending deferred consideration of further state assumption.

The balance of the century (1998 and 1999) was devoted to implementing and digesting both state funding and trial court unification. The status of employees has been a matter of extensive negotiations, and the recommendations of a special Judicial Council Task Force on Trial Court Employees were under consideration as the century closed.[46] Resolution of the facilities question is a longer-term proposition, but the search was well under way for a permanent solution. For example, the Judicial Council, in response to legislative direction,[47] created a Task Force on Court Facilities with the hope that it would facilitate appropriate and adequate facilities for all court operations to the satisfaction of both the courts and the counties.

These are not idle hopes. Shortly following the close of the century, important legislative steps were taken, with Judicial Council support, toward state responsibility for facilities and court responsibility for persons employed in the courts, as discussed in Chapter Fifteen.

In addition to major issues regarding employee status and facilities, implementation of state funding requires a multifaceted transformation in the relationships among the counties, courts, and AOC. At the heart of this transformation is the question of how to acquire for trial courts the support services previously provided by counties, which counties are no longer obliged to perform in the absence of compensation. In the view of one knowledgeable observer, these administrative issues "will ultimately have a bearing on whether the Lockyer-Isenberg Trial Court Funding Act of 1997 is hailed as a success or chastised as a failed attempt of the Legislature to 'get its hands around' the funding and public access issues of the trial courts."[48]

An Advocate: The Judicial Council and the Quality of Justice

Before leaving the subject of court funding, it is imperative to address the vital role played by Judicial Council endorsement and adoption of values regarding the quality of justice. If Proposition 13 was a catalyst and recession was an obstacle, Judicial Council advocacy in this area was a facilitator.

This evolved as part of the Judicial Council's maturation in planning. A critical product of that evolution, discussed in Chapter Four, deserves revisiting. That product is the Strategic and Reorganization Plan adopted by the Judicial Council in 1992 with five explicit goals, including a commitment "to improve access, fairness, and diversity in the judiciary," and "to modernize judicial administration practices."[49]

If the Judicial Council had not committed to these qualitative goals and reaffirmed that commitment, the funding quest could well have remained a repetition of the old refrain that courts need more money and a more reliable source of money. The goals of the new strategic plan raised deliberations to a new level. This was not just renewing the traditional plea for additional funding. Instead, the judicial branch through its governing body was offering assurance that present and future funds would be dedicated to improvement—including improved access, fairness, and diversity—as well as modern judicial administration. Likewise, this commitment propelled the shift from the TCBC to the Judicial Council and the AOC as the primary entities in the funding process.

This obviously struck a responsive chord with the legislature. Similar aspirations had appeared in preambles to various legislative proposals for increased state funding for courts, beginning in the mid-1980s with those introduced by Senator Keene and Assembly Member Robinson. The council's explicit goals in 1992 appeared, for the first time, to create a shared vision.

That vision found its way into various segments of Assembly Bill 233, the ultimate legislation providing for full state funding of California's courts. For example, the Judicial Council is directed to allocate funds from the Trial Court Improvement Fund "to ensure equal access to trial courts by the public, to improve trial court operations, and to meet trial court emergencies."[50] Another example is explicit authorization for Judicial Council rules providing for fairness training of judges and other judicial officers in "racial, ethnic, and gender bias, and sexual harassment."[51] As part of overall state funding, the legislature created and funded the Judicial Administration Efficiency and Modernization Fund with authorization for the Judicial Council, or the AOC as its designee, to expend the fund "to promote improved access, efficiency, and effectiveness in trial courts. . . ."[52]

It was in this spirit and in this manner that state funding as a major monument to the improved administration of justice was achieved during the last half-century.

Notes

1   Chief Justice Ronald M. George, State of the Judiciary Address, California Legislature (March 20, 2001), *www.courtinfo.ca.gov/reference/soj0301.htm.*

2   Judicial Council of California, *Twelfth Biennial Report to the Governor and the Legislature* (1948), p. 15.

3   Id., p. 35.

4   Id., pp. 35–37.

5   Id., p. 54.

6   [California] Select Committee on Trial Court Delay, *Report 4* (February 1972), p. 22.

7   Booz, Allen & Hamilton Inc., *Unified Trial Court Feasibility Study: Final Report* (December 3, 1971), p. 104; Select Committee on Trial Court Delay, *Report 4*, p. 23.

8   Judicial Council of California, *Annual Report to the Governor and the Legislature* (1972), p. 21.

9   Booz, Allen & Hamilton, *Unified Trial Court Feasibility Study*, Appendixes A–B.

10 Id., p. 105, Appendix F.

11 Id., p. 106.

12 Booz, Allen & Hamilton Inc., *California Lower Court Study: Final Report* (September 15, 1971), Appendix A.

13 California Constitution, article XIII A.

14 Kim Turner, *Administrative Implementation of Changes in Intergovernmental Relations Defined in the Lockyer-Isenberg Trial Court Funding Act of 1997: A Summary Report,* March 1999 ([San Rafael, Calif.]: Marin County Superior Court, 1999), p. 3.

15 Judicial Council of California, *Annual Report to the Governor and the Legislature* (1985), part 1, p. 6.

16 Id., p. 3.

17 The Brown-Presley Trial Court Funding Act, California Government Code, section 77000 and following.

18 Id., section 77100(b)–(c).

19 At one point, moneys were placed in this fund but earmarked by the legislature to pay county and other costs incurred in implementing new technology known as STATSCAN.

20 All references are to the first segment of the fiscal year.

21 Judicial Council of California, *Annual Report to the Governor and the Legislature* (1983), part I, p. 39.

22 Id., p. 42.

23 Ibid.

24 Id., pp. 39, 43.

25 Brown-Presley Act, California Government Code, section 77000 and following.

26 Judicial Council of California, *Annual Report to the Governor and the Legislature* (1990), volume I, pp. 44–45.

27 Government Code, section 77301; Judicial Council, *Annual Report* (1990), volume I, p. 46.

28 A county received a supplemental block grant fund if the number of new trial court judgeships in that county created by 1987 legislation exceeded ten positions. This applied to Los Angeles, San Diego, and Santa Clara Counties. The state budgeted $5.8 million for this purpose.

29 Judicial Council of California, *Annual Report to the Governor and the Legislature* (1991), volume 1, p. 51.

30 Id., pp. 52–53.

31 Trial Court Realignment and Efficiency Act of 1991, California Statutes 1991, chapter 90, section 2(a)(4)(B), p. 405.

32 Government Code, section 68112 (1991); Trial Court Realignment and Efficiency Act of 1991, section 6, p. 407.

33 Judicial Council of California, *Annual Report to the Governor and the Legislature* (1993), volume 1, p. 10.

34 California Assembly Bill 1344 (1992); Government Code, section 68502.5.

35 Judicial Council, *Annual Report* (1993), volume 1, p. 11.

[36] Judicial Council of California, *Annual Report to the Governor and the Legislature* (1994), part 1, p. 5.

[37] Id., p. 6.

[38] See Judicial Council of California, *Annual Report to the Governor and the Legislature* (1996), p. 12; minutes (May 17, 1996), pp. 14–16; Task Force on Trial Court Funding, *Final Report to the Judicial Council* (May 3, 1996), p. 3.

[39] To the extent this collaboration could be said to have a beginning date, it appears to be June 2, 1995, when Administrative Director of the Courts William C. Vickrey sent to an array of county and state officials a blueprint titled *State/County Partnership Trial Court Funding Proposal.*

[40] California Statutes 1997, chapter 850.

[41] Judicial Council of California, Administrative Office of the Courts, *Trial Court Funding Resource Manual,* 2d ed. (1998), tab 5, p. 3.

[42] Government Code, sections 77200–77213.

[43] Id., section 77003; California Rules of Court, rule 810.

[44] Government Code, section 77201(b)(1).

[45] Id., section 77201(b)(2).

[46] Id., section 77600.

[47] Id., section 77650.

[48] Turner, *Administrative Implementation of Changes in Intergovernmental Relations Defined in the Lockyer-Isenberg Trial Court Funding Act of 1997,* p. 73.

[49] Judicial Council, *Annual Report* (1993), volume 1, p. xii.

[50] Government Code, section 68502.5(a)(6).

[51] Id., section 68088.

[52] Id., section 77213(a) and (b).

Chapter 7
A System for Judicial Discipline

Overview

he quest for ways to remedy unacceptable behavior by judges, without compromising judicial independence, was quite success-ful during the latter half of the last century.

The techniques available in 1950 for disciplining judges were ineffective: impeachment and conviction by the California Legislature, a recall election, defeat at a regular election, or removal by the governor for disability.

This changed significantly in 1960 when the voters approved a mea-sure proposed by the legislature and endorsed by the Judicial Council to create a Commission on Judicial Qualifications. Under rules of procedure adopted by the Judicial Council, the commission was authorized to rec-ommend to the Supreme Court the retirement of an impaired judge with permanent disabilities or the removal of a judge for misconduct, failure to perform his or her duties, or habitual intemperance. In 1966 public censure was added as a sanction and an additional ground for removal was approved by the voters—conduct prejudicial to the administration of justice that brings the judicial office into disrepute.

Over the years the commission conducted numerous investigations, but it was not until 1973 that the Supreme Court removed a judge on its recommendation.

In 1976 the commission was renamed the Commission on Judicial Performance and its powers expanded to include private admonishment.

The two most prominent proceedings of the commission were recommendations that led to the retirement of a Supreme Court justice and an investigation (without recommendations) of the entire Supreme Court, requested by Chief Justice Rose Elizabeth Bird.

From the beginning and continuing into the 1990s, commission proceedings were, with minor exceptions, private and confidential until such time as a disciplinary recommendation was made to the Supreme Court. This all changed in 1994 when voters approved a legislative proposal to confer independent status on the commission, to reconfigure membership so that a majority were public members, to make formal proceedings public, to grant to the commission the right to promulgate its rules of procedure, and in several ways to expand the commission's jurisdiction and authority.

The work of the commission has been closely linked first with the Code of Judicial Conduct adopted in 1974 by the California Judges Association (CJA) and later with the Code of Judicial Ethics adopted by the Supreme Court.

Both the volume of work and the size of commission operations have grown steadily from inception.

As the first judicial disciplinary body of its kind in the nation, the commission has had a salutary effect on judges' conduct and has inspired establishment of similar entities in every state.

he phrase "judicial performance" implies behavior both positive and negative. In the context of justice administration, however, the phrase had its origin in historical efforts to punish unacceptable actions by judges and judicial officers. From 1950 to 2000, the terminology evolved from judicial removal to judicial discipline to judicial conduct and, at the close of the century, to judicial performance. The actions of judges and judicial officers that came under scrutiny ranged from the contents of an appellate opinion to the solicitation of prostitutes.

Status as a monument in the administration of justice is based upon the great strides made over the past half-century. Those improvements successfully resolved the tension between preserving judicial independence and remedying unacceptable actions by judges and judicial officers. The topic is commendable for the further reason that progress in this area has reflected the philosophy expressed in the 1950s by Chief Justice Phil S. Gibson: "Surely the people have the right to expect that every judge will be honest and industrious and that no judge will be permitted to remain on the bench if he suffers from a physical or mental infirmity which seriously and permanently interferes with the performance of his judicial duties."[1]

Judicial Performance at Midcentury

As of 1950, there were four ways to remove from office a judge whose behavior was unacceptable: impeachment and conviction by the legislature, a successful recall election, defeat at a regular election, or removal by the governor for disability. Each method was flawed. Impeachment had occurred only twice in the state's hundred-year history, and only one of those instances resulted in conviction and removal.[2] Removal by a successful recall election was regarded as cumbersome and expensive, and it apparently had not been successfully used. Defeat at a contested election was likewise rare and expensive, and the outcome was always speculative. The California Constitution[3] and implementing statutes[4] provided that the governor could retire a judge without his or her consent for permanent physical or mental disability. As of 1950 this option had never been exercised and, in the opinion of reputable authorities, probably was unconstitutional.[5] In short, the legislative conclusion at the time was that "present methods for the removal or compulsory retirement of judges are either too cumbersome, too expensive or too time-consuming to be very useful."[6]

The Commission on Judicial Qualifications

Matters changed dramatically in 1960 with creation of the Commission on Judicial Qualifications. The commission was the culmination of coordinated efforts among the Judicial Council, the State Bar, and the legislature. The idea gained serious momentum in 1948 when the State Bar Committee on Administration of Justice approved an earlier recommendation by the Los Angeles Bar Association recommending the establishment of a court to try judges for misconduct or failure to perform the duties of office.[7] Upon approval of that recommendation and principle, the State Bar recommended that the matter be studied by the Judicial Council. Following several years of study, the State Bar and Judicial Council jointly recommended the adoption of a constitutional amendment specifying several causes for removal of judges and a process of investigation and consideration of charges by a Commission on Judicial Qualifications.[8]

The legislature responded by creating in 1957 the Joint Judiciary Committee on Administration of Justice, chaired by Senator Edwin J. Regan. Its reports were filed in 1959 with the most important, for present purposes, being the partial report encompassing the removal of judges. The joint committee introduced its report to the legislature with the observation:

> This committee did not begin its study—nor end it—with the feeling that California judges are a group seriously in need of renovation. The quality of the state judiciary, as a whole, has a high reputation both within the California borders and across the country.
>
> But there is room for improvement.
>
> This fact became increasingly clear to the committee as it undertook to investigate, one after another, complaints made to it by individual attorneys, by bar associations, and by other members of the judiciary. These complaints were directed at certain judges who failed in one way or another to render the service required by their position. Some delayed decisions for months or even years. Some took long vacations and worked short hours, despite backlogs of cases awaiting trial. Some refused to accept assignment to cases they found unpleasant or dull. Some interrupted court sessions to perform numerous marriages, which they made a profitable sideline by illegally extracting fees for the ceremonies. Some tolerated petty rackets in and around their courts, often involving "kickbacks" to court attaches. Some failed to appear for scheduled trials because they were intoxicated—or

they took the bench while obviously under the influence of liquor. Some clung doggedly to their positions and their salaries for months and years after they had been disabled by sickness or age.

It is the eradication of conditions like this that the committee has in mind when recommending improved methods of screening the appointment of judges, more effective procedures for the removal of judges guilty of serious misconduct, and a closer administrative supervision over judges.[9]

The findings and recommendations of the joint committee were that a new Commission on Judicial Qualifications should be created composed of judges, lawyers, and prominent citizens with the power to recommend to the Supreme Court the removal of a judge for cause. Cause was defined as "willful misconduct in office or willful and persistent failure to perform his duties."[10] The joint committee also recommended that the commission be empowered to recommend to the Supreme Court compulsory retirement of a judge if the commission found that the judge was suffering from a disability seriously interfering with the administration of his duties and that the condition was or was likely to become permanent.[11]

This proposal was approved by the legislature and placed before the voters in November 1960 as Proposition 10, part of an overall revision of the judicial article of the California Constitution. The revision was endorsed by the Judicial Council. There were no ballot arguments in opposition, and Senators Regan and Joseph A. Rattigan were able to state that the proposal had been formulated with assistance from the Judicial Council, the State Bar, and the Conference of California Judges as well as having been overwhelmingly approved by both houses of the legislature. In further support of the measure, they asserted that it would "assure real protection against incompetency, misconduct, or non-performance of duty on the Bench."[12] The voters approved the measure, thus formally establishing the Commission on Judicial Qualifications.[13]

As directed by the newly enacted constitutional provisions, the Judicial Council in 1961 adopted rules of procedure for the commission. Likewise, the legislature passed implementing legislation and in the process added another function for the commission. Under this legislation, the commission was authorized to require a medical examination when a judge under sixty-five years of age voluntarily retired due to disability. If the commission determined that a judge was no longer incapacitated, it could conclude that he was subject to assignment to a court by the chair of the Judicial Council.[14]

The implementing constitutional amendment added new sections 1b and 10b to article VI of the constitution. The commission was composed of five judges named by the Supreme Court, two lawyers named by the board of governors of the State Bar, and two citizens named by the governor with the consent of the Senate. This body was authorized to conduct investigations and hear charges against any judge of a California court and to recommend to the Supreme Court removal of a judge for willful misconduct in office, willful and persistent failure to perform duties, or habitual intemperance. The commission also could recommend retirement for permanent disability seriously interfering with the performance of duties. None of the proceedings before the commission were public until and unless it recommended to the Supreme Court the removal or retirement of a judge. In that case, the record filed with the court became public.[15]

The Commission on Judicial Qualifications was busy from the outset. Members took their oaths of office on March 24, 1961, and held meetings in March, June, July, September, and December. The Judicial Council's rules for removal or retirement of judges became effective August 1, 1961. In August the commission appointed Executive Secretary Jack E. Frankel, who in turn employed a stenographer and opened an office in the State Building at 350 McAllister Street in San Francisco. Mr. Frankel was destined to serve the commission as its chief executive for almost thirty years.

Commission High Points

After ten years of operations and with 1,087 authorized judicial positions in California, the commission proposed and the Judicial Council concurred in a general revision of its procedural rules. During 1971, the tenth anniversary year, 217 complaints were filed with the commission of which 162 were closed as unfounded or without merit. In another 54 instances, extensive investigation or inquiry occurred, resulting in 42 written communications to judges. However, no formal hearings were held during the year and no recommendations were made to the Supreme Court.

During that first decade, the California Constitution Revision Commission, in its proposed revision of the judicial article of the constitution, later approved by both the legislature and voters, broadened both the grounds for removal and possible sanctions. The revisions repealed original section 10b and added new section 18, reading in part:

(c) On recommendation of the Commission on Judicial Qualifications the Supreme Court may (1) retire a judge for disability that seriously interferes with the performance of his duties and is or is likely to become permanent, and (2) censure or remove a judge for action occurring not more than 6 years prior to the commencement of his current term that constitutes wilful misconduct in office, wilful and persistent failure to perform his duties, habitual intemperance, or conduct prejudicial to the administration of justice that brings the judicial office into disrepute.[16]

This had the effect of adding as a ground for removal "conduct prejudicial to the administration of justice that brings the judicial office into disrepute." It also added the intermediate disciplinary option of public censure. Removal from office was the only discipline available prior to this change.

During the 1960s the commission recommended disciplinary action only once, but its recommendation of removal from office was rejected by the Supreme Court.[17] However, matters accelerated in the 1970s following the 1966 expansion of the commission's jurisdiction and available sanctions. Between 1970 and 1973 the Supreme Court approved commission recommendations that a judge be publicly censured for conduct prejudicial to the administration of justice that brings the judicial office into disrepute. In 1973 the Supreme Court, for the first time in history, in the case of *Geiler v. Commission*, removed a judge from office following a recommendation of removal by the commission.[18]

Since this was the first occasion in which removal actually occurred, the *Geiler* case is important for procedure as well as result. The Supreme Court used this occasion to establish precedent in the following important areas:

◆ Burden of proof: "[P]roof by clear and convincing evidence sufficient to sustain a charge to a reasonable certainty."[19]

◆ Special masters: If the investigation has involved utilization of special masters to make findings of fact and conclusions of law, the commission has the ultimate power to recommend to the Supreme Court, and the commission therefore is "free to disregard the report of the masters and may prepare its own findings of fact and consequent conclusions of law."[20]

◆ Supreme Court review: The court must make its own independent evaluation of the record and evidence, and "it is to be our findings of fact and conclusions of law, upon which we are to make our determination of the ultimate action to be taken, to wit, whether we should dismiss the proceedings or order the judge concerned censured or removed from office."[21]

The Supreme Court then proceeded to conduct an independent review of the record, ultimately concurring in all respects with the findings of fact and conclusions of law reached by the commission. Specifically, the court concurred that Judge Leland W. Geiler was guilty of misconduct constituting "wilful misconduct in office" and "conduct prejudicial to the administration of justice that brings the judicial office into disrepute" as a result of indiscreet use of vulgar, injudicial, and inappropriate language directed toward court attaches and lawyers and crude and offensive conduct in public places. In addition, it was concluded that the judge had acted in bad faith by interfering with the attorney-client relationship due to petty animosities toward public defenders.[22]

The Commission on Judicial Performance

In 1974, after fourteen years of experience, the commission asserted that "the people of the state are ready for a higher standard of judicial fitness" and as a result recommended to the Judicial Council that "private admonition and Commission reprimand be added to the California Rules of Court as alternative disciplinary measures."[23] The council replied that a constitutional amendment would be required to add these powers.

During the following two years, extensive efforts by the Judicial Council, commission, State Bar, and legislature produced Proposition 7, which was overwhelmingly approved by voters at the November 1976 election.

Proposition 7 changed the commission's name to the Commission on Judicial Performance and expanded its powers.

- ◆ The phrase "habitual intemperance" was refined as a ground for discipline by adding "in the use of intoxicants or drugs."

- ◆ Private admonishment by the commission was authorized if a judge engaged in an improper action or a dereliction of duty.

- ◆ One of the grounds for censure or removal was changed from "wilful and persistent failure to perform his duties" to "persistent failure or inability to perform the judge's duties."[24]

The same amendment also provided for a special tribunal of seven court of appeal justices to be drawn by lot for the purpose of considering any recommendation by the commission for the censure, removal, or retirement of a Supreme Court justice.

McComb v. Commission on Judicial Performance

The ink barely was dry on the constitutional provision for a special tribunal for proceedings involving a Supreme Court justice when it became necessary to consider charges against Justice Marshall McComb. The commission conducted an investigation and hearing on the fitness of the eighty-two-year-old associate justice of the Supreme Court to continue in office. The commission ultimately found that Justice McComb, who had served fifty years as a judge, was suffering from chronic brain syndrome or senile dementia that was detrimental to the performance of his judicial duties, had shown willful and persistent failure to perform such duties, and that his disability was or was likely to become permanent. The commission therefore recommended that he be retired or removed from office.

The special tribunal of seven court of appeal justices convened, considered an array of procedural and substantive objections by Justice McComb, and concluded after an independent evaluation of the evidence that there was clear and convincing evidence that Justice McComb was suffering from a disability that rendered him unable to perform his judicial duties and that the disability was or was likely to become permanent. The tribunal, however, rejected the commission recommendation that Justice McComb be removed from office for conduct prejudicial to the administration of justice. Rather, the tribunal found that his behavior was not willful but symptomatic of senility and ordered the retirement of Justice McComb with the proviso that the retirement be regarded as voluntary.[25]

Investigation of the Seven Justices of the Supreme Court

Less than two years following the proceedings by which Justice McComb was retired from the Supreme Court, all seven justices of the Supreme Court became the objects of an investigation by the Commission on Judicial Performance. The circumstances surrounding this unprecedented investigation of all the members of a single court, let alone the Supreme Court, and the outcome make this the most notorious matter conducted by the commission during the forty years between its creation and the conclusion of the century.

On November 24, 1978, Chief Justice Rose Elizabeth Bird wrote to Justice Bertram Janes, chair of the commission and an associate justice of the Court of Appeal, Third Appellate District, in Sacramento, requesting an investigation. She referred to accounts in the press charging that the Supreme Court had deferred announcing the decision in *People v. Tanner*, a notorious criminal case, until after the November 7, 1978, election. These reports had been accompanied by the suggestion or allegation that announcement of the decision was delayed for fear of adverse effects on the retention elections of Chief Justice Bird, Associate Justice Frank C. Newman, and Associate Justice Wiley W. Manuel, who were on that November ballot for voter approval or rejection.

Chief Justice Bird continued in her letter to Justice Janes that "this charge is totally false." She added that "the deliberative process in *Tanner* was without question incomplete prior to November 7, and indeed remains incomplete to this day. . . ."[26]

Acknowledging speculation that the commission might investigate these allegations, Chief Justice Bird preemptively requested that "the Commission undertake an investigation of the charge that the Supreme Court improperly deferred announcing a decision in the *Tanner* case. . . . I further request that if, after investigation, the Commission finds that circumstances warrant, it consider the issuance of a public report under the authority of rule 902(b)(2), describing the Commission's factual findings and conclusions in sufficient detail to address all issues which have been raised."[27]

Chief Justice Bird also transmitted a twelve-page description of the decision-making process entitled *Description of California Supreme Court Procedures*, which had not previously been made public. She promised "my full cooperation and assistance, and that of my office, in conducting your investigation."[28]

Following the Chief Justice's request for a commission investigation, a storm broke within and outside the Supreme Court.[29] Apparently there were several additional requests for a commission inquiry and, after due consideration, the commission decided to proceed.

One of its first actions was to retain Seth Hufstedler and his law firm to serve as special counsel to the commission in the conduct of the investigation. Mr. Hufstedler was a former president of the California State Bar and a highly respected attorney nationally and in California.

Another early step by the commission was to request on December 18, 1978, that the Judicial Council modify rule 902 of the California Rules of Court, which required confidentiality in most aspects of commission proceedings, to confer upon the commission substantial discretion to make public disclosures about these specific proceedings. In January 1979, the Judicial Council adopted rule 902.5, applicable only to these proceedings, authorizing the commission in its discretion to make appropriate public disclosures. More importantly, however, the new rule 902.5 compelled the commission to conduct a public hearing and restricted the commission by requiring that any decision be based "solely upon evidence presented at the public hearing."[30]

In April 1979, the commission, in effect, ordered public hearings based upon the following findings of fact:

(1) The subject matter is generally known to the public;

(2) There is broad public interest;

(3) Confidence in the administration of justice is threatened due to lack of public information concerning the status and conduct of the proceedings; and

(4) The public interest in maintaining confidence in the judicial office and the integrity of the administration of justice requires that some or all aspects of such proceedings should be publicly conducted or otherwise reported or disclosed to the public.[31]

The procedural scope of the commission's investigation was prescribed by the Judicial Council, chaired by Chief Justice Bird, as follows:

This rule [rule 902.5 of the California Rules of Court][32] shall apply to any investigation or proceeding of the Commission on Judicial Performance relating to any possible improper conduct of any Justice of the Supreme Court of California arising out of (1) any irregularities or delays in handling the *Tanner* case; (2) any irregularities or delays in handling any other case or cases pending before the Supreme Court prior to the election of November 7, 1978, caused or instituted for the purpose of delaying the filing of the Court's decision in any such case until after the date of the election, and/or (3) any unauthorized disclosure of confidential information regarding any of the above pending cases prior to the public release of the decision.[33]

Mr. Hufstedler initiated his investigation on December 27, 1978, and on June 11, 1979, submitted his *Background Report of Special Counsel* in anticipation of a preliminary investigation hearing. The investigation was extensive and included sixty-two depositions under oath, including depositions of all seven justices of the Supreme Court.

The investigative hearing by the commission began on June 18, 1979. Prior to the hearing all seven justices of the Supreme Court were served with subpoenas to appear as witnesses at this public hearing. The commission proceeded, and five Supreme Court justices as well as a number of court personnel testified in public. The proceedings received extensive media coverage.

Justice Stanley Mosk was the last justice on the list of witnesses; he was scheduled to appear before the commission on July 9. Prior to that time, Justice Mosk sought a writ of mandate to quash the commission's subpoena to appear and testify. The issues raised by his petition ultimately were resolved by the Supreme Court, which for this purpose was composed entirely of justices from various courts of appeal sitting pro tem since all the regular justices of the Supreme Court had been recused or disqualified due to conflict of interest.

At the heart of the proceedings was Justice Mosk's position that the Judicial Council did not have constitutional authority to enact rule 902.5 authorizing the public hearing. Rather, he asserted, the constitutional provision that "the Judicial Council shall make rules implementing this section and providing for confidentiality of proceedings" compelled rules guaranteeing confidentiality and did not permit the council to authorize or mandate public hearings.[34] The acting Supreme Court agreed and directed that "Justice Mosk cannot constitutionally be compelled to testify at a public hearing before the commission."[35]

This decision plugged the flow of public information regarding commission proceedings involving the Supreme Court except for a concluding comment by the commission. Following the decision in *Mosk v. Superior Court,* the commission expressed regret at the limitations imposed and stated that "the Commission hereby reports that the status of the investigation is that it is now terminated and the result hereby announced is that no formal charges will be filed against any Supreme Court justice. . . ."[36] What we will never know is whether the commission exercised its power to "privately admonish a judge . . . found to have engaged in an improper action or dereliction of duty."[37]

CHIEF JUSTICES OF CALIFORNIA
Chairs of the Judicial Council
1926–1970

William H. Waste
1926–1940

Phil S. Gibson
1940–1964

Roger J. Traynor
1964–1970

CHIEF JUSTICES OF CALIFORNIA
Chairs of the Judicial Council
1970–Present

Donald R. Wright
1970–1977

Rose Elizabeth Bird
1977–1987

Malcolm M. Lucas
1987–1996

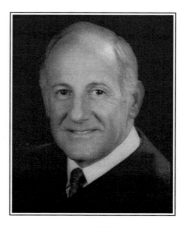

Ronald M. George
1996–Present

ADMINISTRATIVE DIRECTORS
OF THE COURTS
1961–Present

Ralph N. Kleps
1961–1977

Ralph J. Gampell
1977–1986

William E. Davis
1987–1991

William C. Vickrey
1992–Present

State funding achieved. State funding of the trial courts was accomplished through the creativity and cooperation of the judicial, legislative, and executive branches; local governments; and bar groups. Senator Martha M. Escutia (left), former Senator Bill Lockyer (center), and former Assembly Member Phillip Isenberg (right) (all current or former Judicial Council members) were key figures in passage of the Lockyer-Isenberg Trial Court Funding Act of 1997.

Photograph by Leticia Heafey

Judges voted to unify in all fifty-eight counties. Unification of each county's superior and municipal courts into one countywide superior court system was designed to improve services to the public by consolidating court resources, offering greater flexibility in case assignments, and saving taxpayer dollars. The last trial courts were unified on February 8, 2001, when Chief Justice Ronald M. George swore in the four remaining municipal court judges as superior court judges in Kings County. (Shown: Judge Charles R. Johnson.)

The Malcolm M. Lucas Board Room is the symbolic center of the administration of justice in California. The twenty-seven–member Judicial Council convenes in the board room to determine policy for the state judicial branch.

Courts statewide are focused on improving the quality of justice and services to meet the diverse needs of children, youths, and families. Chief Justice Ronald M. George presided over "Adoption Saturday" in the Superior Court of Los Angeles County in 1999.

Courts provide a myriad of support services outside the courtroom.
The family law facilitator program offers free education, information, and
assistance to parents with child support issues. (Shown: Superior Court of
Riverside County.)

**Professional development and continuing education are mandatory for
judicial officers and employees of the judicial branch.** A session of the
California Judicial College in the mid-1980s provided training for judges.

Photograph by Cuauhtemoc Beltran, courtesy of the Imperial Valley Press

A Judicial Council goal is that "members of the judicial branch community will reflect the rich diversity of the state's residents." Presiding Judge Juan Ulloa looked on as Annie M. Gutierrez was installed as a judge in the Superior Court of Imperial County.

Photograph by Jason Doiy

In California, the most linguistically diverse state in the nation with more than 224 languages spoken, court interpreters fill a constitutionally mandated function in the efficient operation of the trial courts. An interpreter assists in understanding court proceedings in the Superior Court of Butte County.

Photograph by Jason Doiy

While protecting privacy rights, the judicial system is working toward integration of court technology systems for more effective information sharing and maximum efficiency. Computers play a vital role in tracking court calendars and the thousands of documents that arrive in a courthouse every day.

Photograph courtesy of the Seaver Center for Western History Research, Los Angeles County Museum of Natural History

In 2002 the state assumed governance, ownership, and maintenance of court facilities, contributing to the goal of access for all residents to safe, secure, and adequate facilities. The Mariposa County Courthouse, completed in 1854, is the state's oldest courthouse in continuous use. It is listed on the National Register of Historic Places.

In all, the Commission on Judicial Performance devoted forty-five days to the Supreme Court investigation between December 1, 1978, and November 2, 1979. Hearings consumed twenty-nine of those days and the remaining sixteen were devoted to meetings.[38]

The resolution of this investigation requested by Chief Justice Bird apparently created frustrations within the commission that led to proposed constitutional changes regarding the review of judicial conduct.

> Based upon its experience and mindful of its role as a watchdog to improve judicial performance and enhance standards of conduct, the Commission early in 1980 will propose to the Legislature changes in Article VI, Sections 8 and 18, of the California Constitution. These changes will deal primarily with the rule-making power for the Commission's proceedings, limited exceptions to confidentiality, and the role of the Supreme Court in reviewing disciplinary actions taken by the Commission.[39]

If these proposals were submitted to the legislature, they apparently were not enacted. The next major constitutional changes concerning the commission occurred nine years later in 1988.

The Commission's Silver Anniversary

Before further changes, however, the commission celebrated its twenty-fifth anniversary in 1985. By this time, the commission had referred a total of twenty-two cases to the Supreme Court for disciplinary action. During the five years leading to the silver anniversary, the commission could point with justified pride to handling an average of 336 complaints and 60 investigations per year, resulting in an annual average of five admonishments, two resignations or retirements while under investigation, and two public censures or removals.[40]

Also by the twenty-five-year mark, the commission had developed a solid set of declarations detailing its policies, procedures, and practices. These were neither duplicative of nor inconsistent with constitutional mandates, statutes, or Judicial Council rules. However, as a public document, they served the beneficial purpose of clearly outlining the commission's investigation procedure, process for formal proceedings, and applications for disability retirement.[41]

Toward Public Proceedings

In November 1988, the people of California passed Proposition 92, as proposed by the legislature, making important changes in the direction of commission openness by allowing:

> [T]he judge to require that a formal hearing be public, unless the commission finds "good cause" for a confidential hearing. . . .
>
> [T]he commission to hold a hearing in public if the charges involve moral turpitude, dishonesty or corruption. . . .
>
> [T]he commission, with the judge's consent, to issue a "public reproval." This is a new level of discipline, more severe than a private admonishment (which the commission can issue by itself), but less severe than a public censure (which requires a formal hearing, argument before the commission, a recommendation by the commission to the Supreme Court, and full review in the Supreme Court). . . .
>
> [T]he commission to issue appropriate press releases in limited circumstances.[42]

Independence and Public Proceedings

The Commission on Judicial Performance became a standalone institution within the judicial branch of government in 1994, and its proceedings shifted dramatically from confidential to public. Proposition 190, proposed by the legislature and approved by the voters in November, provided for major changes that were in effect at the close of the century.[43]

> *Membership*—The membership of the Commission increased from nine to eleven members. The composition of the Commission changed from five judges, two lawyers and two public members to six public members, three judges and two lawyers. The Supreme Court remains responsible for the appointment of the judge members. The Speaker of the Assembly appoints two of the public members; the Senate Rules Committee appoints two public members; and the Governor appoints the remaining two public members as well as the two lawyers. The State Bar Board of Governors no longer appoints lawyer members.
>
> *Open proceedings*—In cases in which formal proceedings are instituted after March 1, 1995, the notice of charges and all subsequent papers and proceedings will be public, including hearings and appearances. Previously, formal proceedings were

confidential except the Commission had discretion to open hearings in cases involving charges of moral turpitude, corruption or dishonesty when an open hearing was in the interests of justice and in the pursuit of public confidence.

Rulemaking—The Commission now has the authority to promulgate its own rules regarding procedures and confidentiality. Previously, rules regulating the Commission were made by the Judicial Council.

Disciplinary determinations—The Commission has the authority to make censure and removal determinations. . . . Previously, the Commission made recommendations for such action to the Supreme Court, which was responsible for determinations regarding censure and removal.

Review of Commission decisions—The Supreme Court has discretionary review of Commission disciplinary determinations; the Court may make an independent review of the record. If the Court does not review the Commission's determination within 120 days after granting a petition for review, the Commission's decision will be final. Previously, censure and removal determinations were made by the Supreme Court, upon recommendation by the Commission, after an independent review of the record.

Public admonishment—The public reproval has been replaced by the "public admonishment." The judge's consent is no longer required.

Interim suspension—The Commission has the authority to suspend a judge, with pay, upon notice of formal proceedings charging the judge with misconduct or disability.

Jurisdiction over former judges—The Commission has the authority to censure and admonish former judges for actions occurring not more than six years prior to the commencement of the former judge's last term in office. A judge's retirement or resignation will not prevent the Commission from completing an investigation or disciplinary proceeding.

Censured former judges barred from assignments—The Commission may "bar" a former judge who has been censured from acting as a judge by assignment, appointment or reference from any California state court.

Supreme Court jurisdiction in proceedings involving the Commission—The Supreme Court has exclusive jurisdiction over proceedings brought by a judge who is a respondent in a Commission proceeding. Requests for injunctive relief or other provisional remedies in these proceedings must be decided by the Supreme Court within 90 days.

Immunity—Commission members and staff have absolute immunity from liability for their conduct in the course of their official duties. In addition, no civil action or adverse employment action can be taken against any individual based on the individual's statements to the Commission.

Disclosure to appointing authorities—The Commission shall provide to any Governor or to the President private admonishments, advisory letters or records of other disciplinary action with respect to any individual under consideration for a judicial appointment.

Budget independence—The Commission's budget is separate from the budget of any other state agency or court.[44]

The Code of Judicial Ethics

This subject is important to the Commission on Judicial Performance, but it has a distinct and somewhat separate lineage.

The first Code of Judicial Conduct was adopted for California judges in 1974 by the California Judges Association. Although the CJA was and is a private membership organization, the Code of Judicial Conduct for many years enjoyed quasi-official status. This status derived in large measure from the Supreme Court, which on one occasion made the following strong supporting statement regarding the code:

> While the canons do not have the force of law or regulation, they reflect a judicial consensus regarding appropriate behavior, and are helpful in giving content to the constitutional standards under which disciplinary proceedings are charged. . . .
>
> We therefore expect that all judges will comply with these canons. Failure to do so suggests performance below the minimum level necessary to maintain public confidence in the administration of justice.[45]

The existence of formal standards of judicial conduct neatly coincides with the past half-century. The original Canons of Judicial Ethics were promulgated by the American Bar Association (ABA) and adopted with modifications in 1949 by the Conference of California Judges, a predecessor to the CJA. In 1972 the ABA substantially revised the canons and adopted them as the Code of Judicial Conduct. These revisions were based in large measure on the work of a special committee headed by former Chief Justice Roger J. Traynor. During the interim, the Conference of California Judges had become the CJA. Effective January 5, 1975, the CJA adopted a new California Code of Judicial Conduct adapted from the ABA's 1972 model.

The ABA model code was further revised in 1990, and a modified version was adopted by the CJA in 1992.

This evolution and the role of the CJA changed dramatically in 1994. As a result of Proposition 190, approved by the voters in November 1994, the Supreme Court was directed to "make rules for the conduct of judges, both on and off the bench, and for judicial candidates in the conduct of their campaigns. These rules shall be referred to as the Code of Judicial Ethics."[46]

In response, the Supreme Court adopted, as an interim measure, the CJA's 1992 Code of Judicial Conduct. This was followed by formal Supreme Court adoption of a Code of Judicial Ethics effective January 15, 1996.

As adopted and modified by the Supreme Court, the code at the end of the century directed each judge to uphold the integrity and independence of the judiciary (Canon 1), to avoid impropriety or the appearance of impropriety in all activities (Canon 2), to perform the duties of judicial office impartially and diligently (Canon 3), and to so conduct the judge's quasi-judicial and extrajudicial activities as to minimize the risk of conflict with judicial obligations (Canon 4). In addition, judges and judicial candidates were mandated to refrain from inappropriate political activity (Canon 5). The Supreme Court made clear that all judges must comply with the code, as must any officer of the state judicial system, including but not limited to magistrates, court commissioners, referees, court-appointed arbitrators, judges of the State Bar Court, temporary judges, and special masters (Canon 6).

The clear implication is that failure by a judge to comply with the Code of Judicial Ethics would constitute grounds for disciplinary proceedings before the Commission on Judicial Performance. This connection between the Code of Judicial Ethics and disciplinary action is echoed in the expectations of the commission. "The Commission's authority is limited to investigation and discipline of judicial misconduct. Judicial misconduct usually involves conduct in conflict with the standards set forth in the Code of Judicial Ethics. . . ."[47]

Resources and Volume

From a part-time executive director and stenographer in 1960, the commission staff, by the year 2000, had grown to twenty-seven authorized positions including sixteen attorneys. The title of the chief executive officer had changed to director–chief counsel, and the remaining staff members were organized into four groups: office of trial counsel, investigation staff, office of commission counsel, and administrative staff. The annual budget for staff and all commission activities was approaching $3 million.[48]

While this growth might surprise some, it is hardly surprising when considering that by 1999 the commission was receiving in excess of 1,000 new complaints per year and producing in excess of 1,000 dispositions annually. For those investigations that warranted disciplinary actions, the commission in 1999 issued thirty advisory letters, three private admonishments, four public admonishments or reprovals, and three public censures; recommended and achieved removal of one judge; and precipitated the resignation or retirement of three additional judges.

Impact of the Commission

The Commission on Judicial Performance clearly has had an impact far beyond the number of formal disciplinary actions it has undertaken. The mere existence of the commission with its clear powers of investigation and array of graduated disciplinary sanctions inevitably must have exercised commendable preventive influence on judges who might otherwise have strayed into areas of misconduct. In addition, there is documented evidence that the mere existence of commission proceedings has over the years served as the catalyst to lead erring judges to either resign, retire, or modify their behavior.

These are the dividends for the citizens of California. The commission has also made an important national contribution. California's commission was the first of its kind. Thanks to its good example and success as an experimental alternative to the cumbersome processes of impeachment and its kin, every state in the union now has a similar judicial disciplinary body. All of them have borrowed in substantial measure from some aspect of California's Commission on Judicial Qualifications and successor Commission on Judicial Performance, whether it be in membership, process, or sanctions. For all of these reasons, the commission has played a major role in establishing judicial performance as a component of the improved administration of justice.

Notes

1   Phil S. Gibson, "For Modern Courts," *Journal of the State Bar of California* 32 (1957), p. 735.

2   California Legislature, "Partial Report of the Joint Judiciary Committee on Administration of Justice on the California Judiciary" (1959) in *Appendix to the Journal of the Senate* (1959 Regular Session), volume 2, [section 1], p. 48.

3   California Constitution, article XXIII, section 1.

4   California Government Code, section 75060.

5   California Legislature, "Partial Report of the Joint Judiciary Committee on Administration of Justice," p. 48.

6   Id., p. 51.

7   Gibson, "For Modern Courts," p. 733.

8   Id., pp. 733–34.

9   California Legislature, "Partial Report of the Joint Judiciary Committee on Administration of Justice," p. 7.

10   Id., p. 51.

11   Ibid.

12   Senators Edwin J. Regan and Joseph A Rattigan, Argument in Favor of Proposition 10, Senate Constitutional Amendment No. 14, submitted to California voters on November 8, 1960.

13   As noted in Chapter Three, the long-standing Commission on Qualifications was continued in existence by Proposition 10, but its name was changed to the Commission on Judicial Appointments in order to avoid confusion with the new disciplinary commission.

14   Government Code, sections 68701–68755 and 75060.

15   Jack E. Frankel, "The Commission on Judicial Qualifications," *Journal of the State Bar of California* 36 (1961), p. 1008.

16   California Constitution (1967), article VI, section 18.

17   *Stevens v. Commission* (1964), 61 Cal.2d 886.

18 *Geiler v. Commission* (1973), 10 Cal.3d 270.

19 Id., p. 275.

20 Ibid.

21 Id., p. 276.

22 Id., pp. 285–86.

23 California Commission on Judicial Qualifications, *1974 Annual Report*, pp. 2–3.

24 California Constitution (1976), article VI, section 18; California Commission on Judicial Performance, *1976 Annual Report*, p. 1.

25 *McComb v. Commission on Judicial Performance* (1977), 19 Cal.3d Special Tribunal Supplement 1.

26 Chief Justice Rose Elizabeth Bird, Letter to the Honorable Bertram D. Janes, Associate Justice, California Court of Appeal (November 24, 1978), in California Commission on Judicial Performance, *In the Matter of Commission Proceedings Concerning the Seven Justices of the Supreme Court of California, Appendix to Background Report of Special Counsel* (June 11, 1979), volume II, exhibit 365.

27 Ibid.

28 Ibid.

29 See, for example, California Commission on Judicial Performance, *In the Matter of Commission Proceedings Concerning the Seven Justices of the Supreme Court of California, Background Report of Special Counsel* (June 11, 1979), exhibits 441–464.

30 Id., p. 19.

31 Id., p. 20; volume II, exhibit 659, "Rule 902.5, California Rules of Court."

32 Repealed effective July 1, 1982.

33 California Rules of Court, former rule 902.5.

34 California Constitution (1976), article VI, section 18(f).

35 *Mosk v. Superior Court* (1979), 25 Cal.3d 474, 499.

36 California Commission on Judicial Performance, *Report of Status and Announcement of Results Regarding Investigation of California Supreme Court Justices* (Novem-

ber 5, 1979), p. 2 (text and attachments provided by staff of the commission in response to the author's request).

37 California Constitution, article VI, section 18(d)(3).

38 California Commission on Judicial Performance, *1979 Annual Report*, p. 2.

39 Id., p. 3.

40 California Commission on Judicial Performance, *1985 Annual Report*, Appendix 2.

41 California Commission on Judicial Performance, *1987 Annual Report*, Appendix 4(C).

42 California Commission on Judicial Performance, *1988 Annual Report*, p. 3; California Constitution (1988), article VI, sections 18(f)(1)–(3) and 18(g).

43 California Constitution (1994), article VI, sections 8, 18, and 18.5.

44 California Commission on Judicial Performance, *1995 Annual Report*, pp. 7–8.

45 *Kloepfer v. Commission on Judicial Performance* (1989) 49 Cal.3d 826, 838 n. 6.

46 California Constitution (1994), article VI, section 18(m).

47 California Commission on Judicial Performance, *1997 Annual Report*, p. 1.

48 California Commission on Judicial Performance, *1999 Annual Report*, pp. 29–30.

Chapter 8
Reduction of Delay in Resolving Cases

Overview

onfirming the emerging reputation of the Judicial Council as a problem solver, the California Legislature in 1949 requested a study of pretrial conferences and their potential to reduce delay and facilitate dispositions. Following research and experimentation, the council reported a favorable conclusion. The legislature, in response, authorized the Judicial Council to adopt rules governing pretrial conferences in civil cases. Pretrial conferences became mandatory in most superior court cases, but attorney opposition ultimately led to repeal of the authorizing legislation.

The Judicial Council returned to the fray in the early 1970s through the Select Committee on Trial Court Delay. This committee issued six reports and, in addition to recommendations on unification and state funding (discussed in Chapters Five and Six), made numerous recommendations ranging from reduced jury size to arbitration. These were considered and partially adopted by the council in the ongoing search for delay reduction.

In the late 1970s, the thinking about delay and the responses to it changed following multistate research that contradicted popular notions about the causes of delay. Experimentation to alter the "local legal culture," as a report of the National Center for State Courts (NCSC) called it, succeeded in reducing delay, which further changed thinking and dialogue.

Time standards for the processing of cases, from filing to disposition, were a tangible product of this new thinking. The standards rested on the premise that it is the responsibility and prerogative of the judge and court, not the attorneys, to control the pace of litigation from commencement to disposition.

Both the standards and premise were attacked by attorneys and judges favoring the traditional view that attorneys should control their cases. However, the new approach continued to gain favor and was widely accepted by the century's end.

The national ferment came home to California with enactment of the Trial Court Delay Reduction Act of 1986. Substantial efforts by the Judicial Council and the Administrative Office of the Courts (AOC) were required to meet the act's provisions for adopting criminal and civil time standards, measuring and reporting compliance, establishing exemplary delay reduction programs in nine superior courts, and training participating judges.

Within three years the Judicial Council reported that among participating courts case processing time had improved dramatically, jury trials had been shortened, and pending cases were younger.

Based upon these results, the Judicial Council recommended early in the 1990s, and the legislature concurred, that the council should undertake a comprehensive and continuing program of delay reduction. Among the specific steps were broadly applicable time standards, improved case-management systems, addressing existing laws that impede delay reduction, and mechanisms for monitoring success. The program explicitly embraced the view that litigation should be managed by the court, from beginning to resolution, within a reasonable time frame. This program became institutionalized and effective even as the Judicial Council, the AOC, and the courts digested unification and the shift to state funding.

*D*elay has long been an ogre in justice administration, and rightly so. Everyone has heard the lament that "justice delayed is justice denied" or that, when it comes to justice, "delay is the most effective form of denial."

Indictments of delay were as virulent as ever during the past half-century. In 1958, Earl Warren, Chief Justice of the U.S. Supreme Court, decried the ravages of delay on justice in an address before the American Bar Association (ABA). "Interminable and unjustifiable delays in our courts are today compromising the basic legal rights of countless thousands of Americans and imperceptibly corroding the very foundations of constitutional government in the United States. Today, because the legal remedies of many of our people can be realized only after they have sallowed with the passage of time, they are mere forms of justice."[1]

Concern about delay in California's judicial processes was pervasive throughout all but a small segment of the period from 1950 to 2000. Significant progress was made in eliminating or reducing delay, thus creating another milestone in improved administration of justice.

California profited from and contributed to national programs. Refining the concepts of delay was a significant component of the national endeavors during this half-century. In prior decades, "delay" had been used rather indiscriminately with the result that an implication evolved that any time consumed in the preparation or prosecution of a pending lawsuit was delay and therefore unacceptable. Matters were clarified in the 1970s by explicit recognition that litigation is not an instantaneous process and that time is required to adequately prepare and to achieve appropriate resolution. The most explicit statement and generally accepted standard was articulated by the American Bar Association: "From the commencement of litigation to its resolution, whether by trial or settlement, any elapsed time *other than reasonably required* for pleadings, discovery, and court events, is unacceptable and should be eliminated." [Emphasis added.][2]

The Judicial Council of California explicitly embraced this standard as the measure of an acceptable pace of litigation.[3]

In the following discussion, "delay reduction" and "reducing delay" are used since they are the phrases commonly applied in this area. In substance, however, the progress in California has revolved around more refined concepts of instituting case management, expediting the pace of litigation, and eliminating lapses in any significant phase of criminal or civil litigation.

Pretrial Conferences in the 1950s

The California Legislature, in 1949, requested that the Judicial Council "make a study of the subject of pretrial practice, including procedures employed in other jurisdictions, with a view to ascertaining whether the adoption of a pretrial system in California would facilitate the disposition of civil cases. . . ."4 This request was based in part on the legislative determination that "the increased volume of litigation in California has resulted in . . . delay in the disposition of civil cases. . . ."5

The Judicial Council responded in its 1954 biennial report to the governor and legislature. While some might say that this was a delayed reply on the subject of delay, that would be an unfair assessment. Two facts should be revisited before reaching judgment. The first is that the Judicial Council was extensively engaged with implementation of the lower court reorganization achieved by constitutional amendment in 1950. Second, the legislature's request preceded by more than a decade the creation of the AOC and the position of Administrative Director of the Courts, thus requiring the Judicial Council to undertake a rather substantial program without the assistance of appropriate staff. Nonetheless, the scope of the Judicial Council's efforts was impressive:

◆ Appointment of two pretrial committees, through the Chief Justice—one for the northern part of the state and the other for the southern part—to study the subject of pretrial hearings

◆ Publication in June 1950 of the results of an examination of all available reports and publications relative to pretrial usage in state and federal courts, titled *Pretrial Procedure Study—Preliminary Report*

◆ Appointment of a special committee, through the Chief Justice, to conduct local experiments in pretrial usage for the purpose of knowing the reception and results of using pretrial procedures in selected courts in California

◆ Launching of an out-of-state survey regarding the operation and conduct of pretrial conferences in leading jurisdictions in the United States

◆ Establishment by 1952 of a program of pretrial conferences in various parts of the state6

In these efforts, the Judicial Council focused on the use of pretrial conferences and acknowledged that the principal objectives were "to reduce the trial to a determination of the basic factual and legal issues that are actually in dispute . . . [which] usually results in a speedier, more efficient trial with a great saving of both time and expense to litigants, witnesses and the courts."[7]

With this explicit commitment to reducing delay, the Judicial Council made the following recommendation to the legislature:

> After careful consideration and discussion of the foregoing findings and recommendations of its Committee on Pretrial Procedure, of the usage and operation of the pretrial system in other states, of the workings of pretrial conferences on an experimental and voluntary basis in this State in the last few years, of the views of various members of the bench and bar, of the work and findings of the Committee on Pretrial Procedure of the State Bar, of the above mentioned action of the Conference of State Bar Delegates, and of the text of the above bill, *the Judicial Council: (1) reports and finds in favor of pretrial conferences, and that the adoption of an effective pretrial system in California, through rules promulgated by the Judicial Council in order to insure and permit of the requisite flexibility as above discussed, should serve to facilitate the disposition of civil cases, to relieve congested court calendars, and otherwise to improve the administration of justice; and accordingly (2) reports and recommends to the Governor and Legislature the enactment into law of the above quoted bill relating to the establishment of pretrial conferences in the state by rules of this council.*[8]

The legislature embraced this recommendation and in 1955 enacted legislation authorizing the Judicial Council to promulgate rules governing pretrial conferences in civil cases in both the superior and municipal courts.[9]

These rules mandated pretrial conferences in every superior court civil case in which a memorandum-to-set-for-trial had been filed by one of the parties. Short causes, with an estimated trial time of less than two hours, were exempted.[10]

Then followed a stormy period of implementation. The resistance of lawyers ran high. Notwithstanding formal support and participation from the State Bar prior to enactment of the pretrial rules, the Judicial Council found itself in continuous conflict with the broader membership of the bar with the result that, after a few years, the Judicial Council acceded and the legislation authorizing control over pretrial conferences was repealed.

Delay Reduction in the 1960s

Aside from continuing efforts to impose pretrial conferences, delay reduction as an explicit Judicial Council priority apparently was dormant during this decade. Certainly, the Judicial Council's plate was full. At the beginning of the decade was the campaign to revise the judicial article of the California Constitution and thereafter implement the changes achieved, such as creating the Commission on Judicial Qualifications and establishing the Administrative Office of the Courts. Later, the Judicial Council also followed closely and contributed to further revision of the judicial article during the work of the Constitution Revision Commission in the latter 1960s.

The Select Committee on Trial Court Delay

Delay reduction returned to an explicit spot on the Judicial Council's agenda in 1972 by creation of the Select Committee on Trial Court Delay. As noted previously in Chapters Five and Six in connection with court organization and funding, this committee made extensive recommendations. However, those were only two of many topics touched on by the committee, which issued six reports during its year of existence. Other recommendations covered a broad range of topics including compulsory establishment of administrators in larger superior courts, prescribed duties of presiding judges, compulsory settlement conferences, limited oral argument, restricted disqualification of judges, sanctions for failure to appear at trial or court conference, reduction of jury size, reduction of peremptory challenges, majority verdicts in selected criminal cases, no-fault automobile insurance, and arbitration in civil cases.[11] This array of proposals was considered and partially adopted by the Judicial Council during ensuing years.

The work of the Select Committee, for the most part, was gathering and sifting the universe of ideas regarding proposed cures for court delay. The resulting proposals were those adopted by the committee after analysis by staff and deliberations by committee members. What was missing from these efforts, both in the Select Committee on Trial Court Delay and in Judicial Council proceedings, was a crucible for determining the real-life efficacy of specific proposals. This all changed in the latter part of the 1970s as a consequence of empirical research and experimentation that furnished the missing crucible.

Delay in State Courts Nationally

Until the 1970s, efforts to reduce delay consisted of advocating and, in some cases, implementing favorite theories in the hope that they would in fact achieve the desired goal of expediting litigation. These were exercises in logic guided more by the principle that "they should work" than by proof that "they would work." Judicial Council adoption of mandatory pretrial conferences was a good example, as was the recommendation of the Select Committee to create a single-level trial court.

In California and throughout the nation, favored theories and proposals were episodic or anecdotal, or both, and lacked reliable, supporting empirical data.

This all began to change in 1978 with a report from the National Center for State Courts titled *Justice Delayed: The Pace of Litigation in Urban Trial Courts*.[12] This report was based on unprecedented empirical measurement of the pace of litigation in urban courts of general jurisdiction in larger states throughout the nation. Among the facts that emerged were these:

◆ Comparable state trial courts processed comparable cases at widely varying speeds and numbers of dispositions per judge.

◆ The time from commencement to disposition was three times longer in some courts than in others; the number of dispositions per judge was three times greater in some courts than in others.

◆ Criminal cases were consistently processed more quickly than civil cases.

◆ Civil cases moved significantly faster in courts with individual calendars.

◆ Neither processing time nor judicial productivity appeared to be improved by extensive settlement programs.[13]

Two broader conclusions of the research were particularly notable. First, the NCSC team stated: "We are persuaded that few of the traditional explanations of trial court delay differentiate faster from slower courts. Delay—or comparatively tardy disposition of civil and criminal cases—does not emerge as a function of court size, judicial caseload, 'seriousness' of cases in the caseload, or the jury trial rate."[14]

Second, the NCSC team advised:

It is our conclusion that the speed of disposition of civil and criminal litigation in a court cannot be ascribed in any simple sense to the length of its backlog, any more than it can be explained by court size, caseload, or trial rate. Rather, both quantitative and qualitative data generated in this research strongly suggest that both speed *and* backlog are determined in large part by established expectations, practices, and informal rules of behavior of judges and attorneys. For want of a better term, we have called this cluster of related factors the "local legal culture." Court systems become adapted to a given pace of civil and criminal litigation. That pace has a court backlog of pending cases associated with it. It also has an accompanying backlog of open files in attorney's offices. These expectations and practices, together with court and attorney backlog, must be overcome in any successful attempt to increase the pace of litigation. Thus most structural and caseload variables fail to explain interjurisdictional differences in the pace of litigation. In addition, we can begin to understand the extraordinary resistance of court delay to remedies based on court resources or procedures.[15]

Interestingly, these research findings appeared to fit California although the overall situation in California was not an explicit focus of the research.[16]

The next stage in national efforts was to determine empirically whether the "local legal culture" could be modified to improve the pace of litigation. For this purpose, experiments were undertaken in several state trial courts around the nation. After these experiments had been in existence for an appropriate period of time and had been subjected to reliable evaluation, the conclusion was announced that delay in litigation is not inevitable and that the following package of ingredients in a delay reduction plan could, and did, both alter the local legal culture and improve the pace of litigation:[17]

First there must be a commitment by the court to control caseflow, followed by identification of the major events in the litigation process which the court must control and measurement of the present pace of litigation between these events. This enables the court to determine whether the time between steps is acceptable and, if not, to specify the maximum permissible time in the typical case, with allowance for exceptional cases. This produces time standards which govern the overall pace of litigation as well as each stage in the process. The court can then implement the plan, with emphasis on monitoring completion of pleadings, early identification of cases subject to alternate dispute resolution processes, monitoring filing of trial readiness documents, development of realistic trial setting policies, and application of a firm continuance policy. This last step is critical in establishing firm trial dates and assuring that cases be tried when scheduled. To execute the plan successfully the court should also have or develop a system to produce the information needed to manage the processing of cases and should, at an appropriate point in the process, consult with the trial bar and other affected public officials, such as the prosecuting attorney.[18]

A new generation of thinking and examination of court delay was prompted by these early efforts. Subsequent assessment and experimentation confirmed, in refined form, the initial findings and conclusions.[19]

Tangible dividends resulted from these national efforts. The most prominent was the adoption of time standards for case processing. The first standards were promulgated by the Conference of State Court Administrators in 1983. These standards basically provided for the conclusion of most felony cases within 180 days of arrest and of misdemeanor cases within 90 days of arrest. Civil cases in which a jury trial was requested were to be tried, settled, or disposed of within eighteen months from the date litigation commenced and, in nonjury cases, within twelve months.[20] In 1984 the American Bar Association adopted similar standards proposed by its Conference of State Trial Judges. These standards provided that 90 percent of all general civil cases should be concluded by settlement or trial or otherwise within twelve months from the date the case was filed. Ninety-eight percent of these cases should be concluded within eighteen months of filing and the remainder within twenty-four months of filing, barring exceptional circumstances.[21]

Also in 1984, the Conference of Chief Justices, consisting of the chief justice from each state supreme court, collectively endorsed the establishment of time standards for case processing in each state judicial system for all categories of civil and criminal cases. In addition, the chief justices endorsed the establishment of monitoring procedures and effective enforcement procedures for time standards.[22]

The time standards were based upon the new premise that the judge and the court have a duty to control the pace of litigation from beginning to disposition and the further responsibility to eliminate any lapse of time in the litigation process other than that reasonably required for court events and preparation. Of course, this flew in the face of the traditional view that the courts were passive receptacles for lawsuits and that the attorneys, not the judge or court, would decide when events occurred and govern the pace of those events. Attorney opposition to both the time standards and the underlying philosophy was virulent. For that matter, opposition among judges who favored that status quo also was vigorous.

Ultimately, the new approach prevailed—thanks in large measure to a group of courageous trial judges and attorneys from around the country who aggressively defended and advocated time standards and the corollary responsibility of judges. They were aided by the empirical research that demonstrated fallacies in past theorizing about delay and the proven success of the new approach in expediting litigation.[23]

California's Trial Court Delay Reduction Act of 1986

This national ferment came home to California in 1986 in the form of the Trial Court Delay Reduction Act.[24] By this act, the California Legislature mandated an exemplary delay reduction program and directed the Judicial Council, on or before July 1, 1991, to report on the results and to recommend whether it should be applied to all superior and municipal courts.[25]

This legislation was based upon the premise that "[d]elay in the resolution of litigation . . . reduces the chance that justice will in fact be done, and often imposes severe emotional and financial hardship on litigants."[26] Sponsored by Attorney General John Van de Kamp, the implementing bill was introduced and endorsed by Speaker of the Assembly Willie Brown. For reasons that are not apparent, the Judicial Council, Chief Justice Rose Elizabeth Bird, and Administrative Director of the Courts Ralph J. Gampell did not take an official position while this legislation was under active consideration by the legislature.

It appears that the legislation was inspired by Attorney General Van de Kamp's participation in an advisory committee of the National Center for State Courts through which he learned of the successful efforts of other states to reduce court delay. The impact of national developments is further reflected by the fact that the legislation he subsequently sponsored contained the generally accepted definitions promulgated by the ABA: "[L]itigation, from commencement to resolution, should require only that time reasonably necessary for pleadings, discovery, preparation, and court events, and that any additional elapsed time is delay and should be eliminated."[27]

Almost coincidentally with enactment of the delay reduction legislation, leadership of the judicial branch of government changed with appointment of Justice Malcolm M. Lucas as Chief Justice and William E. Davis as Administrative Director of the Courts. They both embraced the goals and obligations of the 1986 act. This was an important change from the preceding Judicial Council neutrality because the act imposed major burdens on both the Judicial Council and the courts of California. The new law:

◆ Required the Judicial Council to adopt case processing time standards for the processing and disposition of civil and criminal actions

◆ Mandated that the Judicial Council collect, maintain, and publish statistics on superior courts' compliance with the time standards

◆ Directed the Judicial Council to select nine superior courts that were to establish exemplary delay reduction programs[28]

◆ Required that the exemplary programs start by January 1, 1988, and continue for three years

◆ Directed the Judicial Council to train judges participating in the program

◆ Gave judges who were selected to serve in the pilot programs the responsibility for eliminating delay with authority to assume control over the pace of litigation by actively managing cases from start to finish

◆ Allowed the presiding judge of any superior court to voluntarily establish an exemplary delay reduction program[29]

The Judicial Council and the AOC, working with the National Center for State Courts, promptly swung into action. Time standards were adopted effective July 1, 1987; the mandatory pilot courts were designated by December 1986; ten voluntary delay reduction programs in other courts were established shortly thereafter; and participating judges in mandatory pilot courts undertook the legislative obligation to "actively monitor, supervise and control the movement of all cases assigned to the program from . . . filing . . . through final disposition."[30] In addition, rules were adopted to implement new procedures, and the pilot programs were evaluated on an ongoing basis.

By 1991, it was possible for the Judicial Council to report that:

◆ *Case processing time had improved dramatically:* Ninety percent or more of case dispositions in 1990 were achieved within two years of filing in all nine mandatory pilot courts, compared to 1987, when it took more than three years. For the cases disposed of most quickly (the fastest 50 percent), all nine pilot courts showed improvement; four pilot courts cut the median time to disposition in half.

◆ *Trial time for jury trials had been shortened:* Seven of the nine pilot courts had cut the length of jury trials, and five had completed at least half of their jury trials in one week.

◆ *Pending cases were younger:* Five of the pilot courts cut in half the percentage of cases pending more than two years. In all nine mandatory pilot courts, the age of cases pending was substantially less than the age of cases pending before the program began.[31]

Judicial Council Charter for Delay Reduction

In response to the Trial Court Delay Reduction Act of 1986, the Judicial Council reported to the legislature in 1991 the following groundbreaking recommendations, which were substantially enacted during the 1990s and which are set forth in some detail at this point to underscore the importance of delay reduction as a milestone in the improved administration of justice. The Judicial Council advocated for taking the following steps:

1. Adopt rules or standards that would furnish courts with supportive delay reduction guidance, including:

    ◆ Litigation should be managed by the court, from beginning to resolution, within a reasonable amount of time.

    ◆ Expeditious and timely resolution of cases is the goal, after full and careful consideration of the facts and consistent with justice.

    ◆ Delay could reflect a failure of justice and undermine the public's confidence in the courts.

    ◆ A continuous delay reduction effort in California is in the public interest.

    ◆ Trial courts have the responsibility to manage their caseloads to reduce delay.

2. Adopt standards or rules that give trial courts flexibility in developing case-management systems, which should have the following characteristics:

    ◆ Early and continuous case monitoring from the point of filing

    ◆ Assignment of cases to different case-management tracks depending on their characteristics and monitoring needs

    ◆ The use of sanctions

    ◆ Firm trial dates

    ◆ Trial proceedings management

3. Ask the Chief Justice to appoint an advisory committee to review existing statutes and rules to find out which procedures prevent

the courts from meeting case-management time standards and to modify those that are prohibitive.

4. Adopt a rule or standard to encourage trial courts to annually assess their compliance with time standards and to identify procedures, rules, California Rules of Court, and statutes that are obstacles to meeting standards.

5. Retain the superior court delay reduction case-management time standards.

6. Adopt Standards of Judicial Administration for trial court presiding judges and court administrators to emphasize new leadership and case-management roles as a result of delay reduction programs.

7. Adopt standards or rules that provide the resources and training needed for trial courts to monitor and manage their caseloads.

8. Develop a municipal and justice court delay reduction program by identifying procedures that prevent trial courts from meeting the case-management time standards and modifying those that are found to be prohibitive.[32]

Notes

1   U.S. Chief Justice Earl Warren, speech to opening assembly of the American Bar Association annual meeting (1958), quoted in Thomas C. Yager, "Justice Expedited—A Ten-Year Summary," *U.C.L.A. Law Review* 7 (1960), p. 57 n. 1.

2   American Bar Association, Judicial Administration Division, *Standards Relating to Trial Courts*, Standards of Judicial Administration, volume 2 ([Chicago]: American Bar Association, 1992), section 2.50, p. 76.

3   California Standards of Judicial Administration, section 2, Caseflow Management and Delay Reduction—Statement of General Principles, adopted effective July 1, 1987.

4   Assembly Concurrent Resolution No. 92—Relating to requesting the Judicial Council to study pretrial practice and procedure (July 2, 1949), California Statutes 1949, chapter 191, pp. 3406–7.

5   Id., p. 3406.

6   Judicial Council of California, *Fifteenth Biennial Report to the Governor and the Legislature* (1954), part 1, pp. 13–14.

7   Id., p. 15.

8   Id., p. 21.

9   California Statutes 1955, chapter 632, p. 1130; California Code of Civil Procedure (1955), section 575. Rules relating to pretrial conferences were adopted by the Judicial Council in 1956, effective January 1, 1957; Judicial Council of California, *Seventeenth Biennial Report to the Governor and the Legislature* (1959), part 1, p. 54.

10   Judicial Council of California, Amendments to Rules for the Superior Courts (1956), rules 8–9.5, 47 Cal.2d 3, pp. 3–9.

11   [California] Select Committee on Trial Court Delay, *Report 6* (June 1, 1972).

12   The underlying research for this study was funded by the federal Law Enforcement Assistance Administration (LEAA) as part of its national initiative to improve state courts. It also was undertaken jointly by the National Center for State Courts and the National Conference of Metropolitan Courts.

13   Thomas Church, Jr., et al., *Justice Delayed—The Pace of Litigation in Urban Trial Courts* (Williamsburg, Va.: National Center for State Courts, 1958), "Executive Summary," précis.

[14] Id., p. 5.

[15] Id., p. 54.

[16] Larry L. Sipes, "Managing to Reduce Delay," *California State Bar Journal* 56 (1981), p. 104.

[17] Larry L. Sipes et al., *Managing to Reduce Delay* (Williamsburg, Va.: National Center for State Courts, 1980). This study, too, was funded by the LEAA.

[18] Larry L. Sipes, "Reducing Delay in State Courts—A March Against Folly," *Rutgers Law Review* 37 (1985), p. 305.

[19] One of many examples is John Goerdt, *Re-examining the Pace of Litigation in 39 Urban Trial Courts* (Williamsburg, Va.: National Center for State Courts, 1991).

[20] Sipes, "Reducing Delay in State Courts," p. 310.

[21] American Bar Association, *Standards Relating to Trial Courts*, standards 2.50–2.55, p. 76.

[22] Sipes, "Reducing Delay in State Courts," p. 311.

[23] Contrary to the practice elsewhere in this book, the author personally acknowledges the indispensable contribution of Judge Robert Broomfield to reducing trial court delay. At the time of these developments he was the presiding judge of the superior court in Maricopa County (Phoenix), Arizona. He sponsored the most ambitious and successful experiment, in which a group of volunteer judges in his court demonstrated the efficacy of time standards and judicial control over the pace of litigation. As president of the National Conference of Metropolitan Courts, he championed the new knowledge. As chairman of the American Bar Association's Conference of State Trial Judges, he was instrumental in gaining adoption of the association's time standards for case processing. Judge Broomfield was subsequently appointed to the U.S. District Court in Phoenix.

[24] Trial Court Delay Reduction Act of 1986, California Statutes 1986, chapter 1335, p. 4743; California Government Code, sections 68600–68620.

[25] Passage of this legislation was facilitated by the fact that the superior court in San Diego County and a few others had embraced the ABA standards as goals for delay reduction.

[26] Assembly Bill 3300; California Statutes 1986, chapter 1335, section 68601(b), pp. 4743–44.

[27] California Government Code, section 68603(a).

28 These courts were to be those with the highest numbers of at-issue civil cases, pending more than one year, per judicial position. Four of these courts were to have more than eighteen judges, and five were to have more than eight judges.

29 Judicial Council of California, Administrative Office of the Courts, *Prompt and Fair Justice in the Trial Courts: Report to the Legislature on Delay Reduction in the Trial Courts* (July 1991), volume 1, p. 3.

30 Trial Court Delay Reduction Act of 1986, California Statutes 1986, p. 4745.

31 Judicial Council, *Prompt and Fair Justice in the Trial Courts*, volume 1, p. 7.

32 Id., pp. 10–12.

Part 3
Enhancing Justice

The search for improvement during the "golden era" was not confined to monumental milestones. Indeed, important progress was achieved across the spectrum of justice administration. Although these achievements may have spanned less than a half-century or impacted only a focused aspect of the system, they contributed significantly, especially in the areas of families and children in the courts, judicial education, alternative dispute resolution, fairness and equality, interpreter services, and technology.

Chapter 9
Families, Children, and the Courts

Overview

ases involving families and cases of juvenile delinquency are major components of the workload in California courts. Prominent are marriage dissolution, child and spousal support, and child custody and visitation, as well as actions by juveniles that would be criminal if committed by an adult.

This has been an area in which judicial branch concerns have been supplemented by an unusually high level of policy and other interventions by the California Legislature and federal government.

Termination of marriages was simplified by substituting dissolution for divorce. Major steps were taken to eliminate domestic violence. Protection of children's welfare was strengthened. Judicial control over juveniles at risk was reinforced.

The U.S. Supreme Court also intervened with decisions assuring that defendants in juvenile delinquency proceedings are entitled to various constitutional protections such as the right to counsel.

Justice was further enhanced by the identification of the battered child syndrome, introduction of mediation in family proceedings, and creation of special advocates to protect the interest of children involved in court proceedings.

Efforts of the Judicial Council and the Administrative Office of the Courts (AOC) also were notable, culminating in the creation of the AOC's Center for Families, Children & the Courts.

*T*he phrase "litigation explosion" was spawned during the latter half of the 1900s and along with it predictions of calamity as well as a cornucopia of cures. Whether the increases in case filings were aberrational in relation to population increases and other demographic factors was a debate that also flowed from the hue and cry surrounding the alleged litigation explosion.

One fact was indisputable then and now. Civil cases involving families and noncivil cases involving juvenile delinquency compose a major part of the workloads in California courts. For example, during the decade from 1988 to 1998, family law filings in the state's superior courts consistently exceeded the number of civil filings involving personal injury, death, and property damage.[1] Indeed, family law filings in 1997–1998 were more than double the total number of filings for personal injury, death, and property damage. During that same decade, noncivil filings involving juvenile delinquency or dependency came very close each year to equaling the total number of criminal filings in California's superior courts.[2]

The national experience in state courts further confirmed that if there was a litigation explosion it was occurring in cases involving families and juveniles. Over a significant period of time in the 1980s and 1990s, civil filings in state courts increased by 34 percent, but the rate of domestic relations filings increased by 77 percent.[3] While criminal filings increased by 45 percent, quasi-criminal proceedings involving juveniles increased by 68 percent.[4]

What types of cases are involved? Traditionally, civil cases involving families include divorce or dissolution of marriages, spousal and child support, child custody and visitation, guardianship, adoption, nonfamily placement of dependent children, termination of parental rights, or establishment of paternity. In more recent periods these categories have been augmented by proceedings involving abuse directed at spouses, children, and elders. Conservatorships and trusteeships ordinarily involve adults and more specifically elderly adults. Noncivil proceedings typically involve conduct by juveniles that if committed by an adult would be regarded as criminal.

This returns us to the main point—cases involving families and juveniles are a major part of court business in California and elsewhere. In general, civil filings involving families and noncivil filings involving juveniles constitute more than a third of the total caseload of California's superior courts.[5]

The importance and extent of these cases did not pass unnoticed in California during the past quarter-century. Major steps are outlined below that establish the importance of this area as a milestone in the improved administration of justice.

Before proceeding, however, it must be noted that, more than in any of the areas considered to this point, the actions and policies of the federal government had major impact. Likewise, actions and policy initiatives by the California Legislature probably have been at least as prominent as in other areas.

Marriage

Termination of the marriage relationship has been the largest single category of court filings in the area of domestic relations. Prior to 1970 California provided the traditional remedy of divorce. However, in 1969 California joined the movement to "no-fault divorce" by permitting dissolution of the marriage relationship without establishing fault or misfeasance by either spouse. This simplified marriage termination.[6]

Domestic Violence

The need to curb domestic violence and protect spouses and former spouses from abuse always existed, but thanks to the efforts of many legal, judicial, and citizen leaders during this period the problem began to receive the attention it deserved. In 1977, the California Legislature by statute gave courts authority to grant temporary restraining orders in domestic violence cases[7] and financed shelters for battered women.[8] Shortly thereafter the legislature made it a crime to rape one's spouse.[9] A statutory presumption also was created against awarding child custody to a batterer.

The federal government contributed in 1994 by enacting the Violence Against Women Act, which, among other things, created causes of action assertable in state courts and provided significant federal funding for local domestic violence prevention efforts.[10]

The California Legislature continued by emphasizing criminal legislation that encouraged arrest in domestic violence cases,[11] eliminating the option of diversion for defendants charged with domestic violence in criminal cases,[12] and permitting law enforcement officers to arrest in domestic violence cases based on "reasonable cause" even if the officer did not witness the offense.[13]

Children

The welfare of children is a vital concern in dysfunctional families, but especially in the context of divorce or dissolution. Court proceedings devoted to protecting the welfare of children were refined during this period to encompass determining which parent receives custody when a marriage is terminated, visitation of the children by the noncustodial parent, financial and other support, protection against abuse or neglect, termination of parental rights, and placement outside the family through either temporary foster home care or permanent adoption.

Juvenile Delinquency and Dependency

California has an elaborate statutory scheme governing judicial jurisdiction over children. The court can determine that a minor is a "dependent child of the court" if the welfare of that child is in jeopardy, through no fault of the child.[14] For example, if there is a substantial risk that the child will suffer serious physical harm as a result of action or failure to act by his or her parent or guardian, the court can declare the child to be a dependent of the court. Likewise, if the conduct of a parent or guardian could result in the minor suffering serious emotional damage, the child can be declared a dependent child of the court. Other grounds for such a declaration include sexual abuse by a parent, guardian, or other member of the household; severe physical abuse by any person known to the parent if the parent knew or reasonably should have known of the abuse; leaving the child without any provision for support; acts of cruelty by a parent, guardian, or other member of the household; or abuse or neglect of a minor sibling.[15]

The court can also determine that a minor is a ward of the court as a result of the minor's own conduct. "Any person who is under the age of 18 years when he violates any law of this state or of the United States or any ordinance of any city or county of this state defining crime . . . is within the jurisdiction of the juvenile court, which may adjudge such person to be a ward of the court."[16] Habitual disobedience or truancy can also lead to a judicial determination that a minor is a ward of the court.[17] These matters are placed within the jurisdiction of the superior court with the legislative direction that when exercising this jurisdiction actions taken shall be described as actions by the "juvenile court."[18]

Major State and Federal Initiatives[19]

1974   Federal statute enacted requiring as a condition of receiving federal funds that a guardian ad litem be appointed to represent the child in every case involving an abused or neglected child that results in a judicial proceeding.[20]

1975   Compact created by federal law to govern adoptive placement of children between member states of the compact, including independent (private) adoptions. California has been a member of the Interstate Compact on the Placement of Children (ICPC) since January 1975.[21]

1975   Federal Child Support Enforcement Program began as mandated by Title IV-D of the Social Security Act.

1980   States encouraged by federal guidelines and funds to prevent unnecessary foster care and to provide children with permanent homes as quickly as possible.[22]

1981   California Legislature mandated that all custody and visitation issues in dispute must proceed to mediation with a court-provided mediator before the matter can be set for a hearing.[23]

1982   Child welfare services restructured by statutes with four major goals: (1) prevention of unnecessary foster care placements, (2) family reunification if possible, (3) reduction in number of long-term foster care placements, and (4) stable and most familylike setting for those who must remain in foster care long term.[24]

1984   Federal law required expedited processes for establishing and enforcing child support orders. California established minimum child support amounts.[25]

1988   Legislature required Judicial Council to establish (1) guidelines encouraging the development of local Court Appointed Special Advocate (CASA) programs, which assist abused and neglected children who are the subjects of judicial proceedings, and (2) a grant program to assist in creating and expanding CASA programs.[26]

1990   Judges required to consider any history of spousal abuse by a parent before determining child custody or child visitation rights for that parent.[27]

1991 Legislature required Judicial Council to develop standards of practice for mediation.[28]

1992 California Family Code adopted effective January 1, 1994.[29]

1993 Congress allocated funds to state courts for improving the handling of cases involving child abuse and neglect.[30]

1996 Multifaceted juvenile court legislation enacted in California to protect children from the effects of domestic violence. It gave courts the authority to remove a battering parent or guardian from the home, prohibit visitation by the battering parent if it would jeopardize the safety of the child, and create a "safety plan" option in cases where the child is removed from the home of the battered parent.[31]

1996 Federal grant funding provided to all states for noncustodial access and visitation programs.[32]

1996 Legislature provided for child support commissioners and family law facilitators in each county, supported with significant federal funding.[33]

1997 Judicial Council established an interagency agreement with the California Department of Social Services to award federal grant funding for noncustodial access and visitation programs.[34]

1997 Congress acted to promote the primacy of child safety and timely decisions while continuing efforts to prevent the removal of children and to reunify families when possible.[35]

1998 Legislature directed Judicial Council to create a one-year pilot project to provide that in any child custody proceeding, including mediation and other proceedings, the court would appoint an interpreter to interpret the proceedings at court expense if one or both of the parties is unable to participate fully in the proceeding due to a lack of proficiency in the English language and the court determines that the parties are financially unable to pay the cost of an interpreter.[36]

1999 Legislature established the California Department of Child Support Services as the managing agency for child support programs and required that local child support agencies take over support programs from the district attorneys by January 1, 2003.[37]

1999   Judicial Council required by statute to develop standards for full
        and partial court-connected evaluations, investigations, and assess-
        ments related to child custody.[38]

1999   Administrative and funding requirements for the Access to Visitation
        Grant Program amended to provide that the grants' main focuses
        are (1) supervised visitation and exchange services, (2) education
        about protecting children during family disruption, and (3) group
        counseling for parents and children.[39]

Major Judicial Decisions

Three decisions by the U.S. Supreme Court contributed to the inter-
twining of federal actions and the administration of juvenile justice in California. The court held in *In re Gault* [40] that minors in juvenile delinquency
proceedings are protected by various provisions of the U.S. Constitution's
Bill of Rights, including adequate notice of charges; representation by counsel, including the right to court-appointed counsel; the right against self-
incrimination; and the right to confront and cross-examine witnesses. A short
time later, the U.S. Supreme Court held that the appropriate standard of
proof in juvenile delinquency proceedings is "beyond a reasonable doubt."[41]
In *Breed v. Jones* the Supreme Court held in 1975 that the prohibition against
double jeopardy set forth in the Fifth Amendment to the U.S. Constitution
applies in juvenile court proceedings.[42]

Overarching Developments

Several events also are noteworthy because of their general effect upon
the improved administration of justice in this area.

The first was completely separate from the courts or judicial process,
but it had a profound influence upon subsequent statutory enactments and
judicial proceedings. That event was publication of the landmark article "The
Battered Child Syndrome" by Dr. C. Henry Kempe in the *Journal of the
American Medical Association.*[43] Published in 1962, this article first exposed
the reality that significant numbers of parents and caretakers batter their
children. Within five years following publication of Dr. Kempe's report,
all states had adopted child abuse reporting laws.

Another noteworthy event was the introduction of mediation in the context of various judicial proceedings involving families. In 1963, the Association of Family and Conciliation Courts was founded to promote conciliation,

and subsequently mediation, as an alternative to litigation. This contributed to California legislation in 1984 directing the Judicial Council to assist counties in implementing mediation and conciliation proceedings and to administer a grant program for research and demonstration projects that included "[t]he development of conciliation and mediation and other newer dispute resolution techniques, particularly as they relate to child custody and to avoidance of litigation."[44]

Development of special advocates to represent the interests of children in various court proceedings also was important. First established in the Superior Court for King County, Washington, in 1977, both the concept and the program, which came to be known as Court Appointed Special Advocate or CASA, grew in California and elsewhere. In 1988 several major steps were taken in California. First, the legislature directed the Judicial Council to establish guidelines encouraging the creation, development, and expansion of local CASA programs to assist abused and neglected children in judicial proceedings. Second, the Judicial Council adopted guidelines for awards to local CASA programs. Finally, in 1991, the Judicial Council awarded the first ten CASA grants to local jurisdictions.

In 1996, another important development was legislation to create in California the positions of child support commissioner and family law facilitator.[45] The Judicial Council established statewide programs to implement the legislation. These positions were intended to overcome inadequacies in the existing arrangements regarding child and spousal support orders by providing "an expedited process in the courts that is cost-effective and accessible."[46] To achieve this, each superior court was directed to have child support commissioners, and to have a sufficient number, to hear child support actions and related matters involving enforcement services of the district attorney's office (now the local child support agency).[47] In addition, the legislature created the new family law facilitator positions, to be filled by attorneys, to provide free education, information, and assistance to parents with child support issues.[48]

At several points the Judicial Council and the AOC took steps to ensure that the governance institutions of the judicial branch were effectively organized to promote improved justice in the area of families, children, and the courts. For example, in 1985 the Judicial Council established the Statewide Office of Family Court Services in the AOC. In 1988 separate Judicial Council advisory committees were created for family and juvenile law. In 1992 the Judicial Council, as part of its strategic planning process, established the Family and Juvenile Law Advisory Committee.

In 1997 a new Center for Children and the Courts was formed within the AOC. Shortly following the end of the century, this Center for Children and the Courts was merged with the Statewide Office of Family Court Services to create within the AOC the Center for Families, Children & the Courts. In this way, both the Judicial Council and the AOC ensured that appropriate resources would be available for research, services, advice, and general support as the courts of California continued to strive to meet the challenges posed by both the substance and volume of judicial proceedings involving families and children.

Notes

1   Judicial Council of California, Administrative Office of the Courts, *Annual Report* (1999), *Court Statistics Report—Statewide Caseload Trends 1988–1989 through 1997–1998 and Caseload Data for Individual Courts 1996–1997 and 1997–1998,* p. 47.

2   Id., p. 53.

3   Brian J. Ostrom and Neal B. Kauder, eds., *Examining the Work of State Courts, 1997: A National Perspective from the Court Statistics Project* (Williamsburg, Va.: National Center for State Courts, 1998), p. 7.

4   Ibid.

5   Judicial Council, *Annual Report* (1999), *Court Statistics Report,* pp. 47, 53.

6   California Civil Code, section 4000.

7   Domestic Violence Prevention Act of 1977, California Statutes 1977, chapter 720, p. 2304.

8   Domestic Violence Center Act of 1977, California Statutes 1977, chapter 892, p. 2670.

9   California Statutes 1979, chapter 994, p. 3384.

10 Violence Against Women Act of 1994, 42 U.S.C.A., section 13931 and following.

11 California Statutes 1995, chapter 246.

12 California Statutes 1995, chapter 641.

13 California Statutes 1996, chapter 131.

14 California Welfare and Institutions Code, section 300.

15 Ibid.

16 Welfare and Institutions Code, section 602.

17 Welfare and Institutions Code, section 601.

18 Welfare and Institutions Code, section 245.

19 Substantial segments of the material in this section were prepared by staff of the AOC's Center for Families, Children & the Courts, including a timeline of major events prepared for the Family and Juvenile Law Advisory Committee.

20 Child Abuse Prevention and Treatment Act of 1974 (CAPTA), Pub.L. No. 93-247 (1974).

21 California Family Code, sections 7900–7910; Adoptions Interstate Compact on the Placement of Children.

22 Federal Adoption Assistance and Child Welfare Act of 1980.

23 Child Custody Mediation Statutes (1980), Family Code, sections 3160–62; former Civil Code, sections 4607 and 4607.1.

24 Adoption Assistance and Child Welfare Act of 1980, Pub.L. No. 96-272 (1982); California Senate Bill 14.

25 Agnos Child Standards Act of 1984.

26 Welfare and Institutions Code, sections 100–109.

27 Assembly Bill 2700 (1990) (Roybal-Allard).

28 Family Code, section 3162.

29 California Statutes 1992, chapter 162.

30 Federal Omnibus Reconciliation Act of 1993, also known as the Family Preservation and Support Act.

31 Assembly Bill 2647 (1996) (Kuehl).

32 Personal Responsibility and Work Opportunity Reconciliation Act of 1996 (PRWORA), Pub.L. No. 104-139 (1996) 110 U.S. Statutes 2258, Title III, Subtitle I—Enhancing Responsibility and Opportunity for Nonresidential Parents.

33 California Statutes 1996, chapter 957; PRWORA.

34 Pub.L. No. 104-193 (1997) 110 U.S. Statutes 2258.

35 Adoption and Safe Families Act of 1997 (ASFA).

36 California Statutes 1998, chapter 981.

37 California Statutes 1999, chapter 478; California Statutes 1999, chapter 480.

38 California Statutes 1996, chapter 761; adoption of standards and guidelines by January 1, 1999, was required.

39 California Statutes 1999, chapter 1004; California Family Code, sections 3201–4.

40 *In re Gault* (1967), 387 U.S. 1.

41 *In re Winship* (1970), 397 U.S. 358.

42 *Breed v. Jones* (1975), 421 U.S. 519.

43 C. Henry Kempe, "The Battered Child Syndrome," *Journal of the American Medical Association* 181 (1962), pp. 17–24.

44 California Statutes 1984, chapter 893, p. 3004.

45 California Statutes 1996, chapter 957; Family Code, sections 4250–53.

46 Family Code, section 4250.

47 Family Code, section 4251.

48 See Family Code, sections 10002, 10007.

Chapter 10

Education for Members of the Judicial Branch

Overview

 here were no formal programs for judicial education in California or elsewhere at midcentury. This was corrected by the California Judges Association (CJA) and the Judicial Council.

Overcoming opposition from members, the CJA launched a program of educational seminars for California judges in 1959 and established California's annual judicial college in the mid-1960s.

On roughly the same timetable, the Judicial Council through the Administrative Office of the Courts (AOC) sponsored judicial workshops— first for municipal court judges and subsequently for justice and superior court judges.

These separate efforts merged in the mid-1970s by creation of the Center for Judicial Education and Research (CJER), with collaborative oversight by the CJA and the Judicial Council. Permanent funding was achieved in the latter 1970s as part of the California Legislature's appropriation to the Judicial Council and AOC.

The curriculum, judicial student body, educational materials, and staffing expanded significantly during the first decade.

During the concluding decade of the century the organization was transformed. The Governing Committee of the Center for Judicial Education and Research was incorporated into the Judicial Council's system of auxiliary bodies as an advisory committee. The Judicial Council added education as one of its major goals. The CJER developed a long-range strategic plan. It was consolidated with the AOC's education unit, relocated to offices within the AOC, and given responsibility for nonjudicial staff training throughout California.

As the century concluded, the education program had completed new initiatives on the subject of fairness in the courts and was planning expansions in staff training, distance learning, comprehensive curricula, ethics training, and futures planning.

*A*t midcentury the subject of judicial education was not only a clean slate; there was no slate. Indeed, the entire area of continuing education for attorneys was in its infancy. California's Continuing Education of the Bar (CEB) program was formally established in 1947 by joint agreement of the State Bar and the University of California at Berkeley for the purpose of providing refresher courses to lawyers returning from military service during World War II.

Judicial education began to emerge nationally in the early 1960s. Through the efforts of the judicial administration section of the American Bar Association (ABA), the first session of the National College of State Trial Judges was held in 1964. From that early beginning evolved the National Judicial College, which at the close of the century was offering, from its base in Reno, Nevada, residential and regional courses to judges under the auspices of a governing body appointed by the ABA.

The story of education for nonjudicial court personnel began even later. Probably the most significant early development was the establishment of the Institute of Court Management around 1970 for the purpose of training court executive officers and other managers to perform the growing number of nonjudicial, administrative functions in the courts of the country.[1]

Judicial Education in California

This is a story of two streams that eventually merged. One consisted of the efforts of the California Judges Association.[2] The other consisted of efforts by the Judicial Council and AOC.[3]

Not only was there no judicial education in California at midcentury, there was opposition to the concept. Indeed, as late as 1958, the CJA at its annual membership meeting received a recommendation from a special committee on the activities of the conference that the organization should not "conduct [nor] cause to be conducted . . . symposiums, seminars or refresher courses for judges."[4] Notwithstanding this recommendation, the CJA, in collaboration with Boalt Hall School of Law at the University of California at Berkeley, sponsored a two-day institute for California judges in June 1959. The subject was "the judge and the jury trial," and four dozen judges from superior and municipal courts in nineteen counties attended the institute. Similar institutes were held in each of the next two years. The format changed somewhat in 1962 when an all-day seminar on trial procedure was offered the day before the opening of the CJA annual meeting.

At the same time the CJA's Municipal Court Committee sponsored an all-day workshop for municipal court judges on the subject of sentencing, with sessions in both Southern and Northern California. At the northern session, Ralph N. Kleps, the relatively new Administrative Director of the Courts, offered that the Judicial Council and AOC would organize future workshops, which was favorably received by the municipal court judges. With this development we can see the headwaters of the two streams that subsequently merged in this field: the CJA on one hand and the Judicial Council and AOC on the other.

Role of the California Judges Association

By 1963 the CJA annual meeting included a two-day, in-depth educational seminar featuring a variety of subjects. The success of these seminars and other CJA-sponsored programs suggested that trial court judges were ready for judicial education by the mid-1960s.

Several California judges attended the initial session in 1964 of the ABA's National College of State Trial Judges and returned with the idea of fashioning something similar in California. This idea matured to the point that by the latter part of 1965 the CJA executive board approved a proposal, contingent on financing, to establish a California college for judges with a contemplated two-week session available to municipal and superior court judges.

After a search among private foundations for funding, the CJA, through its recently formed subsidiary foundation, received a grant of $125,000 in 1966 from the Ford Foundation for the purposes of establishing and operating for three years California's own judicial college. It has been said that this was the nation's first statewide judicial education program. The CJA made arrangements for the college to be conducted at the newly constructed Earl Warren Legal Institute, part of Boalt Hall School of Law at the University of California at Berkeley.

The fledgling California College of Trial Judges overcame the challenges of developing curriculum, selecting faculty, and gathering course materials. The first session took place between August 20 and September 1, 1967, with eighty judges in attendance. For the next year and several years thereafter, the CJA employed the services of a part-time administrator to assist with the many aspects of planning and executing the college sessions.

As the end of the Ford Foundation grant neared, the CJA turned successfully to the federal government's Law Enforcement Assistance Administration (LEAA) as a new source of funding and obtained from the

California Council on Criminal Justice (a state agency that distributed the federal funds) a three-year grant to defray substantially all of the college's expenses. (These agencies are discussed at length in Chapter Four.)

While the CJA was nurturing its new college, it also was busy sponsoring workshops both on a standalone basis and in conjunction with the annual meeting. There were four such seminars or workshops in 1969 alone.

Role of the Judicial Council and the AOC

After offering Judicial Council and AOC sponsorship of municipal court workshops in 1962, Ralph N. Kleps on behalf of the Judicial Council successfully proposed legislation in 1963 that launched a series of annual institutes for municipal and justice court judges. Soon thereafter, annual sentencing institutes for superior court judges were offered, as well as programs for juvenile court judges and the presiding judges of metropolitan superior courts.

By 1969 the Judicial Council and the AOC, similar to the CJA, also conducted four judicial education workshops or seminars around the state.

Creation of the Center for Judicial Education and Research

The CJA recognized in the early 1970s that a permanent funding source was needed for the judicial college. With the looming conclusion of the LEAA grant in 1972, the CJA's incumbent president called a meeting of representatives of the CJA, CEB, and AOC to explore options. Bernard E. Witkin, the distinguished legal scholar and early supporter of the CJA's college, also was invited to attend.[5]

The outcome of this and subsequent meetings was creation of the Center for Judicial Education and Research. This solution was modeled after a 1971 agreement between the State Bar and the University of California to perpetuate the CEB for attorney education. With respect to the CJER, the Judicial Council would serve the same role as the University of California's Board of Regents did for the CEB by becoming the official sponsor and funding entity through which state funds would flow. The CJA would serve in a capacity similar to the State Bar Board of Governors in the CEB by drawing upon its members for faculty, curriculum, and materials.

Following ratification by both the CJA and the Judicial Council, the AOC successfully obtained a first-year grant of LEAA funds in the amount of $210,000 for establishment of the CJER in 1973, with the tentative commitment of similar funding for 1974 and 1975.

The governing committee of the CJER consisted of four persons nominated by the CJA and four representatives of the Judicial Council, all appointed by Chief Justice Donald R. Wright. A full-time, professional staff was hired in the summer of 1973.[6]

The Judicial Council transferred all of its educational activities to the CJER with the exception of two annual workshops for presiding judges. The CJA relinquished to the CJER administration of the college, which was renamed the California Judicial College in 1978.

Although the CJER continued to receive federal grants for several years, the program was placed on solid financial footing in 1976 when the California Legislature, with concurrence by Governor Ronald Reagan, included the bulk of the CJER budget, including the California Judicial College, in the Judicial Council's annual appropriation.

From a staff of two professionals and an office manager in 1973, the CJER by 1987 had grown to a thirty-member staff with an annual budget approaching $3 million. The program conducted by the staff in the late 1980s included:

◆ The annual two-week judicial college still held in July at Boalt Hall School of Law at the University of California at Berkeley

◆ Eight continuing education institutes (two and one-half to three days) for new and experienced judges to discuss current legal developments, updates on substantive law, and information on standardized court practices

◆ Twelve orientation programs for new judges, of one week each

◆ Three graduate programs known as the Continuing Judicial Studies Programs, of one week each

Participation had reached a total of 2,000 enrollments each year from a total judiciary of approximately 1,500 judges and 300 judicial officers. In addition, the publications produced by the CJER included benchbooks, benchguides, and manuals on many aspects of judicial responsibilities; fifty audiotapes, many of which presented lectures delivered at the judicial college; and 100 instructional videotapes, including lectures and specially produced programs.

The CJA itself decided in the mid-1980s that there was an ongoing need for an educational program in addition to that offered by the CJER. This conclusion led to retention of the CJA's seminars held in conjunction with annual and midyear meetings, as well as occasional one-day work-shops on problems of particular interest to groups within the judiciary. By century's end, such programs had covered a broad spectrum of topics including employment litigation, expert witnesses, justice in the public eye, jury management and relations, and coping with change.

Systemic Education in the 1990s

Maturation of the CJER accelerated during the last decade of the century. Every aspect of the organization from governance to mission was impacted.[7]

Governance

The role of the Governing Committee of the Center for Judicial Education and Research and its relationship to the Judicial Council were revised and formalized in August 1993 with the adoption of rule 1029 (now rule 6.50) of the California Rules of Court. The governing committee was added as one of the advisory committees to the Judicial Council and charged with "maintaining a high quality and independent judicial education arm of the California judicial system."[8] The committee still consisted of eight judicial officer members appointed by the Chief Justice, with bifurcation of board representation between the CJA and the Judicial Council. Bernard E. Witkin had for many years served as an advisory member and continued to do so. He was joined by the president of the CJA and the Administrative Director of the Courts, who were added as advisory members.

At its July 1996 strategic planning session, the governing committee invited an array of interested parties to examine the relationships among the leaders in California judicial branch education and to revisit and discuss issues surrounding governance. The participants reached consensus on the following issues: (1) a single governing board should oversee and provide policy guidance for judicial branch education, including both judicial and administrative education; (2) the membership of the governing committee of the CJER should be expanded to include three court administrators or executive officers as voting members; and (3) the Judicial Administration Institute of California, concerned with court administration training, should become one of the primary planning committees reporting to the governing committee. The governing committee recommended appropriate amendments to rule 1029 of the California Rules of Court to implement these changes. The Judicial Council concurred, adopting the amendments effective January 1, 1997.

Planning

Following the lead of the Judicial Council, which held its first strategic planning meeting in 1993, the governing committee of the CJER held its first strategic planning workshop in December of that year. Subsequent annual workshops resulted in development of a long-range strategic plan for judicial education, which was approved by the Judicial Council.

The Judicial Council in 1995 added education as one of the five strategic goals: "Achieve the goals of the Judicial Council through judicial branch education and professional development."[9]

Administration

In August 1994, the AOC undertook a major reorganization of workload and personnel, and the AOC's administrative education unit was consolidated with the CJER. Along with the unit's four staff members and budget came a new expansion of the CJER's responsibility beyond judicial education.

After having its offices in or near Berkeley for twenty-two years, the CJER moved its offices in August 1995 to the AOC in San Francisco. As part of an AOC and Judicial Council reorganization, the CJER became the Education Division of the AOC, with responsibility for staffing the governing committee of the CJER but also for a broader role as an integrated part of the AOC. The CJER director became part of the AOC management team, with shared responsibility for the whole organization. Moving the CJER's offices to San Francisco with the AOC facilitated these changing roles and increased opportunities for collaboration between the CJER and other AOC divisions.

Program for Judges

By 1990, most states had gone to some form of mandatory judicial education. California had adopted mandatory continuing legal education for attorneys, and the legislature was discussing mandating judicial education by statute. The Governing Committee of the Center for Judicial Education and Research undertook an exhaustive study of the issue and, after a lively debate on the subject over the course of eighteen months, recommended that the Judicial Council require education for new judges and justices. The council adopted rule 970 of the California Rules of Court, effective January 1, 1996, to implement that recommendation.[10]

Judicial education is also now required for judges new to a family law assignment[11] or a juvenile dependency assignment.[12]

In 1999, the governing committee recommended, and the Judicial Council adopted, sections 25–25.6 of the California Standards of Judicial Administration, which set forth more comprehensive suggested (nonmandatory) standards for participation of judges and court staff in education and training. These standards acknowledge the importance of judicial branch education in improving the fair, effective, and efficient administration of justice and state that judges should consider participation in educational activities to be part of their official duties.

Program for Court Staff

When the CJER consolidated with the AOC's education unit in 1994, its initial responsibility, beyond judicial programs, was administrative education for presiding judges, court executive officers, and some middle managers. However, by century's end, responsibility for administrative education expanded to all aspects of court management and to the more than 20,000 trial and appellate court staff.

Fairness

In 1997 Chief Justice Ronald M. George announced a fairness education initiative in which he strongly encouraged California courts to make broad-based training in racial, ethnic, gender, and disability fairness available to all judicial officers by June 30, 1998, and to all court staff by the end of 1999. The Chief Justice called on the AOC and CJER to provide the technical assistance necessary to carry out the effort. The CJER had offered programs on judicial fairness education since 1981. It had been a primary part of the one-week orientation program for new judges, which had been mandatory for new judicial officers since 1996.

In response to the Chief Justice's initiative, the CJER specifically developed a "Fairness in the California Courts" curriculum, supplemented by a videotape, for judicial officers that was provided to all trial and appellate courts, along with train-the-trainer programs and other technical assistance for local court fairness education programs. The CJER next developed "Beyond Bias: Assuring Fairness in the Workplace," a curriculum for court staff that again was provided to all courts with train-the-trainer programs and other technical assistance.

Fairness education continues to be an important focus of the CJER's work and has been integrated into substantive law programs, offered in freestanding courses specifically devoted to some aspect of fairness, and made a part of all faculty training programs.

Breadth

The statewide education program for judicial officers and court staff at both the trial and appellate court levels includes orientation programs for new judicial officers and court clerks; continuing education programs for judicial officers, court administrators, and managers; annual statewide conferences for judicial officers and court administrators; videotapes and audiotapes; and judicial benchbooks, benchguides, and practice aids, in both electronic and print form. The education services cover all areas of judicial and administrative practice, including criminal, civil, juvenile, family, domestic violence, probate, mental health, complex litigation, genetics, and environmental law. They also include skill building in areas such as decision making, trial management, juror treatment, sentencing, technology, personnel management, leadership, budgeting, and fairness on the bench and in the workplace. Special programs are provided for judges from rural counties and for retired judges who sit on court assignment.

Beyond 2000

These achievements over the past several decades certainly create a milestone in the improved administration of justice. It seems entirely likely that the pace and quality of achievement will continue when one considers the endeavors that were in progress as the new millennium began:

- ◆ The development and broadening of court staff education. Because the audience is so large (20,000), most court staff education must be delivered by distance education methods. A training coordinator network is also being developed, with the goal of each court location eventually having a training coordinator who is the point of contact for the CJER.

- ◆ Distance education projects:

  - ✓ A court staff Web site is under development, which will include an online version of the *Basic In-Service Training Manual,* a comprehensive list of staff training programs offered through the AOC, and a number of commercial online courses that have been purchased.

  - ✓ Online self-directed courses for judges and court staff.

  - ✓ Videoconferencing.

  - ✓ Satellite broadcast.

  - ✓ Electronic publication of judicial benchguides, both on CD-ROM and via the Internet.

◆ A comprehensive curriculum development project. Education committees in every area of subject matter expertise are developing a complete curriculum for judicial officers, from entry level to career mastery.

◆ The development and delivery of an ethics training program for all judicial officers. The Judicial Council has sponsored a Commission on Judicial Performance defense insurance program, and each judicial officer must participate in a qualifying training program every three years in order to be covered by the program.

◆ The Futures Conference in June 2000, organized by the governing committee of the CJER. The focus was on how judicial branch education can meet the changing needs of the courts in the next ten years within the Judicial Council's strategic vision.

Notes

1 "Education" and "training" in the court context often are used interchangeably for judicial and court personnel. However, "education" will be used in this discussion to encompass both.

2 The predecessor to the CJA was the Conference of California Judges, but for convenience all references are to the CJA.

3 A substantial portion of the information used in this section is derived from Cameron Estelle Andersen, *The Story of the California Judges Association: The First Sixty Years* (San Francisco: Bancroft–Whitney, 1992), but the text will not be burdened with repeated citations. Readers interested in more detail should consult the excellent discussion of judicial education, pp. 112–47.

4 Id., p. 113.

5 Bernard E. Witkin continued, until his death in 1995, to play a prominent role in both the college and judicial education. In recognition of his many contributions, financial and otherwise, the college was renamed in 1996 as the Bernard E. Witkin Judicial College of California.

6 The first director was Paul Li, an attorney in the AOC who had been assistant director in charge of legal research, who would go on to serve for twenty years as the CJER's steward.

7 The substance of this section was prepared by James Vesper of the CJER, and his research has been used extensively in crafting this text.

8 California Rules of Court [1994], rule 1029 (repealed January 1, 1999; now rule 6.50).

9 Judicial Council of California, *Annual Report to the Governor and the Legislature* (1995), part 1, p. 4.

10 This was in addition to section 25 of the California Standards of Judicial Administration, adopted in 1990, suggesting nonmandatory guidelines for judicial education.

11 California Rules of Court, rule 1200.

12 California Welfare and Institutions Code, section 304.7; California Standards of Judicial Administration, section 25.2(c).

Chapter 11
Alternative Dispute Resolution

Overview

Alternative or appropriate dispute resolution (ADR) became a part of court operations between 1970 and 2000, both in California and elsewhere. Congestion and delay, the traditional demons, were driving forces.

Although many approaches are enveloped within ADR, arbitration and mediation were the two major areas of court-annexed ADR in California. In arbitration, litigants submit their respective causes to a neutral third party, who is empowered to render a decision on the merits. It is the most formalized alternative to court adjudication. Mediation and its sibling, conciliation, are informal processes in which the neutral third party assists the litigants in searching for a mutually acceptable settlement but has no power to impose a solution.

Arbitration came first. At the urging of local bar groups, both the Los Angeles and San Francisco Superior Courts established arbitration programs in 1971 for smaller personal injury cases. The Judicial Council approved.

By the mid-1970s arbitration was legislated in California for smaller personal injury cases in larger superior courts, and it became mandatory by the late 1970s.

The Judicial Council studied the arbitration system and concluded in the mid-1980s that its effects were favorable. Mandatory arbitration subsequently was perpetuated by the California Legislature, and the monetary limit on eligible cases was increased.

By the close of the century, arbitration's impact was difficult, if not impossible, to quantify, but it continued to be viewed favorably and was the most extensively used form of court-annexed ADR.

Mediation also was imposed by statute. Beginning in 1993, mediation in civil cases became mandatory in Los Angeles County for an experimental period of five years. Other courts were given the option of adopting the program. The Judicial Council was directed to report on the effects and savings, if any. Well before the end of the experiment, the Judicial Council reported that mediation had exceeded both the cost savings and time savings specified by the legislature. This led to expansion of mediation in the trial courts and the start of mediation experiments in the appellate courts.

Several years prior to mediation in civil cases, mediation was available in California family cases, and by the century's end it was in universal use.

*T*he concept of alternative dispute resolution, or appropriate dispute resolution as it is called by some,[1] is simple: attempt to resolve disputes by means other than traditional, adversarial litigation in the courts.

The concept is simple but not new. Without delving into ancient history, one need only look to the American Arbitration Association and its extensive involvement in privately negotiated agreements for examples of arbitration rather than litigation of disputes. This model has been replicated in a number of other contemporary contexts such as health care, employment, and purchases or sales of corporate securities. Moreover, the concept is certainly not new in California. As early as 1927 California had a statute permitting the enforcement of arbitration agreements as well as awards made pursuant to them.[2] This statutory scheme not only was endorsed but strengthened by recommendations of the California Law Revision Commission in 1960.[3]

What was new nationally and in California, from 1950 to 2000, was the concept and rather extensive implementation of court-sponsored ADR programs. Both the birth and growth of court-sponsored ADR occurred in two rather different settings. The first was cases involving family matters and the formal recognition of conciliation courts. The second began in small civil cases. Pennsylvania broke new ground in 1952 when the legislature empowered courts of common pleas to establish compulsory arbitration to expedite small claims and relieve delay. The jurisdictional ceiling originally was $1,000, but in a relatively short time it was raised to $3,000 and then to $10,000. Pennsylvania's lead was followed by several other states, such as Ohio and Alaska.

These new court programs had three key characteristics that distinguished them from then-existing private ADR such as arbitration. First, court arbitration was mandatory rather than voluntary. Second, the parties did not have the right to select the third-party neutral who would serve as arbitrator. Third, the arbitration decision was not final because the universal right to a trial entitled a party who disagreed with the arbitration decision to seek judicial review or retrial.

By the end of the century, ADR, both within and outside courts, had grown extensively. Programs outside the courts, such as "private judging" or "rent-a-judge" businesses, will not be addressed here for a variety of reasons, not least of which is the dearth of readily available or reliable information.[4]

Programs in courts spanned a broad continuum by the century's end: negotiation, mediation, neutral evaluation, mini-trials, summary jury trials, settlement conferences, neutral fact finding, arbitration, referral to private judges, confidential listening, and facilitation by ombudspersons.[5]

As a practical matter, only arbitration and mediation were broadly used within the courts of California and elsewhere. As we embark upon the journey into these areas, it should be kept in mind that those who passed this way before us, both recently and decades ago, have lamented the lack of information to light the way. This is especially true regarding the impact of ADR in California.[6]

Arbitration

The first courts in California to officially venture into this field were the superior courts in Los Angeles and San Francisco Counties. In 1971, representatives of the Los Angeles Trial Lawyers Association and the Association of Southern California Defense Counsel, with the support of the presiding judge of the Los Angeles Superior Court, initiated the Attorneys' Special Arbitration Plan for smaller personal injury cases. The board of supervisors provided financial support, and staff of the superior court were designated to administer the program.

Shortly thereafter, representatives of the San Francisco Trial Lawyers Association and the Association of Northern California Defense Counsel, again with the support of the superior court presiding judge, initiated a virtually identical system for San Francisco Superior Court in 1971.[7]

The impetus for arbitration in the courts came from two traditional demons, congestion and delay, which are well indicted by the following excerpt from a resolution adopted by the California Senate in 1971:

> Whereas, There is presently an excessive burden of litigation in the courts in California; and
> Whereas, The entire judicial process in California is overloaded causing extensive delay to citizens who are entitled to speedy justice; and
> Whereas, This overloading of the courts also seriously increases the costs of civil litigation; and
> Whereas, Court procedures must be studied and streamlined; now, therefore, be it
> Resolved by the Senate of the State of California, That the Senate Rules Committee enter into a contract with the Judicial Council

to conduct a study of the possible role of the use of arbitration in the judicial process and that such study be concluded by November 20, 1972. . . . [8]

Following the study requested by the Senate, the Judicial Council approved in principle the use of arbitration in small personal injury cases as a means of reducing superior court caseloads but reserved judgment on whether arbitration proceedings should be compulsory.[9]

Concerns about congestion and delay were not fanciful. Court filings, especially in civil cases, had increased dramatically during the 1960s and 1970s, as had the backlog of pending cases. Concurrently, the ratio of dispositions to filings was declining while the time to trial was significantly lengthening, whether measured from filing or from certification by counsel that a case was ready for trial.[10]

As a promising form of relief, arbitration was embraced by the California Legislature, which in 1974 adopted a plan for uniform statewide arbitration in the superior courts. The legislature acted with the support of the Judicial Council and the California Trial Lawyers Association. However, Governor Ronald Reagan vetoed the bill because it required the state to bear the cost of administration, including arbitrators' fees. These fiscal concerns also reflected fear within the executive branch of government that this would be a first step toward state funding of local trial courts, which Governor Reagan's administration opposed.[11]

The following year California had a new governor: Edmund G. "Jerry" Brown. Over the objections of his own Finance Department, he signed legislation similar to that previously vetoed by Governor Reagan. Implementing the legislation, the Judicial Council promulgated rules requiring arbitration in superior courts with ten or more judges. Optional adoption was permitted in other courts. The parties could stipulate to arbitration by mutual agreement, but plaintiffs could unilaterally elect arbitration in cases valued up to $7,500. In effect, plaintiffs could force defendants into arbitration so long as plaintiffs accepted a ceiling of $7,500 on the award. Both parties were given the right to reject the arbitrator's award and pursue the litigation in court (trial de novo) regardless of whether the arbitration was elected or stipulated.[12]

Rather than an end, the new plan was merely the beginning. In 1978 the legislature created fifty-four new, permanent judicial positions, but the legislation was vetoed by Governor Brown. Mandatory arbitration was advanced as an alternative to the expense of creating this substantial number of new judgeships. The concept was embraced by Governor Brown and his staff, and in early 1978 legislation was introduced on his behalf to create a system of mandatory arbitration.[13] Following extensive legislative maneuvering and deliberations by a broad array of interested parties, the legislation was passed in September and signed by the governor.[14] The plan thus created had the following key characteristics:

◆ There were three methods for referring a case to arbitration: stipulation, plaintiff's election, or court order.

◆ Court-ordered arbitration was required in superior courts with ten or more judges if the amount in controversy did not exceed $15,000.

◆ Mandatory arbitration applied only to civil suits for monetary compensation.

◆ Arbitration by plaintiff's selection was limited to awards not exceeding $15,000.

◆ Arbitration hearing dates were set no later than sixty days after assignment to an arbitrator.

◆ An arbitrator had to be either a member of the State Bar or an active or retired judge.

◆ Arbitrators were paid $150 per day.

◆ Any party could request a court trial within twenty days after an arbitration award was filed.

◆ If the judgment following court trial was not more favorable than the arbitration award, the party requesting the trial had to pay the arbitrator's fee plus other specified costs.[15]

Hopes were high for the new program, and proponents envisioned several benefits.

◆ Congestion and backlog in large superior courts would be reduced by diverting smaller cases from trial.

◆ Judicial workloads would be reduced, requiring fewer new judgeships and thereby reducing court costs.

◆ Arbitration would be more expeditious, less costly, and more satisfying to litigants.

◆ With more expeditious handling of small civil cases, pressure to abolish the jury system would be reduced or eliminated.[16]

An evaluation of the program by the Rand Corporation after only one year of operation concluded that those who hoped for sharp reductions in court congestion "should temper these hopes somewhat."[17] Moreover, "the effect of arbitration on court costs [was] highly uncertain."[18] And the effects of arbitration on litigants in lawsuits involving small sums were unclear.[19]

The 1978 plan had two additional provisions. First, it required the Judicial Council by January 1, 1984, to report to the governor and the legislature regarding the effectiveness of mandatory arbitration. Second, the statutory scheme of mandatory arbitration was to "sunset" on January 1, 1985 (later extended to 1986), in the absence of continued statutory authorization.[20]

In response to these provisions, the Judicial Council established an advisory committee that conducted an in-depth study of the arbitration system, including its effects on the courts and users. As part of its report, this committee offered the following conclusions and recommendations, adopted by the Judicial Council on November 19, 1983:

> The committee finds that judicial arbitration is a valuable dispute resolution mechanism which has favorably affected the cost, complexity, and time associated with litigating smaller civil cases. The users of the program—litigants and their attorneys—confirm that dispositions resulting from judicial arbitration generally tend to be more prompt, inexpensive, and predictable, and are frequently more satisfactory to all parties.
>
> The program has emerged as an essential calendar management tool for the courts, permitting the disposition of civil active cases, including those not ordered to arbitration, to occur on the whole more quickly and economically, while providing litigants in smaller civil cases with a desirable alternative to conventional litigation.
>
> Based on its study of the effects of the judicial arbitration program, the committee recommends that legislation be enacted indefinitely retaining judicial arbitration beyond its current repeal date of January 1, 1986.[21]

Mandatory arbitration not only was perpetuated, it was propelled by the legislature's Trial Court Delay Reduction Act of 1986 (discussed in Chapter Eight), which required courts to identify cases suitable for ADR.[22] In 1987, the monetary limit on cases subject to mandatory arbitration was increased to $50,000.[23]

In 1989 the Rand Corporation updated its earlier assessment, which had been made after the program was in operation for only one year. With the benefit of six years of operation, Rand reached generally favorable conclusions.

> The results of our survey indicate that California's judicial arbitration program appears to be satisfying many, if not all, of its proponents' original objectives. For instance, the program is well accepted by local court officials, who consider arbitration an effective calendar management tool. It has also proved quite flexible, enabling counties to adapt the program to local needs and circumstances.
>
> Most significantly, arbitration continues to offer litigants a speedier alternative to trial. This benefit has been achieved with no observable dissatisfaction among attorneys or litigants, as reflected in the low rate of actual trials *de novo*.
>
> In spite of arbitration's success in some areas, it has not proven to be a panacea for dealing with crowded civil calendars. In contrast to significant growth in civil filings since 1979, arbitration caseloads have not grown proportionately and appear to be in a stagnant period. It may be that the recent doubling of the jurisdictional limit to $50,000 will prove an impetus to growth.
>
> In our opinion, the program's greatest need is for an ongoing means of monitoring and evaluating its performance. Although many courts maintain some program statistics, there is no general requirement that they do so, nor is there a central place for reporting and disseminating these data. In light of the recent debate in the legislature concerning arbitration and the program's substantial cost, it seems only prudent to report periodically on the arbitration program. Since arbitrated cases now represent a significant fraction of the courts' civil damage caseload, we recommend that local courts resume the reporting of data to the California Judicial Council for compilation and analysis in the council's annual report.[24]

As California entered the final decade of the last century, the need persisted to reduce delay and cost for litigants. As knowledgeable experts observed:

> Over 90 percent of all civil cases filed in California settle prior to trial. A high percentage of these settlements occur "on the courthouse steps," or shortly before trial. Dispute resolution mechanisms currently incorporated into court procedures, such as nonbinding arbitration, are helpful in settling many cases, but

they come after cases are filed and after parties have invested considerable sums in the litigation. California's challenge is to create a system of civil justice and appropriate dispute resolution that encourages satisfactory settlements early in the process, that minimizes costs for both the parties and the state, and that results in informed decisions and perceived fairness.[25]

The same needs that had earlier motivated creation of mandatory arbitration obviously still existed. The number and variety of ADR programs in California, however, had greatly expanded, as had the amount of work performed by ADR providers.[26] By 1999 it appears there were fifty-one civil ADR programs in California courts in addition to judicial arbitration. Superior court arbitration programs existed in forty-four counties.[27] Although it was possible to identify these court-related programs, the conclusion regrettably was that "we know very little about most of them."[28]

Even with that reservation, a subcommittee of the Judicial Council was able to conclude at the close of the century that civil ADR processes positively furnished a greater choice of dispute resolution methods, accommodated a broader range of interests and concerns than possible within the confines of formal litigation, provided a broader range of available remedies, offered the possibility of earlier and faster resolution of disputes, reduced costs, and appeared to provide litigants with greater satisfaction with dispute resolution processes and outcomes.[29] These positive effects were offset to some extent by fewer procedural protections, secrecy, and the fact that ADR does not create legal precedent by which attorneys and future litigants might be guided.[30]

When the focus was confined to California's judicial arbitration program, the effects at century's close were "unclear."[31] This was true with respect to time savings, cost savings, impacts on court workload, and impacts on court costs as well as public perception of the courts."[32] Arbitration, nonetheless, had by the end of the 1900s become the most common form of court-sponsored ADR.[33]

Mediation

Mediation programs were the second most prevalent form of court-sponsored ADR in California.[34] Just as the search for a solution to court congestion and delay led the California Legislature to arbitration, these same concerns led the legislature in 1993 to mediation. At that time the legislature adopted and the governor signed the Civil Action Mediation Act.[35] Declaring that it was in the public interest for mediation to be encouraged and used by the courts, "the Legislature found that mediation is an effective process for reducing the cost, time, and stress of dispute resolution that affords parties a greater opportunity for participating directly in resolving their disputes and may help to reduce the backlog of cases burdening the judicial system."[36]

This legislation created a five-year pilot project that was mandatory in the courts of Los Angeles County. Optional adoption of the program by other courts was authorized. At the heart of the plan was the prerogative of the presiding judge, or his or her designate, to refer to mediation any civil action that otherwise would be subject to mandatory judicial arbitration.

This act also contained a sunset provision effective January 1, 1999, with the further direction to the Judicial Council to report by January 1, 1998, regarding the effects and savings, if any, realized by the courts and parties. The legislature announced in advance that the pilot mediation programs would be regarded as a success if they resulted in savings of at least $250,000 to the courts, with corresponding savings to the parties. Within three years mediation programs were operative in the superior courts of Los Angeles, San Diego, and El Dorado Counties as well as in the municipal courts of San Diego, San Mateo, and Mono Counties. After only *two years* of operation the Judicial Council announced that "savings to the parties have been more than five times the legislative benchmark for the *five-year* pilot project" and the "estimated savings to the courts for two years . . . was more than eleven times the Legislature's $250,000 target."[37]

This permitted the Judicial Council comfortably to offer the following conclusion and recommendation: "The pilot project created by the Legislature for cases submitted under the Civil Action Mediation Act has exceeded the cost- and time-savings goals of that act and has won strong approval from reporting parties and their counsel. By removing the sunset clause and ending the pilot project early, the Legislature would recognize mediation, whether court-ordered or voluntary, as an effective process for reducing the cost, time, and stress of dispute resolution."[38]

By the end of the century the legislature expanded mediation by authorizing the creation of civil mediation pilot programs in four additional courts, with authorization in two of them to make mandatory referrals of civil cases to mediation and compensate the mediators from court funds.[39] It should also be noted that late in the 1990s experimentation had begun with mandatory mediation in appellate litigation under a program authorized by the Judicial Council in the First Appellate District of the Court of Appeal (San Francisco).[40]

Use in Cases Involving Families and Juveniles

Mediation in cases involving family relationships and juveniles requires special attention. In many ways ADR in the court context began with attempts in divorce cases to achieve conciliation between estranged spouses. Those efforts sometimes even occurred prior to commencement of formal divorce proceedings and were offered as a service by the court. Building upon a 1939 statutory enactment,[41] superior courts, by 1980, were statutorily authorized to exercise jurisdiction as a "family conciliation court"[42] and to do so for the purposes of protecting the rights of children; promoting public welfare by preserving, promoting, and protecting family life and matrimony; and providing means for the reconciliation of spouses and the amicable settlement of family controversies.[43]

It appears that conciliation and mediation have blended in terms of techniques, and in this sense mediation in family matters has been on a growth trajectory in California courts.

Among the notable developments during the latter part of the last century was the direction to the Judicial Council in 1984 to oversee mediation and conciliation court services in family matters.[44] In 1990 the Judicial Council adopted uniform standards of practice for child custody mediation as well as for disputes over visitation.[45] In 1993 the California Legislature mandated separate mediation in cases involving domestic violence, with the further provision that parties participating in these mediation sessions were entitled to be accompanied by a support person.[46]

By the end of the century, the use of mediation in family cases had become universal throughout California.

Observations

Court-related alternative dispute resolution in California didn't really start until the final quarter of the last century, and the start was slow. Moreover, the impetus was external to the courts—beginning first with local bar associations and then continuing by legislative mandates. While ADR mandates from the legislature and governor may have been cast in terms of aiding litigants and courts, the original motivation may have been driven more by the desire to avoid the expense of creating new, permanent, and costly judgeships.

Even so, the avowed purposes of saving litigants time, money, and anguish are commendable, as are the institutional goals of improving the quality of justice by furnishing alternatives to conventional litigation, reducing congestion, expediting case processing, and better utilizing precious judicial resources. While verifying the achievement of these commendable ADR objectives may still elude the judicial system, both the purposes and the effort create a milestone in the administration of justice.

Notes

1   For instance, [Judicial Council of California], Commission on the Future of the California Courts, *Justice in the Balance, 2020: Report of the Commission on the Future of the California Courts* (1993), p. 40.

2   California Statutes 1927, chapter 225.

3   California Law Revision Commission, *Recommendation and Study Relating to Arbitration* (December 1960).

4   See, for example, Janice A. Roehl, Robert E. Huitt, and Henry Wong, *Private Judging: A Study of Its Volume, Nature, and Impact on State Courts: Final Report* (Pacific Grove, Calif.: Institute for Social Analysis, 1993).

5   California Judicial Council, Center for Judicial Education and Research, *Judges Guide to ADR* (1996), pp. 14–17.

6   Deborah R. Hensler, Albert J. Lipson, and Elizabeth S. Rolph, *Judicial Arbitration in California: The First Year*, Rand Publication Series R-2733-ICJ ([Santa Monica, Calif.]: Institute for Civil Justice, Rand Corporation, 1981), pp. xvi–xvii; Judicial Council of California, Task Force on the Quality of Justice, Subcommittee on Alternative Dispute Resolution and the Judicial System, *Alternative Dispute Resolution in Civil Cases: Report* (August 1999), pp. v–vii.

7   John G. Fall, project director, *A Study of the Role of Arbitration in the Judicial Process* (Judicial Council of California, 1972), pp. 18–26.

8   California Senate Resolution 139 (Moscone), 2 *California Senate Journal* (1971 regular session), pp. 2766–67, 2933.

9   Fall, *Role of Arbitration*, [preface].

10 Id., pp. 9–15; Hensler, Lipson, and Rolph, *Judicial Arbitration in California*, pp. 4–8.

11 Hensler, Lipson, and Rolph, *Judicial Arbitration in California*, p. 10.

12 Id., pp. 10–11.

13 California Senate Bill 1362 (Smith); California Statutes 1978, chapter 743, p. 2303.

14 Hensler, Lipson, and Rolph, *Judicial Arbitration in California*, pp. 13–23, 105–7.

15 Id., pp. 22–23.

16 Id., pp. 12–13.

17 Id., p. 93.

18 Id., p. 94.

19 Id., p. 96.

20 California Statutes 1978, chapter 743, sections 1141.29 and 1141.32, p. 2307; Hensler, Lipson, and Rolph, *Judicial Arbitration in California*, p. 2.

21 Judicial Council of California, *Annual Report to the Governor and the Legislature* (1984), pp. 5–6; California Statutes 1983, chapter 1253, section 1141.32, p. 4944. By the time of the Judicial Council's report, the repeal date had been extended by legislative amendment to January 21, 1986.

22 California Government Code, section 68607(d); Trial Court Delay Reduction Act of 1986, California Statutes 1986, chapter 1335.

23 California Code of Civil Procedure, section 1141.11; California Statutes 1987, chapter 1204, section 1, p. 4298.

24 David L. Bryant, *Judicial Arbitration in California: An Update*, Rand Publication Series N-2909-ICJ ([Santa Monica, Calif.]: Institute for Civil Justice, Rand Corporation, 1989), pp. x–xi.

25 Robert Barrett, Jay Folberg, and Joshua Rosenberg, *Use of ADR in California Courts: Report to the Judicial Council of California Advisory Committee on Dispute Resolution* (University of San Francisco School of Law, December 1991), p. 5.

26 Id., p. 35.

27 Judicial Council of California, Task Force on the Quality of Justice, Subcommittee on Alternative Dispute Resolution and the Judicial System, *Alternative Dispute Resolution in Civil Cases*, p. 50.

28 Ibid.

29 Id., pp. 7–15.

30 Id., pp. 15–16.

31 Id., pp. 62–64.

32 Id., pp. 62–65.

33 Judicial Council of California, *Civil Action Mediation Act: Results of the Pilot Project, Legislative Report* (November 1996), p. 7. Attributable to the statutory

mandate compelling arbitration in civil cases involving less than $50,000 in larger courts and the supplemental discretionary authority in smaller courts to also compel arbitration. Code of Civil Procedure, section 1141.11(a)–(b).

[34] Judicial Council, *Civil Action Mediation Act*, p. 7.

[35] California Statutes 1993, chapter 1261, p. 7323.

[36] Judicial Council, *Civil Action Mediation Act*, p. 1.

[37] Id., pp. 2–3.

[38] Id., p. 9.

[39] California Statutes 1999, chapter 67.

[40] Judicial Council of California, Task Force on Appellate Mediation, *Mandatory Mediation in the First Appellate District of the Court of Appeal: Report and Recommendations* (September 2001).

[41] California Statutes 1939, chapter 737, p. 2261.

[42] California Statutes 1980, chapter 48, section 1740, p. 126.

[43] California Family Code, section 1801; see also California Statutes 1980, chapter 48, section 1768, p. 131.

[44] California Family Code, sections 1850–1852; see also California Statutes 1984, chapter 893, section 5180, p. 3004.

[45] Judicial Council of California, *Annual Report to the Governor and the Legislature* (1991), volume 1, pp. 90–91.

[46] California Family Code, sections 3170 and 6303; see also California Statutes 1993, chapter 219, section 116.8, pp. 1628–29, and section 154, pp. 1659–60.

Chapter 12
Fairness and Access to Justice for All

Overview

ublic attitudes toward courts were measured nationally and in California during the closing quarter of the last century. The results were discouraging. Americans were dissatisfied with court performance and had unfulfilled expectations about courts providing equality and fairness. Most Californians viewed courts as "poor" or "only fair" and felt that both access and treatment were unequal.

Nationally, a consortium was formed of state court entities devoted to combating the several forms of bias in courts.

California began with an attack on gender bias that led to the Judicial Council's establishment of the Advisory Committee on Gender Bias in the Courts in 1987. This committee reported in 1990 that gender bias in the courts was a significant problem and submitted sixty-eight recommendations to insure fairness.

A special committee, charged with acting on these recommendations, reported in 1996 that one-third had been substantially implemented.

Following the initial report of the gender bias committee, a companion committee was established by the Judicial Council to address racial and ethnic bias. By 1994 it was apparent that a comprehensive effort was required, and the Access and Fairness Advisory Committee was created by the Judicial Council.

This umbrella committee divided into six subcommittees: access for persons with disabilities, gender fairness, racial and ethnic fairness, women of color, sexual orientation, and education and implementation.

These various subcommittees utilized a similar array of research techniques including opinion polls, surveys, public hearings, and interviews. By the end of the century, all but the sexual orientation subcommittee had completed sufficient research to advise the Judicial Council that there were opportunities in each area to improve fairness.

*P*ublic attitudes regarding courts were surveyed at several points in the last quarter-century. Results were discouraging both nationally and in California. Public confidence was not high. At the national level, a survey commissioned by the National Center for State Courts produced these insights, among others, in 1978:

- ◆ The general public and community leaders were dissatisfied with the performance of courts and ranked courts lower than many other major American institutions.

- ◆ The public's concern about courts stemmed from the feeling that basic expectations, including equality and fairness, had not been met.[1]

Toward the end of the century, a survey of public attitudes in California provided similar and equally alarming results.[2] A majority of Californians had an "only fair" or "poor" opinion of the state's courts.[3] Californians believed, in general, that "some people get treated better than others" and, specifically, that "[p]oor people do not have equal access[,] . . . minorities are not treated as well as whites, and white males receive the best treatment."[4]

There were both national and California responses to this new knowledge.

National Response

The most significant development nationally was state-by-state establishment of commissions or similar bodies dedicated to combating various forms of bias. The objectives were bias eradication and demonstrable equality for all persons involved in court processes.

Gender bias may have been the first target, thanks to the efforts of the National Association of Women Judges and other groups. A national conference sponsored by the National Center for State Courts in 1981 apparently inspired the creation of the first gender bias task force, also in 1981, within the New Jersey court system.

Ultimately these antibias entities joined forces as a national consortium that enabled them to share information, techniques, and inspiration. California played a prominent role in this consortium, with notable contributions by individual judges.

California's Response

Within California, the efforts of many dedicated persons ensured that the pursuit of fairness would be a milestone in the improved administration of justice.

Following the national conference on gender bias, a steering committee was formed composed entirely of women lawyers, law professors, and judges. This group urged Chief Justice Rose Elizabeth Bird to establish a gender bias task force in California, as had been done in New Jersey and elsewhere. The Chief Justice responded by appointing, in 1986, a special committee to review issues of gender bias in the courts. This appeared to be the first formal response to bias in California's courts. Based upon the work of that committee, the Judicial Council in 1987 created the Advisory Committee on Gender Bias in the Courts. This was supplemented in 1991 when the Judicial Council created the Advisory Committee on Racial and Ethnic Bias in the Courts.

It became apparent in a relatively short time that an all-encompassing effort was both needed and appropriate. The Judicial Council therefore created in 1994 the Access and Fairness Advisory Committee "to review and make recommendations about fairness issues in the courts related to race, ethnicity, gender, persons with disabilities, and sexualorientation."[5]

At the close of the century this umbrella committee had organized itself into six subcommittees respectively concerned with access for persons with disabilities, gender fairness, racial and ethnic fairness, women of color, sexual orientation, and education and implementation.

Both the creation of the Access and Fairness Advisory Committee and its activities are embraced by the Judicial Council's mission for the judiciary, which emphasizes fairness and accessibility in the resolution of disputes arising under the law. More specifically, the first goal of the Judicial Council, incorporated into its strategic plan, stresses "equal access to the courts" as well as "fair and just" treatment in the courts.[6]

Gender

The original Advisory Committee on Gender Bias in the Courts submitted in 1990 a draft report advising that "gender bias was a significant problem in the courts as it was throughout society." The committee also submitted for consideration sixty-eight recommendations "designed to insure fairness for all participants in the court system."[7]

Utilizing an array of research techniques, as well as public hearings, the committee examined the potential for gender bias in five substantive areas: family law, domestic violence, juvenile and criminal law, court administration, and civil litigation and courtroom demeanor. In each area the committee concluded that gender bias existed or had the potential to exist. For example, in the family law area the extent and level of gender bias led the committee to recommend, among other things, changes in child and spousal support, custody, division of assets, assignment of judges, training of family lawyers, and mediation.[8] With respect to domestic violence, the committee noted: "because 95 percent of the victims of domestic violence are women, the judicial system's unequal and inadequate treatment of such victims and of the crime of domestic violence raised serious issues of gender bias."[9]

The committee found in the area of juvenile and criminal law three major areas of concern: appointment of attorneys to represent defendants, treatment of female offenders, and operation of juvenile courts. The committee concluded that "gender bias affects the ways in which the criminal and juvenile courts operate, both directly and indirectly."[10] Within the courts themselves, the committee found potential for gender bias in administration in view of the fact that California courts employ women predominantly in lower-paid classifications.[11] The committee rather forcefully concluded that gender bias was unacceptably high in the courtroom environment— flowing from judicial conduct in the form of either actions by judges or the failure of judges to control courtroom interactions in which other participants, such as attorneys or court employees, exhibited gender-biased behavior.[12]

After review and consideration by a special subcommittee, the Judicial Council unanimously adopted the recommendations of the committee and formally issued the report in 1996.

The landmark work of the advisory committee in the area of gender bias was accompanied by the work of another Judicial Council group, the Gender Fairness Subcommittee of the Access and Fairness Advisory Committee, charged with implementing the gender fairness proposals. Thanks to the work of this group, it was reported that by 1996 approximately one-third of the sixty-eight original proposals submitted to the Judicial Council in 1990 had been substantially implemented.[13]

Minorities

The Judicial Council's Advisory Committee on Racial and Ethnic Bias in the Courts approached its task directly by conducting public hearings. Between November 1991 and June 1992, thirteen days of public hearings were conducted in twelve cities throughout California. In addition to open invitations to individuals and groups to testify, on a public or confidential basis, people were invited to submit written testimony or observations. By the conclusion of this process, 249 people testified, resulting in 2,600 pages of testimony, and 94 people made written submissions totaling 1,000 pages.[14]

From this mass of information the advisory committee concluded that issues of fairness existed in a broad array of areas ranging from access to justice to minority employment within courts.

Recognizing that the testimony and statements elicited during the course of public hearings did not necessarily reflect a representative sampling of the California population, the advisory committee subsequently conducted an opinion survey for the purpose of determining whether the opinions of those who testified could be objectively verified as views held by the general public. The results of that survey were submitted to the Judicial Council in 1994. The clearest conclusion was that there are two distinct perceptions of the judicial system in California. "One system is experienced primarily by judicial officers, and to some extent nonjudicial court personnel, while the 'other' system is the domain of racial and ethnic minorities."[15] The second distinct conclusion from the survey was that "racial and ethnic minorities do not share a monolithic view of the courts."[16]

Persons with Disabilities

The Access and Fairness Advisory Committee elected to provide special focus on persons with disabilities and did so by creating a subcommittee responsible for "studying and addressing issues related to the availability of all aspects of the judicial system to persons with disabilities and chronic medical conditions."[17] To discharge this responsibility, the subcommittee undertook a multistage research program composed of public hearings, telephone and mail surveys, and in-person interviews.

The primary areas of inquiry concerned attitudes, architecture, communications, environment, transportation, and employment. Admitting that the objective was to ascertain perceptions and experiences, the subcommittee during the course of its work apparently did not attempt to document barriers to access for disabled persons.

The committee in 1997 submitted for the Judicial Council's consideration an array of recommendations—all in support of the objective of increasing access to the judicial process for persons with disabilities.[18]

At the heart of the recommendations were proposals for extensive education both within and beyond the courts to familiarize court officials with the Americans with Disabilities Act (ADA) and to heighten awareness of access problems for persons with disabilities. The subcommittee also urged that the Judicial Council help courts assess court capacity to assist persons with disabilities; require an ADA coordinator in all courts; adopt a standard of judicial administration to provide flexible scheduling to accommodate disability-related problems of stamina or time limitations; and undertake a compliance review to quantify the extent to which persons with disabilities face physical barriers to participation in the legal system.

Sexual Orientation

The subcommittee responsible for issues related to sexual orientation was in the midst of its initial research as the century ended. Surveys were being used extensively, as they had been used by the other subcommittees. The threshold objective was to examine the experiences of court users with the goal of identifying procedures that have been especially successful in promoting access and fairness for lesbians and gay men. The second objective was to examine the experiences of court employees in order to assess the courts as a workplace for gay men and lesbians as well as to determine ways in which the work environment can be improved.

Notes

1   Yankelovich, Skelly and White, Inc., "Highlights of a National Survey of the General Public, Judges, Lawyers, and Community Leaders," in *State Courts: A Blueprint for the Future: Proceedings of the Second Annual Conference on the Judiciary*, National Conference on the Judiciary ([Denver]: National Center for State Courts, 1978), p. 5.

2   Yankelovich, Skelly and White/Clancy Shulman, Inc., "Surveying the Future: Californians' Attitudes on the Court System," in *2020 Vision: Symposium on the Future of California's Courts: Research Papers* (December 10–11, 1992).

3   Id., p. [1] 5.

4   Id., p. [2] 10.

5   Judicial Council of California, California Courts Web site: [Programs: Access and Fairness: Background Information], *www.courtinfo.ca.gov/programs/access/about/htm.*

6   Judicial Council of California, *Leading Justice Into the Future: Strategic Plan* (March 2000), p. 9.

7   Judicial Council of California, Advisory Committee on Gender Bias in the Courts, *Achieving Equal Justice for Women and Men in the California Courts* (1996), p. xiii.

8   Id., p. 7.

9   Id., p. 11.

10 Id., p. 13.

11 Id., p. 15.

12 Id., p. 17.

13 Judicial Council of California, Access and Fairness Advisory Committee, Gender Fairness Subcommittee, *Gender and Justice: Implementing Gender Fairness in the Courts: Implementation Report* (1996), p. 1.

14 Judicial Council of California, Advisory Committee on Racial and Ethnic Bias in the Courts, *1991–92 Public Hearings on Racial and Ethnic Bias in the California State Court System* (1993), p. 2.

15 Judicial Council of California, Advisory Committee on Racial and Ethnic Bias in the State Courts, "Report on Fairness in the California Courts: A Survey of

the Public, Attorneys, and Court Personnel," Administrative Office of the Courts Report Summary (June 28, 1994), in *Reports and Recommendations* (July 7, 1994), tab 2, p. 6.

16   Ibid.

17   Judicial Council of California, Advisory Committee on Access and Fairness in the Courts, Access for Persons with Disabilities Subcommittee, *Public Hearings Report: Access for Persons with Disabilities* (1997), p. 1-1.

18   Judicial Council of California, Advisory Committee on Access and Fairness in the Courts, Access for Persons with Disabilities Subcommittee, *Summary of Survey and Public Hearing Reports* (1997), pp. 16–24.

Chapter 13
A Response to Diversity—
Interpreter Services

Overview

 f a person's knowledge of the English language is inadequate for understanding court proceedings, he or she is vulnerable, particularly as a defendant in a criminal case. The plight of these persons received substantial attention and assistance in the last quarter-century.

Two important events occurred in the 1970s. The California Constitution was amended in 1974 to provide that "[a] person unable to understand English who is charged with a crime has the right to an interpreter," which clarified a murky area of law. Several years later, in response to a request from the California Legislature, the Judicial Council reported major findings regarding needs and recommendations to improve interpreter services.

The legislature replied in 1978 by directing the State Personnel Board to certify qualified interpreters to the superior courts, and the Judicial Council to report statistics on interpreter utilization and adopt standards governing the need for interpreters in individual cases, interpreter competence, and interpreter conduct.

This sufficed through the 1980s, but more was needed. On recommendation of the Judicial Council, the legislature in 1993 directed the council to implement a comprehensive court interpreter program. The council complied by addressing training, testing, certification, performance evaluation, recruitment, management, and other aspects of interpreter services. In the 1990s the Judicial Council promulgated professional ethics for interpreters and campaigned for a legislative increase in interpreter compensation.

Achievements in this area appropriately are measured against conditions in California. As reported by the Judicial Council in 1995, 224 languages were in use in California. The top 10 foreign languages used in criminal proceedings were Spanish, Vietnamese, Korean, Armenian, Cantonese, Farsi/Persian, Tagalog, Cambodian, Laotian, and Russian. Of the 1,675 certified court interpreters, 1,536 were certified in Spanish—by far the most frequently used foreign language in the courts. Annual expenditures for interpreter services exceeded $58 million per year by the year 2000.

his milestone in the administration of justice warrants several introductory observations. First, the focus is on assistance for persons involved in court proceedings whose knowledge of the English language is nonexistent or so limited that they are unable to comprehend the proceedings without the assistance of an interpreter who can translate into a language known to the person. Individuals with impaired hearing, vision, or speech have significant problems that are receiving attention, but the number of persons with language problems is far greater.

Second, the focus is on criminal defendants because life, liberty, or property, in the form of bail or fines, is at stake in the legal proceedings confronting them. This does not minimize serious needs, as well as progress, in civil and juvenile proceedings, but they are not at the heart of this milestone.

Third, this is an area in which there has been extensive, interactive direction from the California Legislature to the judicial branch. This characteristic is shared with other milestones such as families and juveniles in the courts, delay reduction, and alternative dispute resolution.

Finally, there is a deceptive simplicity when considering interpreter services. If a defendant does not speak English, the obvious response would seem to be to provide a person to interpret who speaks the defendant's language. But lurking beneath the surface are devilish issues.

◆ Who determines the extent of a defendant's proficiency or lack of proficiency in English: the defendant, the defendant's counsel, a third party, or the judge?

◆ Is a defendant entitled to an interpreter at all phases of criminal proceedings, such as the preliminary hearing, or only at trial?

◆ At trial, is the defendant entitled to translation of only the testimony of the witnesses or of all proceedings that transpire?

◆ Must the translation furnished to the defendant be verbatim, or may it be a summary?

◆ Should the translation be simultaneous with a witness's testimony or consecutive, following the witness's testimony?

◆ Is a defendant entitled to have documents translated?

◆ Is a defendant entitled to an interpreter to facilitate communications with counsel?

◆ When interpreter services are provided, is the defendant entitled to exclusive use of an interpreter, or may that interpreter be shared with other defendants or even the prosecution?

◆ Outside the courtroom, is the defendant entitled to interpreter services for consultations with counsel or other matters related to the criminal proceedings?

◆ Are interpreter services to be provided only for indigent defendants?

With respect to the interpreters themselves, there are significant issues regarding qualifications, testing, certification, recruitment, availability, compensation, and status (independent contractor versus employee), to name a few.

Not all of these issues were resolved by century's end, but the courts of California under Judicial Council and Administrative Office of the Courts (AOC) leadership made sufficient progress during the last quarter-century to make assistance to non-English-speaking persons a milestone in the improved administration of justice.

Where to Begin?

Obviously interpreters were used in court proceedings prior to the 1970s, but an appropriate point to begin this story is 1973, when the California Legislature adopted Assembly Concurrent Resolution 74, which, among other things, stated that communication difficulties of non-English-speaking citizens and residents "frequently jeopardize access to equal justice under the law and threaten the liberty and property rights"[1] of these persons. Based on these and other propositions, the legislature directed that the "Judicial Council shall immediately undertake a comprehensive research study to identify and evaluate, at every stage of the judicial process, both criminal and civil, the language needs of non-English-speaking citizens and residents."[2] To ensure that the Judicial Council understood the meaning of "comprehensive," the legislature also directed that the study include:

(a) Identification of tasks and responsibilities of interpreters at various stages of the judicial process;
(b) Identification of documents and forms that need to be provided in languages other than English;
(c) Standards of qualifications and competency for interpreters at various stages of the judicial process;
(d) The needs faced by non-English-speaking citizens and residents in contact with all justice-related units of government, including,

but not limited to, police and sheriffs' offices, district attorneys' offices, public defenders' offices, all courts and the offices of county clerks;

(e) The development, design, and conduct of training programs for interpreters;

(f) Development of an interpreter utilization model suitable for use in both urban and rural settings;

(g) Identification of both urban and rural justice systems receptive to testing a developed interpreter utilization model for a one-year period;

(h) Development of a suitable system to fully evaluate the effectiveness of any developed model.[3]

Close on the heels of the legislature's request for the Judicial Council's study, the voters of California in 1974 adopted a proposal of the Constitution Revision Commission that amended the California Constitution to provide: "A person unable to understand English who is charged with a crime has a right to an interpreter throughout the proceedings."[4]

This was a fundamental change in the explicit law of California and was offered for these reasons: "The Commission also recommends adoption of a provision for an English interpreter at State expense to persons accused of a crime who cannot understand English. Although furnishing interpreters is customary, the Commission does not believe that the law adequately provides for them. Given the large numbers of persons living in California who do not speak English, the Commission feels that the opportunity for equal treatment under the law is enhanced by a constitutional right to an interpreter."[5]

While the appropriateness of this addition to the constitution seems apparent in today's world, prior to 1974 the state of the law regarding access to interpreter services was chaotic at best. In fact, one analyst concluded that prior to 1974 "the rights of the non-English speaking criminal defendant, as such, were largely ignored and the only recognition given to the problems raised by the non-English speaking defendant were subsumed under the California Evidence Code section 752, which reads[:] 'When a witness is incapable of hearing or understanding the English language or is incapable of expressing himself in the English language so as to be understood directly by counsel, court, and jury, an interpreter whom he can understand and who can understand him shall be sworn to interpret for him.'"[6] Even this statutory provision suggests rather clearly that the purpose is to provide interpreter services for the judge, attorneys, and jury who may not be able to understand a witness. It also suggests that a non-English-speaking defendant would have received interpreter assistance only when the defendant was a witness and not otherwise during the course of a trial.

A Study of the Language Needs of Non-English-Speaking Persons

A three-part, two-year study, titled *A Report to the Judicial Council on the Language Needs of Non-English Speaking Persons in Relation to the State's Justice System*, was prepared at the request of the Judicial Council by the consulting firm of Arthur Young & Company in 1976–1977. It was the direct response to the legislature's request and was both the first examination of this area and an appropriately detailed examination.[7]

What were the results? At the threshold were the facts that, as of the mid-1970s, there were more than one million non-English-speaking persons in California. The majority of this group spoke Spanish (83 percent), but there were at least seventy other languages spoken in the state.[8] Corollaries to these findings in the court context were that the utilization of Spanish interpreters was five times greater than the utilization of interpreters for all other languages combined, and the greatest utilization of courtroom interpreters was in Southern California.[9]

As part of the methodology for the study, public hearings were held, and numerous persons within and beyond the court system were surveyed for their experiences and perceptions. The broad opinion expressed was that "the present types and levels of courtroom interpreting services provided in criminal matters do not always result in an understanding between non-English speaking and English speaking persons."[10] The reasons for this rather alarming conclusion were that procedures at the time did not ensure that those needing interpreting services would receive them, the ability of persons selected to perform courtroom interpreting varied, multiple defendants were seldom furnished with separate interpreters, procedures such as verbatim translation had the potential to impede undestanding, and procedures did not exist to ensure accuracy of interpretation.[11]

The researchers concluded there were multiple needs regarding courts and criminal proceedings: improvement in the method of determining when a courtroom interpreter was required; provision of qualified interpreters in all languages; ensured availability; testing, certification, and evaluation of court interpreters; provision of courtroom interpreters to defendants in criminal proceedings at no expense to the defendant; and improvement in the procedures for accepting a defendant's waiver of an interpreter.[12]

These were the conclusions submitted to the Judicial Council, and subsequently the legislature, as of January 1976 (Phase I). The second report was submitted in May 1976 (Phase II) and addressed the tasks and responsibilities of court interpreters, certification and testing models for delivering interpreting services, court interpreter training, and the use of bilingual forms.

The final segment of the study was submitted to the Judicial Council in January 1977 (Phase III). The consultants first offered the following supplemental findings:

◆ The roles, relationships, and responsibilities of court reporters are largely undefined.

◆ Establishment of a central licensing authority and statewide certification process for court interpreters would be costly and inflexible.

◆ Interpreter training classes are an effective method of increasing the proficiency of interpreters.

◆ Written and oral interpreter training programs are feasible and can screen qualified from unqualified interpreters.

◆ Existing compensation practices for interpreters are at times inconsistent with commonly accepted wage and salary principles.

◆ Court interpreter assignment procedures vary significantly and do not always meet the courts' needs.[13]

Although the resulting recommendations extended well beyond criminal proceedings, the recommendations all clearly applied to criminal cases.

◆ The Judicial Council should adopt the proposed court interpreters' standards of conduct and professional responsibilities.

◆ Legislation should be enacted for the training and testing of court interpreters in California.

◆ Judicial Council rules should be adopted for establishment of a list of recommended interpreters in designated counties.

◆ The Judicial Council should adopt guidelines for the qualification of court interpreters.

◆ Courts should continue to determine whether an interpreter is needed, but such determinations should be subject to application of Judicial Council guidelines.

◆ Existing laws should be clarified regarding public payment of court interpreters.

◆ Legislation should be enacted requiring periodic review of court interpreters.

◆ Legislation should be enacted to require the Judicial Council to collect and publish pertinent interpreter utilization statistics.

◆ A countywide interpreter fee schedule should be established by local court rule in each county.

◆ County employees assigned additional duties as courtroom interpreters should be reclassified with commensurate paid adjustment.

◆ Courts experiencing difficulty in locating or assigning court interpreters should consider use of a coordinator at the county level who is responsible for obtaining interpreter services when needed.

◆ The Judicial Council should distribute a handbook on court interpreter utilization to judges, attorneys, and interpreters.[14]

Interpreters in the 1970s

This report arrived against a backdrop of rather sparse interpreter services. The State Personnel Board was legislatively mandated to test and certify proficiency in foreign languages. This did not mean certification or qualification as a court interpreter but only testing and certification in knowledge of a language.

The new information developed in the three-stage study subsequently was supplemented, establishing, by the end of the 1970s, that Spanish was used forty times more frequently than all other languages combined in connection with court interpreter services. Those services were utilized 94 percent of the time in criminal cases. More than half of all court interpreter services were used in the three Southern California counties of Los Angeles, Orange, and San Diego.[15]

Initial Standards

Following the Judicial Council's submission to the California Legislature of the final report on language needs, the legislature in 1978 enacted legislation addressing court interpreter services.[16] The legislature recognized "the need to provide equal justice under the law to all California citizens and residents and the special needs of non-English-speaking persons in their relations with the judicial system."[17] The legislature further found that "[p]rovision of competent interpreter services in courts and judicial agencies would be facilitated by a coordinated effort to provide testing programs and to assure adequate interpreter services to all California citizens and residents."[18]

The operational portions of the legislation imposed new duties on the State Personnel Board and the Judicial Council. The personnel board was directed to establish minimum standards of language proficiency, both written and oral, in English and the language to be interpreted. In addition, the personnel board was directed to administer appropriate examinations and annually certify to the superior courts a list of qualified interpreters. The superior courts in the thirty-three larger counties were directed to compile from the list published by the State Personnel Board a list of recommended interpreters for use by all trial courts throughout these counties.[19]

The Judicial Council was directed to report pertinent interpreter utilization statistics to the governor and legislature by December 31, 1980. In addition, the Judicial Council was to implement the legislation by establishing standards for determining the need for a court interpreter in particular cases, for ensuring an interpreter's understanding of court terminology and procedure, and for the professional conduct of court interpreters. Periodic review of each court interpreter's skills and removal of those who failed to maintain skills also were required.

The Judicial Council responded by directing each superior court to establish procedures for review of the performance and skills of court interpreters.[20] The Judicial Council further adopted Standards of Judicial Administration that, among other things, provided guidance in determining the need for a court interpreter, the procedures to be followed during interpreted proceedings, techniques for ensuring interpreter understanding of court terminology, and professional standards of conduct for interpreters.[21]

These standards, combined with the legislature's directives, apparently sufficed through the 1980s.

Interpreters in the 1990s

In the 1990s, court interpreter services received renewed attention. Chief Justice Malcolm M. Lucas advised the State Bar in his 1990 State of the Judiciary Address that he had appointed an Advisory Committee on Court Interpreters because "[w]e must provide qualified interpreters to all who need them to assure every Californian access to justice."[22] This committee was directed to "work toward ensuring early identification of the need for an interpreter, improving the quality of interpreting, and increasing the number of available qualified interpreters."[23] More specifically, the committee was directed to delve into a broad array of topics: developing interpreter training and certification programs; administering interpreter resources; conducting statistical studies; recording interpreted proceedings; evaluating interpreter performance; using technology to provide interpreter services; certifying interpreters for the hearing impaired; training judges, attorneys, and court personnel regarding interpreter services; and proposing comprehensive revisions in the statutes governing interpreters.[24]

The balance of the 1990s produced a steady flow of responsive measures. The Judicial Council in 1991 sponsored legislation, for example, to provide comprehensive interpreter services to the courts and to non-English-speaking persons in the courts. This proposal included creation of a Certified Interpreters Board to take responsibility for testing, certification, and regulation in this area. The proposed legislation also permitted California courts to use federally certified interpreters without regard to state examinations.[25]

By 1993 the legislature had directed the Judicial Council to implement a comprehensive court interpreter program with an extensive set of components ranging from recruitment to continuing education.[26] In June 1993 Chief Justice Lucas appointed the Court Interpreters Advisory Panel,[27] which was a natural extension of his 1990 Advisory Committee on Court Interpreters.

The major thrust of activities to this point was to provide interpreter services for Spanish-speaking persons. This is understandable in view of the overwhelming number of cases in which Spanish interpreters were required. However, beginning in 1993, the Judicial Council through its advisory committee began exploring the development of new proficiency testing for Arabic, Cantonese, Japanese, Korean, Portuguese, Tagalog, and Vietnamese.[28]

In response to the earlier legislative directive, the Judicial Council in 1995 submitted to the governor and legislature a substantial report entitled *Court Interpreter Services in the California Trial Courts*. At this point, 224 different languages were spoken in California. Embedded in this number were fascinating facts revealing the language diversity in the state.

◆　The top languages (in order of usage in the courts) were (1) Spanish, (2) Vietnamese, (3) Korean, (4) Armenian, (5) Cantonese, (6) Farsi/Persian, (7) Tagalog, (8) Cambodian, (9) Laotian, (10) Russian, (11) Mandarin, (12) Arabic, (13) Hmong, and (14) Japanese.

◆ Los Angeles County was the major provider of interpreter services in every major language except Laotian and Hmong.

◆ Spanish remained the most widely used language.

◆ Vietnamese replaced Korean as the second most widely used language.

◆ Armenian was reported as a language with "some usage" in 1992. However, by 1995 it had jumped into fourth place—ahead of Cantonese, Tagalog, and Japanese.

◆ Farsi/Persian, another newcomer, was ranked sixth on the list of the most widely used languages, ahead of Tagalog, Arabic, and Japanese.

◆ Cambodian, Laotian, Russian, and Mandarin each accounted for around $250,000 worth of interpreter services statewide, yet none of these languages was among the group of languages designated for certification testing.

◆ Portuguese, with expenditures of $51,514, did not demonstrate wide usage, although it was a language requiring certification.[29]

In addition to these intriguing data, the Judicial Council reported that the trial courts were spending approximately $32 million per year on interpreter services; there were 1,675 certified court interpreters in 1995, of which 1,536 were certified in Spanish; and, in order to retain certification, court interpreters were required to register with the Judicial Council, annually complete thirty hours of continuing education, and be able to prove forty professional assignments every two years.[30]

The Judicial Council explicitly noted that the information furnished was confined to criminal proceedings. This comment was accompanied by a recommendation for "further investigation into the use of interpreters in the civil sector."[31]

The next major step was promulgation, in 1997, by the Judicial Council and AOC of a comprehensive statement titled *Professional Ethics and the Role of the Court Interpreter.*[32] By the end of the century, Judicial Council concerns and actions extended to campaigning successfully for legislative increases in the rate of compensation for interpreters. This was precipitated by important facts. First, the number of continued or delayed proceedings due to the unavailability of interpreter services doubled from 1997 to 1998. In addition, 224 languages were spoken in California, and yet certification for court interpreters was available in only eight languages—Arabic, Cantonese, Japanese, Korean, Portuguese, Spanish, Tagalog, and Vietnamese.

Finally, the Judicial Council reported that "[t]rial courts often must turn to uncertified interpreters, cope with a growing number of continued or delayed interpreted proceedings, and pay more than established pay rates for interpreters."[33]

In 2000, the council designated an additional five languages for certification—Armenian, Khmer, Mandarin, Punjabi, and Russian—and began developing certification examinations for those languages. By that year, annual expenditures for the interpreter program had risen to more than $58 million, with 1,116 certified interpreters in designated languages and 245 additional interpreters registered in nondesignated languages, for a total of 1,361 interpreters.[34]

Reflections

In many ways the story of court interpreter services in California revolves around Los Angeles County. Not only is it the most populous county in the state, it also has a significant number of residents who are Spanish-speaking. More specifically, the courts in Los Angeles County, led by the superior court, were the first to confront needs in this area by creation of a centralized list of interpreters for use by courts throughout the county.[35] Certification was based on extensive written and oral testing programs that included mock trials.[36] Toward the close of the century, the cost of interpreter services in Los Angeles County accounted for approximately 50 percent of statewide expenditures for interpreter services.

While sheer size and demographics will continue to ensure that Los Angeles County has a prominent place in this story, considerable statewide effort and concern in providing appropriate interpreter services warrant designation of this achievement as a milestone in the improved administration of justice.

Notes

1   Assembly Concurrent Resolution 74; California Statutes 1973, Resolution Chapter 179, p. 3301.

2   Id., p. 3302.

3   Ibid.

4   California Constitution, article I, section 14 (added November 5, 1974).

5   California Constitution Revision Commission, *Proposed Revision of the California Constitution*, part 5 (1971), p. 22.

6   Arthur Young & Company, *A Report to the Judicial Council on the Language Needs of Non-English Speaking Persons in Relation to the State's Justice System* (January 1976), Phase I, pp. III-1–III-2.

7   The scope of this study extended to agencies beyond the courts, such as law enforcement agencies and probation departments, which was in the spirit of the California Legislature's request. It also extended to civil litigation and administrative proceedings.

8   Arthur Young, *Report*, Phase I, p. II-3.

9   Id., p. IV-3.

10   Id., p. V-4.

11   Id., pp. V-4–V-16.

12   Id., pp. II-5–II-12.

13   Arthur Young & Company, *A Report to the Judicial Council on the Language Needs of Non-English Speaking Persons in Relation to the State's Justice System* (January 1977), Phase III, pp. 10–14.

14   Id., pp. 16–32.

15   Judicial Council of California, *Annual Report to the Governor and the Legislature* (1981), pp. 15–34.

16   California Government Code sections 68560–68563 (since superseded); California Statutes 1978, chapter 158, pp. 388–90.

17   Government Code, section 68560(d) (since superseded); California Statutes 1978, chapter 158, pp. 388–90.

18 Government Code, section 68560(e) (since superseded); California Statutes 1978, chapter 158, pp. 388–90.

19 Government Code, section 68562 (as of 1978); Judicial Council, *Annual Report* (1981), p. 15.

20 California Rules of Court, rule 984 (as of July 1, 1979); Judicial Council, *Annual Report* (1981), p. 31.

21 California Standards of Judicial Administration, sections 18–18.3 (as of 1979); Judicial Council, *Annual Report* (1981), pp. 31–34.

22 Judicial Council of California, *Annual Report to the Governor and the Legislature* (1991), p. 3.

23 Id., p. 83.

24 Id., pp. 83–84.

25 Judicial Council of California, *Annual Report to the Governor and the Legislature* (1992), p. 24.

26 Senate Bill 1304; California Statutes 1992, chapter 770.

27 California Courts Web site, *www.courtinfo.ca.gov/programs/courtinterpreters /generalinfo.htm.*

28 Judicial Council of California, *Annual Report to the Governor and the Legislature* (1994), p. 7.

29 Judicial Council of California, *Court Interpreter Services in the California Trial Courts* (1995), pp. i–ii, 1.

30 Id., p. ii.

31 Id., p. iii; see also Judicial Council of California, *Annual Report to the Governor and the Legislature* (1996), pp. 29–34.

32 Judicial Council of California, Administrative Office of the Courts, *Professional Ethics and the Role of the Court Interpreter* (1997).

33 Judicial Council of California, Administrative Office of the Courts, *Foundations for a New Century: Annual Report* (2000), p. 7.

34 Judicial Council of California, Administrative Office of the Courts, *Report to the Legislature on the Use of Interpreters in the California Courts* (2001), pp. 5–7.

35 Even in the 1970s the Los Angeles Superior Court supplied certified Spanish interpreters to all trial courts in the county. See Arthur Young, *Report*, Phase I, p. V-8.

36 Ibid.

Chapter 14
The Power of Technology

Overview

echnology came into use in a variety of court contexts during the past quarter-century, but in the 1990s the Commission on the Future of the California Courts lamented that developments had "left the judiciary behind" and that "the courts are lagging."

Technology in California's courts, nonetheless, is commendable even though the record is fragmented, progress is slow, and the promise still lies substantially in the future.

Certainly by century's end one or more courts were applying technology to perform a wide array of functions including case management, calendars, juries, records, exhibits, and statistics. Accounting and legal research were additional areas of notable technology utilization. Implementation efforts were under way in an even broader array of applications, ranging from interactive video to electronic data interchange.

The first statewide application began in the mid-1980s with automation, in stages, of the appellate courts. This was followed by a Judicial Council and Administrative Office of the Courts (AOC) effort to develop statewide court automation standards. The futures commission offered extensive recommendations to create a "preferred future" for the judicial branch in which use of technology would, among other things, greatly increase Californians' access to and information about justice.

In partial response, the Judicial Council in 1995 created the Court Technology Advisory Committee. By century's end this committee submitted and the council adopted both a *Strategic Plan for Court Technology* and a *Tactical Plan for Court Technology*. The combined thrust of these plans was to shift from local to state perspectives on court technology and, with the advent of full state funding of trial courts, to achieve a systemic technology plan for the entire judicial branch.

*T*n 1950 a court or an attorney desiring to prepare multiple copies of a document, such as a judicial opinion or written interrogatories, had two choices: employing a printer to set type and print copies or "cutting stencils" by manual typewriter in preparation for mimeographing the copies. Neither word processors nor photocopying machines were commercially available.

The next breakthroughs were IBM Selectric self-correcting typewriters and photocopying machines, which became available in the late 1950s and led to creation of the verb "xerox." While these events in speeding production of paper documents were unfolding, the potential of electronics was emerging. Following creation of the first mainframe computer by Univac in 1952, IBM introduced the "360" computer in 1963, followed by the minicomputer in 1964. The first pocket calculator became available in 1971 and the first personal computer in 1975. The Apple II computer was introduced in 1977 and, after a lag of four years, the IBM personal computer was offered. Shortly thereafter inexpensive laser printers also reached the market.[1]

The result was that by century's end the electronic creation, reproduction, storage, and transmission of documents were widespread within the legal community and to a fair extent within the courts. Technology, of course, is much broader than documents.

Technology, particularly in the quarter-century from 1975 to 2000, came into use in a variety of court contexts, with a profound impact on the administration of justice. Most of that evolution in court technology applications was scattered among California's several hundred courts with little or no statewide direction until the end of the century. There was scant coordination or cooperation among courts and no systematic documentation. These realities severely frustrate any conscientious effort to document the growth of technology in courts.

Even granting full credit to the pioneering innovations in dozens of trial courts around the state, courts both in California and nationwide generally have been slow to join the technology parade and certainly have not caught up. In 1993 the Commission on the Future of the California Courts observed: "Despite some degree of automation in most California courts today, in the adoption of new information technologies the private sector and other branches of government have left the judiciary behind. While manual clerical work is rapidly disappearing from the workplace, the courts are lagging the field."[2]

Even though the history is fragmented, progress has been slow, and significant fulfillment of technology's promise still is in the future for courts, the efforts made nonetheless justify recognition of technology applications as a milestone in the improved administration of justice.

Technology Applications

Although there is no compiled history of technology applications in California courts, we do know that in one or more courts automation was utilized for the following functions by the year 2000:

- ◆ *Case management:* online indexes; register of action/docket; case status; related parties, attorneys, etc.; correspondence/notice generation

- ◆ *Calendaring:* scheduling of hearings and events; production of calendars; automated differentiated case management

- ◆ *Accounting:* collection of fees and fines; production of receipts; automatic allocation among accounts; audit trail

- ◆ *Arbitration:* selection of arbitrators; automated conflict recognition; automated notification and notice generation

- ◆ *Jury management:* source list processing; cumulative history of service; panel selection; juror notification and response; automated payment calculation

- ◆ *Case filing:* case intake; front-counter operations; automatic case assignment; workload balancing

- ◆ *File tracking:* tracking of current locations of case files

- ◆ *Records management:* preparation and updating of case files; storage and retrieval; archiving; records destruction

- ◆ *Exhibits management:* tracking of current locations of exhibits

- ◆ *Statistics and reports:* production of required reports for the Judicial Council and other agencies; case status reports; monitoring of judicial performance; generation of caseload reports; generation of ad hoc queries and reports

- ◆ *Legal research:* provision of online indexes[3]

It also appears that in 2000 an appreciable number of trial courts had implemented or were working on implementing the following applied technologies:

- ◆ Interactive video (for example, video arraignments)

- Telephone retrieval of database information

- Innovative data capture (such as bar coding, optical character recognition [OCR] scanning)

- Remote filing (such as fax filing)

- Image-based records management

- Remote access to court records

- Innovative user interfaces (such as kiosks)

- Video recording of trial proceedings

- Electronic mail, bulletin boards, or groupware

- Electronic data interchange with other agencies and departments

- Judicial decision support software

- Other expert systems

- Electronic legal research[4]

Appellate Court Automation

The first systemwide automation began in 1984 with a pilot project in four divisions of the courts of appeal. This was part of a comprehensive automation program to modernize administration of California's appellate courts. This inaugural effort consisted of first providing automated assistance to the clerks' offices followed by developing automated systems for the justices and their staffs.[5] This was preceded somewhat by shifting secretarial services from Selectric typewriters to word processors. By 1986 document preparation had been further transformed by use of personal computers tied to a network available to justices, research attorneys on the court staff, and support staff.[6]

This proved to be a prolonged effort. In the early 1990s the AOC was still grappling to define "the information needs of the appellate courts and their support agencies—clerks' offices, chambers, appointed counsel, libraries, administrative systems, and public information systems—and to find a way to integrate judicial information between the groups."[7]

Systemwide Technology

The first truly statewide venture into technology applications in California's courts apparently occurred in 1991 when Chief Justice Malcolm M. Lucas appointed the Advisory Committee on Financial Reporting and

Automation Performance Standards.[8] This development was driven in large measure by the legislature's Trial Court Realignment and Efficiency Act of 1991 (discussed in Chapters Five and Six). Among the many other provisions in this legislation was the requirement that 2 percent of all fines, penalties, and forfeitures collected in criminal cases be set aside for an automation fund to be used exclusively to pay the costs of automating court record keeping and case management systems for criminal cases, with the further provision that these systems must comply with Judicial Council performance standards.[9] To implement this portion of the legislation, the Judicial Council approved a rule of court, effective March 1, 1992, requiring compliance with the approved Trial Court Automation Standards developed by the AOC.[10]

Several additional events of statewide significance were unfolding. Fourteen municipal courts were engaged in a pilot project experimenting with interactive video for arraignments in criminal cases. The AOC was conducting a pilot project to test electronic and video recording as an alternative in creating the verbatim record of court proceedings. The Judicial Council adopted interim rules governing the filing of court documents by facsimile transmission (fax).[11]

The next major contribution of systemwide significance was made by the Commission on the Future of the California Courts. At the conclusion of its work the commission offered a "preferred future" for the judicial branch of government. The commission proposed that by the year 2020 all Californians be able to access justice information and law in a language of their choosing from public information kiosks, online, or by interactive television in their homes. Physical presence would no longer be required in most justice proceedings. Paper would have nearly vanished from the courts, and technology would have made justice more efficient, more accessible, more understandable, and higher in quality. Rather than dehumanizing justice, technology would "rehumanize" dispute resolution. At the same time, it would unburden judicial branch personnel of most routine, mechanical tasks, freeing them to focus on the needs of court users.[12]

To achieve this vision of the future, the commission offered for consideration by the Judicial Council and others ten specific recommendations.

> Justice information should be easily accessible through common, well-understood technologies. . . .
> To promote efficiency, access, convenience, and cost reduction, interactive video technology should be incorporated into all justice proceedings. . . .

Courts must become paperless. . . .

A comprehensive and integrated data distribution network should be created to connect and serve the entire judicial branch, other agencies, and the public. . . .

Standards to ensure the integrity of justice data must be developed and carefully implemented. . . .

The judicial branch should install case management systems as soon as feasible. . . .

As the technology evolves, proves itself, and demonstrates its utility for judicial decision makers, the courts should be prepared to integrate expert systems into their work. . . .

In the justice system of the future, local innovation should be encouraged, supported, acknowledged, and rewarded. . . .

The judicial branch should create a standing advisory committee on technology. In its oversight role, such a body should develop branch-wide policies and procedures for the use of technology in judicial administration and decision making. . . .

Judicial officers should receive ongoing education on the use of justice system technology and play leadership roles in the modernization of court information systems. As necessary, staff should be retrained for nonmechanical functions.[13]

In response to these recommendations, a Court Technology Task Force was created to advise the Judicial Council and the AOC on the "design, charge, and procedural structure for a permanent governing body to oversee the planning for and implementation of technology in the California trial and appellate courts."[14] Following rather extensive investigation and deliberations, this transitional group presented extensive information regarding the technologies then in use in California's courts, as well as user reactions to those technologies. But its major contribution was recommending establishment of a standing court technology committee charged to "promote, coordinate, and facilitate the application of technology to the work of the California courts."[15] On the assumption that the recommended committee would indeed be established, the task force offered extensive guiding principles and goals for the new committee.

The Judicial Council adopted the recommendations of the task force in 1995 and created the Court Technology Advisory Committee with the mandate to improve justice administration through the use of technology and to foster cooperative endeavors to resolve common technology issues with stakeholders in the justice system.[16]

This technology committee also was given more specific duties:

(1) Recommend standards to ensure compatibility in information and communication technologies in the judicial branch;
(2) Review and comment on requests for the funding of judicial branch technology projects to ensure compatibility with goals established by the council and standards promulgated by the committee;
(3) Review and recommend legislation, rules, or policies to balance the interests of privacy, access, and security in relation to court technology;
(4) Make proposals for technology education and training in the judicial branch;
(5) Assist courts in acquiring and developing useful technologies;
(6) Maintain a long-range plan.[17]

In response to these mandates, the Court Technology Advisory Committee produced two important reports, both of which were adopted by the Judicial Council: the *Strategic Plan for Court Technology*[18] in 1998 and the *Tactical Plan for Court Technology*[19] in 2000.

The strategic plan addressed the "logically discrete but complementary" subjects of planning, infrastructure, court management systems, information, and communications.[20] More specifically, the technology advisory committee included among its extensive objectives and recommendations the following broad goals:

◆ Development and maintenance of a strategic plan for the effective application of technology to the needs of the judicial branch and justice system

◆ Establishment of an infrastructure to meet the information technology needs of the judicial branch

◆ Technical assistance to courts to improve management of operations and resources

◆ Technology applications enabling courts to acquire and utilize information needed to process cases, manage resources, and meet public needs

◆ Implementation of technology programs to meet the information needs of the judicial branch, its partners in the justice system, the public, and others with legitimate needs[21]

This strategic plan approximately coincided with establishment of full state funding of the trial courts (see Chapter Six). For technology in the courts, state funding meant the proverbial rubber had hit the road. This new reality drove the subsequent *Tactical Plan for Court Technology* that was unveiled two years later with a much sharper focus than the earlier strategic plan.

The Court Technology Advisory Committee was frank from the outset, noting that there had been "historic underfunding of technology in the judicial branch" and that "the judicial branch has been unable to articulate a comprehensive plan for technology that includes clear objectives and measurable outcomes."[22] The tactical plan was designed "not only to obtain funding for statewide technology initiatives but also to move trial courts forward toward more coordinated and integrated technology solutions."[23]

Translated, this meant that the days when each trial court followed its own technology path were drawing to a close, as was the existing patchwork of individual court technology applications spawned in all fifty-eight counties by local funding. At the heart of the tactical plan were managing funding related to court technology at the state level, limiting the number of available solutions for common court technology problems, and grouping trial courts according to characteristics and technology problems shared in common.[24] The courts within each of the groups would be "expected to choose from established menus when their existing technology has reached the end of its useful life," with the clear implication that state funds would be provided only for items on the menu for the group in which a court had been placed.[25]

The technology committee advised that this new approach was built upon certain guiding principles:

- ◆ **Functionality:** Judicial Council-approved technological solutions must allow courts to meet state requirements . . . ; must provide for public access to court data; and must ensure effective communications with partners in the justice community.

- ◆ **Economy:** To contain information technology expenditures, court groups must identify the minimum number of alternative technological solutions that meet group or regional needs and achieve state objectives.

- ◆ **Consistency:** Technology should foster a common experience of the court system, irrespective of court size or location.

- ◆ **Innovation:** Individual courts should be encouraged to develop innovative technological solutions that can be replicated cost-effectively within their region or throughout the state.

◆ **Proven Solutions:** Proven technologies should be favored when they minimize risk of failure and reduce costs. Custom-built solutions should be funded when there is no proven alternative, risk is reasonable, and the likelihood of attaining objectives can be demonstrated through a project plan.

◆ **Existing Investment:** Technology should be used as long as it functions effectively.[26]

The Judicial Council was further advised by the Court Technology Advisory Committee that the tactical plan, with its overarching components and proposed implementation steps:

◆ Integrates the technology strategic planning process with the branchwide strategic planning and funding initiatives;

◆ Funds technology from the statewide, rather than the local, perspective;

◆ Coordinates funding for technology;

◆ Achieves economies by encouraging collaborative approaches and common solutions to technology issues;

◆ Provides the foundation for a multiyear implementation plan; and

◆ Maintains flexibility to encourage innovation among trial courts.[27]

As the new millennium opened, extensive efforts were in progress by the AOC and others to make the tactical plan a reality. Regional groups were formed. Local and group technology plans were in development. A branchwide plan was in sight, accompanied by budget implications if enacted.

Viewed collectively, the steps taken by the judicial branch in the 1990s offer an encouraging commitment to more vigorous and systemic exploitation of technology. That commitment, the creation of the advisory committee, the strategic and tactical plans, and serious efforts toward implementation all suggest a milestone in justice administration.

Notes

1   Institute for the Future, "The California Future Databook" in *2020 Vision: Symposium on the Future of California's Courts: Research Papers* (December 10–11, 1992), p. 42.

2   [Judicial Council of California], Commission on the Future of the California Courts, *Justice in the Balance, 2020: Report of the Commission on the Future of the California Courts* (1993), p. 103.

3   Judicial Council of California, *Report of the Court Technology Task Force* (January 25, 1995), appendix B, p. B-8.

4   Ibid.

5   Judicial Council of California, Administrative Office of the Courts, *A.O.C. Newsletter* (August–September 1984), pp. 1–2.

6   Dee Ziegler, "Rose Bird Automates the Supreme Court," *The Recorder* (December 1, 1986), pp. 1, 15.

7   Judicial Council of California, *Annual Report to the Governor and the Legislature* (1992), volume 1, p. 21.

8   Id., pp. 10–11.

9   Id., p. 11.

10 California Rules of Court, rule 1011 (as of 1992).

11 Judicial Council, *Annual Report* (1992), pp. 19–20.

12 Commission on the Future of the California Courts, *Justice in the Balance, 2020*, p. 101.

13 Id., pp. 105–15.

14 Judicial Council, *Report of the Court Technology Task Force*, p. 7.

15 Id., p. 11.

16 California Rules of Court, rule 6.53.

17 Ibid.; Judicial Council of California, *Annual Report to the Governor and the Legislature* (1995), p. 8.

18 Judicial Council of California, Court Technology Advisory Committee, *Strategic Plan for Court Technology* (August 14, 1998).

19 Judicial Council of California, *Tactical Plan for Court Technology* (January 26, 2000).

20 Judicial Council, *Strategic Plan*, p. i.

21 Id., pp. 1, 2, 4, 6, and 7.

22 Judicial Council, *Tactical Plan*, p. 1.

23 Ibid.

24 Id., p. 3.

25 Ibid.

26 Id., pp. 9–10.

27 Id., p. 4.

Part 4

Looking Beyond:
the Next Half-Century

*I*mproving the administration of justice is a quest without end. Nelson Mandela in his autobiography spoke of the long walk to freedom; his sentiments echo on the road to justice:

> I have walked that long road to freedom. I have tried not to falter; I have made missteps along the way. But I have discovered the secret that after climbing a great hill, one only finds that there are many more hills to climb. I have taken a moment here to rest, to steal a view of the glorious vista that surrounds me, to look back on the distance I have come. But I can rest only for a moment, for with freedom come responsibilities, and I dare not linger, for my long walk is not yet ended.

Chapter 15

The Next Fifty Years: 2000 to 2050

Overview

California ever changes—a work in progress. But several developments seem inevitable: continued rapid growth in population,
increased diversity with no ethnic majority, growth in the number
of languages in use (224 in 2000), new population centers that overshadow
Los Angeles and the San Francisco Bay Area, and an increase in the numbers
of youth and the elderly.

Public distrust of government and politics, cyclical economies, and inadequate infrastructure also appear likely. An array of socioeconomic problems
will persist.

California courts, in addition to operating in this milieu, will be confronted with a set of traditional challenges ranging from caseload increases
to deficient resources.

The judicial branch, through Judicial Council leadership, is preparing
itself by strategic planning. There are multiple products of these preparations, but at the heart are the strategic goals.

At the intersection of judicial branch preparations and the contours of a future California is the fact that major trends and problems in California are beyond the power of the judicial branch to alter. Nonetheless, the judicial branch can follow, and has followed, the advice of futurists and strategists by positioning itself to be anticipatory and by fashioning a preferred future toward which to work.

There will be challenges or obstructions to implementing the major goals of the strategic plan, and some of these can already be anticipated in quality of justice, access and fairness, resources, administration, education, and technology. But each of these areas also offers opportunities for abundant improvements in the future administration of justice.

*W*e now move from the golden era of justice administration to the future of justice administration in the Golden State. What is the societal and governmental context in which the judicial branch is likely to function during the next half-century? As one thoughtful commentator has aptly remarked: "California is a work in progress. The state has experienced many periods of rapid growth and change over the past 150 years. There will be no pause for reflection at the millennium. Forces and trends are converging that will, by the middle of the twenty-first century, transform California into a very different state from the one we know today. How California will cope with the challenges it faces is far from clear."[1]

Predicting the future is folly, but our thinking can be informed by an apparent consensus on several major characteristics of California in the decades ahead.[2]

◆ *Population:* Continued rapid growth—doubling to more than sixty million persons by 2050, fueled largely by foreign immigrants with higher birthrates.[3]

◆ *Ethnic diversity:* No ethnic majority at the beginning of the century, but Hispanics pass whites as the largest group in the 2020s and probably become an outright majority before midcentury.[4]

◆ *Language:* The number of languages other than English spoken in California grows from 224 at the beginning of the century to even greater numbers.[5]

◆ *Regionalism:* The dominance of Los Angeles County and the San Francisco Bay Area as the most populous parts of the state is superseded by population growth in Orange County, the Central Valley, and the Inland Empire (Riverside and San Bernardino Counties).[6]

◆ *Age diversity:* The number of Californians under fifteen increases by more than 68 percent and the number over sixty by more than 154 percent, creating a growing population of dependent residents and a shrinking percentage of working-age Californians.[7]

A strong case also can be made for the following projections.

◆ *Political distrust:* The voter revolt expressed by the passage of Proposition 13 in the 1970s continues in the form of declining voter registrations, declining participation in elections by registered voters, term limits, and increased direct legislation by voters through the initiative process—all of which underscore citizen alienation from establishment politics and government.[8]

◆ *Economy:* California's economy continues the pattern of cyclical boom or bust, but the distribution of good times and bad times continues to vary significantly among the five major regions of California.[9]

◆ *Infrastructure:* At the beginning of the century, California ranks near the bottom among the fifty states in spending on infrastructure other than prisons: highways, number 48; higher education, number 37; public schools, number 31. The infrastructure is inadequate to accommodate the needs of the exploding population for roads, schools, sewers, water, bridges, and governmental buildings (including courthouses), but government officials are unwilling or unable to invest the funds necessary for adequate infrastructure.[10]

Closer to home for the judicial branch of government are socioeconomic trends projected for the coming decades: increased violence, continued illegal drug trade, persistent poverty cycles, weakening of the family, continued handgun availability, more children in poverty, more parental abdication of responsibility for children's conduct, and a widening gap between rich and poor.[11]

At the doorstep of tomorrow's courthouses are these projected trends: caseload growth, prison overcrowding, insufficient court funding, escalating litigiousness, court-linked family needs, correction system failures, and deficient judicial compensation. The only bright spot is increased alternative dispute resolution.[12]

Where to go from here? In the words of a perceptive observer who graduated from a California law school: "I would not presume to tell you *what* to think about the future. I will venture only thoughts on *how* to think about it." [Emphasis added.][13]

Preparations for the Future: Process

In many respects preparation for the future by California's judiciary began when Chief Justice Malcolm M. Lucas advised the State Bar in 1990: "We need to anticipate change and plan for action. We need to lead and not wait to be led into the next millennium."[14] Then followed a steady sequence of events (discussed in earlier chapters) of preparing for the future. They reflect *how* the judicial branch is thinking about the future.

◆ 1992—The Judicial Council adopts the first strategic plan for the judicial branch.

◆ 1993—The Commission on the Future of the California Courts concludes its work and publishes *Justice in the Balance, 2020.*

◆ 1994—The Judicial Council assesses and prioritizes the recommendations of the Commission on the Future of the California Courts.

◆ 1995–1996—The Judicial Council refines the strategic plan.

◆ 1997—*Leading Justice Into the Future*, the long-range strategic plan by the Judicial Council, is published for the first time.

◆ 1998—The emphasis shifts to local planning within the judicial branch of government.

◆ 1999—*Leading Justice Into the Future* is updated and revised.

◆ 2000—The Judicial Council adopts a multiyear planning cycle, integrating state and local planning efforts, and provides for action plans to implement strategic plans.

Preparations for the Future: Products

As the governing body of the judicial branch, the Judicial Council, by the end of the last century, had produced and revised a strategic plan consisting of missions both for itself and for the judicial branch of government, as well as guiding principles, goals, policy directions, and plans for implementation.

Although addressed previously in Chapter Four, the six strategic goals of the Judicial Council warrant reexamination here, for they validate the process of preparing for the future and bear on whether, as products of that process, they are adequate for the future.

Goal I. Access, Fairness, and Diversity All Californians will have equal access to the courts and equal ability to participate in court proceedings, and will be treated in a fair and just manner. Members of the judicial branch community will reflect the rich diversity of the state's residents.

Goal II. Independence and Accountability The judiciary will be an institutionally independent, separate branch of government that responsibly seeks, uses, and accounts for public resources necessary for its support. The independence of judicial decision making will be protected.

Goal III. Modernization of Management and Administration
Justice will be administered in a timely, efficient, and effective manner that utilizes contemporary management practices; innovative ideas; highly competent judges, other judicial officers, and staff; and adequate facilities.

Goal IV. Quality of Justice and Service to the Public Judicial branch services will be responsive to the needs of the public and will enhance the public's understanding and use of and its confidence in the judiciary.

Goal V. Education The effectiveness of judges, court personnel, and other judicial branch staff will be enhanced through high-quality continuing education and professional development.

Goal VI. Technology Technology will enhance the quality of justice by improving the ability of the judicial branch to collect, process, analyze, and share information and by increasing the public's access to information about the judicial branch.[15]

Intersection: Courts and the Future

The major characteristics and trends forecast for California are largely beyond the control of the judicial branch of government. Courts cannot stem the tide of immigration, ethnic diversity, or the extensive use of languages other than English. Courts cannot alter the evolution of new regions in California as the exploding population creates new hubs other than San Francisco and Los Angeles. Courts cannot decrease the rise in either youths or the elderly among California's residents. Courts cannot compel greater citizen participation in elections or do much, if anything, to reduce citizen alienation from politics and government. Aside from specific judicial decisions that might have an economic impact, courts likewise can do little about economic cycles and varying regional impacts. And, aside from court facilities, courts can do little, if anything, about filling present or future deficits in infrastructure.

Even with issues more closely tied to the administration of justice it is difficult to perceive how the judicial branch can significantly impact growing violence, trade in illegal drugs, poverty, weakening of the family, handgun availability, parental default, or the gap between rich and poor. The same appears true for the following, all of which are driven by forces *external* to the courts: caseload growth, overcrowded prisons, insufficient funding, escalating litigiousness, court-related family needs, corrections failures, and inadequate judicial compensation.

This does not mean the judicial branch shall be paralyzed or without recourse. Confronted with an array of projections ranging from vast to specific that have the potential for enormous impact on courts, the preferred course is to determine *how* to think about the future, not *what* to think about the future.

At this point two key responses advocated by futurists and strategic planners are to (1) strategically position the institution by being anticipatory rather than reactive in identifying and confronting problems and (2) fashion a preferred future toward which to work while dealing with problems both anticipated and unforeseen.

California's judicial branch appears to have done just that in both the process and products of preparations for the future. The judicial branch has committed to achieving access, fairness, independence, accountability, modern administration, public service, and all the other values in its goals and will strive for success no matter what the future presents in terms of population explosion, diversity, intergenerational conflict, socioeconomic maladies, or their several possible companions. The value of these preparations is proven by the fact that progress is well under way in many areas of the strategic plan.

The following are among the more notable areas of progress since 2000 and the commencement of the new millennium. Each confirms the abiding dedication by the Judicial Council, with leadership by Chief Justice Ronald M. George and Administrative Director of the Courts William C. Vickrey, to *Leading Justice Into the Future.*

Court Facilities

Passage of the Trial Court Facilities Act of 2002, sponsored by the Judicial Council in conjunction with the California State Association of Counties, reversed more than 150 years of precedent by shifting governance, ownership, and maintenance of court facilities from local government to the state.[16] This resolves one of the two major issues left for future attention following enactment of state funding for trial courts. While a complicated transition lies ahead, the symbolic and practical effects of this historically significant step will contribute importantly to the judiciary's goal of access for all in California to safe, secure, and adequate court facilities without regard to where a person resides.

Employees

In addition to facilities, the status of local government employees working in trial courts was left for future resolution when state funding was enacted. Thanks again to Judicial Council leadership, substantial progress was made early in the new millennium with passage in 2001 of the Trial Court Employment Protection and Governance Act, which transferred responsibility for employees from counties to courts,[17] accompanied by increased local assistance from the Human Resources Division of the Administrative Office of the Courts (AOC). This advances the goal of modernizing management and administration.

Fiscal Administration

The goal of responsibly using and accounting for public resources allocated to courts will be directly supported by AOC implementation in 2002 of a new, automated financial system. Developed in collaboration with the executive branch's Department of Finance and the Legislative Analyst's Office, the system will for the first time enable the judicial branch to reliably compile and monitor costs of the entire court system as well as develop prospective budgets integrating current expenditure data, strategic goals, and state government's revenue projections. Internal fiscal administration is being strengthened by a statewide accounting and reporting system.

Technology

The new financial system also promotes the Judicial Council's commitment to utilize technology to "collect, process, analyze, and share information."[18] Further progress was made in 2002 with expanded public access to electronic trial court records.[19]

Juries

Notable advances in the jury system between 2000 and 2002 promote strategic goals ranging from access to quality of justice. The burdens of jury service were both lightened and more fairly distributed in 2002 when statewide implementation of the Judicial Council's "one-day or one-trial" plan was completed.[20] This means that a citizen appearing for jury service need serve as a prospective juror for only one day. If the person is chosen to sit on a trial jury, service is completed at the conclusion of that trial. In addition, progress was made toward the Judicial Council's objective of compensating jurors at $40 per day. The rate was increased by the California Legislature in 2000 to $15 per day.[21] While far short of $40 per day, this was the first increase in forty-three years and is attributable to judicial branch tenacity. The process of summoning prospective jurors is being streamlined while both education and information for jurors are undergoing enhancement during the early days of the new century.

Legal Assistance

In 2001 the Judicial Council inaugurated an online Self-Help Center designed to guide California residents through the legal system and to assist them in locating free or low-cost legal assistance.[22] With a focus on California's increasing number of self-represented litigants, the service provides practical information on a large number of matters, including family law, juveniles, domestic violence, guardianships, conservatorships, small claims, and traffic violations. A version in Spanish will be available in 2003. This initiative bodes well for continued commitment to improved access, fairness, diversity, quality of justice, and service to the public.

Challenges

Again borrowing from the futurists, there obviously are "inhibitors" between the Judicial Council strategic plan and implementation. However, without resorting to use of a crystal ball, it seems that these inhibitors can be anticipated and addressed now by the judiciary. The following examples are offered for illustration.

The Quality of Justice

In order for the judicial branch to be "responsive to the needs of the public,"[23] the reality of volume must be confronted. It seems fair to assume that doubling the population of California by 2050 will at least double the number of criminal, civil, and juvenile lawsuits. Perhaps the most promising response to this inhibitor is to begin full-fledged experimentation with the "multidimensional justice system" envisioned by the Commission on the Future of the California Courts.[24] While there has been encouraging movement in several areas specified by the commission, it has been more episodic than systematic. The launching of new components of a multidimensional justice system will require a coordinated expansion of dispute resolution options; the creation of multioption justice centers; the development of guidelines for assessing disputes and referring them appropriately; the creation of new processes; the promulgation of standards to ensure quality, efficiency, and fairness; the injection of new resources; and perhaps an imposition of penalties for inappropriate use of publicly financed dispute resolution mechanisms.

Even if extraordinary success is achieved with multidimensional justice, volume will engulf the system if the judicial branch suffers, as it has in the past, resource starvation or malnutrition. It will not be sufficient for the judiciary to merely seek and be granted more judges, more judicial officers, more staff, and more courtrooms—although all of those will be essential.

The judicial branch may very well have to assume its rightful responsibility as an interdependent branch of government and support, without supplanting, the efforts of the legislative and executive branches to reduce caseloads. Surely the judicial branch has much to contribute on vexing issues confronting all three branches.

Is our criminal system, with its notably high rate of incarceration and ever-rising caseloads, appropriate for California of the future? Is our system of dealing with family relationships appropriate in view of the complex human, cultural, economic, and legal factors that are involved? Is our civil system of liability and compensation the best we can do to redress loss and allocate responsibility?

While the independence of the judiciary must be preserved, participating in the resolution of these and the many societal issues awaiting California undoubtedly will be explored. Chief Justice George and Administrative Director Vickrey already have taken the judiciary to a new plateau in collaborative searches for solutions to problems that extend beyond the boundaries of courts. Programs involving drug courts, dependency, and mental health are prime reassurances, among many, of continued participation of this caliber.

Access and Fairness

How can a person have "equal access to the courts and equal ability to participate in court proceedings"[25] without assistance of counsel? The constitutional right to counsel in criminal proceedings, regardless of ability to pay legal fees, has already been assured.[26] For some time now there have been proposals to assure free representation in civil proceedings as well.[27] Progress has been made, but have we made all possible progress? If not, what contribution can the judicial branch make?

Resources

Replacing the fractured system of local/state funding of trial courts removed troubling threats to adequate court funding caused by disparate and insufficient appropriations. With full state funding, the judiciary nonetheless faces inhibitors to obtaining the "public resources necessary for its support."[28] The judicial branch, more than ever, must resist being "viewed as just another unit in the executive branch of government" and be prepared for "increased attention on the part of legislative and executive branches of government."[29] Second, the annual budgeting and appropriation mechanism will be controlled by legislators who are subject to term limits and governors who can serve for only two terms, all of which suggest that funding decisions will be the product of a short rather than a long field of vision. Finally, neither the legislative nor executive branch has a long-range strategic plan comparable to that of the judicial branch of government. However, implementation of the judiciary's strategic plan will be severely impeded if held hostage in the annual budgeting process.

To remove these inhibitors, it seems wise to begin a collaborative search with members of the legislature, the governor, and other leaders for a stable and long-range funding mechanism for the judicial branch. This endeavor should be assisted by the commitment to values and problem solving embedded in the judicial branch's mission and plans. Likewise, the implicit willingness to be accountable for progress, as well as utilization of resources devoted to implementing those plans, should justify creation of a multiyear funding system more appropriate for the challenges confronting the judiciary now and well into the future.

Modern Administration

If justice is to be administered using "contemporary management practices . . . [and] highly competent judges,"[30] the threshold ingredient is judicial leadership. Research has demonstrated repeatedly that reform is destined to fail without the institutions of justice and judges willing to take a leadership role, in terms of both policy and implementation.[31] To ensure that the California courts have judges capable of such leadership, it may be appropriate to rethink various aspects of the judicial position.

For example, the only existing legal qualification for becoming a judge in California is membership in the State Bar for ten years.[32] This minimal qualification has been supplemented somewhat by the statutory requirement that, prior to filling a judicial vacancy by appointment, the governor must submit potential appointees for evaluation by the Commission on Judicial Nominees Evaluation of the State Bar. The State Bar is directed to consider the candidate's "industry, judicial temperament, honesty, objectivity, community respect, integrity, health, ability, and legal experience."[33] The evaluation in no way restricts the governor's power to appoint whomever he or she wishes.

Are more qualifications needed to ensure that California has judges with leadership skills who are capable of functioning effectively in the governance context created by the Judicial Council's strategic plan? Perhaps a profile of the desired qualifications of future judicial appointees should be developed. The candidate's legal experience and personal characteristics could be measured, and also the candidate's potential to contribute to implementation of the goals of the judicial branch. A companion to such a profile could, and perhaps should, be an outline of the needed qualifications in each court so that when vacancies arise the court's needs can be assessed in the process of selecting an appropriate judge for the vacancy.

The appointments and election system for trial court judges has been in place for 150 years. At the beginning of the new millennium there are tensions in this system that could very well thwart the Judicial Council goals of a judiciary that "will be an institutionally independent, separate branch of government" with "highly competent judges."[34] The first tension is not new, but it seems to have reached new levels: the extent to which judges, once appointed, will reflect or even carry out the policy positions of the incumbent governor who made the appointment. The second tension is the increase in the number of contested elections for trial court positions and the escalating cost of these elections. These tensions inevitably are inhibitors to obtaining the qualifications and independence contemplated by the Judicial Council goals.

Finally, there are increasing laments regarding the difficulty of recruiting persons willing to serve as judges. The leading deterrent appears to be compensation compared to the rewards of private law practice.

Perhaps it is time to confront these inhibitors by rethinking the career path to judicial office. There are precedents in other nations with judicial systems that have, in effect, created a career judiciary by offering a path that begins in law school and leads ultimately to judicial service.

Education

California has a well-developed and extensive system for education and training of judges, as discussed in Chapter Ten. However, the thrust of the extensive curricula is aimed at legal proficiency. This is reflected in the abundant courses on the rules of evidence, procedure, and substantive law. Measured in terms of achieving the goals of the Judicial Council's strategic plan, worthwhile additions to the curriculum would be techniques for judges to function in a pluralistic, multicultural society; development of leadership skills appropriate for governance and achieving institutional goals in the third branch of government; and development of skills appropriate for the judicial role in a multidimensional justice system.

Technology

The Judicial Council appropriately seeks to better use technology to facilitate the ability of the judicial branch "to collect, process, analyze, and share information" and increase the public's access to that information.[35] But the threshold question for future technology, as a goal within the judicial branch, is whether the focus on "information" is sufficiently ambitious. It would seem appropriate to begin now to fashion a vision for making use of technology that passes well beyond the mere gathering and dissemination of information. Examples already exist of technologies that enable us to create virtual courtrooms in which hearings are conducted with all of the participants (judge, witnesses, counsel, and parties) in different locations but nonetheless able to see and communicate with one another. Anticipating which future technologies will be spawned from those that already exist is a worthy added dimension to the Judicial Council's preparations for the future.

Closing Thought

There will be significant new improvements in the administration of justice between now and 2050 if the laudable aspirations in the present and future plans of the judicial branch are pursued. The number and magnificence of improvements will in large measure turn on whether the Judicial Council, the Administrative Office of the Courts, and the judicial branch build upon the foundation of self-governance begun in 1926 with the creation of the Judicial Council, strengthened in 1961 by establishment of the AOC, and expanded in the 1990s by taking responsibility for charting the course of justice.

Notes

1 Mark Baldassare, *California in the New Millennium* (Berkeley: University of California Press, 2000), p. 1.

2 There are two primary sources for the descriptions in this chapter regarding California's characteristics during the coming decades. The first is Mark Baldassare, *California in the New Millennium*, which is based upon focus group and survey research. The second is *Justice in the Balance, 2020* by the Commission on the Future of the California Courts, which also was based upon an array of techniques for identifying and pooling opinions regarding California in the future.

3 Baldassare, *California in the New Millennium*, pp. 2–3; [Judicial Council of California], Commission on the Future of the California Courts, *Justice in the Balance, 2020: Report of the Commission on the Future of the California Courts* (1993), pp. 9–10.

4 Baldassare, *California in the New Millennium*, p. 3; Commission on the Future of the California Courts, *Justice in the Balance*, pp. 9–10.

5 Commission on the Future of the California Courts, *Justice in the Balance*, pp. 9–10.

6 Baldassare, *California in the New Millennium*, pp. 3–6; Commission on the Future of the California Courts, *Justice in the Balance*, p. 9.

7 Baldassare, *California in the New Millennium*, p. 6; Commission on the Future of the California Courts, *Justice in the Balance*, p. 10.

8 Baldassare, *California in the New Millennium*, pp. 26–34, 46–49, 69–73, and 80–87.

9 Id., pp. 6–8.

10 Id., pp. 8–9.

11 Commission on the Future of the California Courts, *Justice in the Balance*, pp. 6–7.

12 Id., p. 7.

13 Michael E. Tigar, "2020 Vision: A Bifocal View," in *Alternative Futures for the State Courts of 2020* (State Justice Institute and the American Judicature Society, 1991), p. 115. Mr. Tigar graduated from the law school of the University of California at Berkeley.

14   Chief Justice Malcolm M. Lucas, State of the Judiciary Address, State Bar Conference of Delegates (August 26, 1990), reported in Judicial Council of California, *Annual Report to the Governor and the Legislature* (1991), pp. 1, 5.

15   Judicial Council of California, *Leading Justice Into the Future: Strategic Plan* (March 2000).

16   Senate Bill 1732, effective January 1, 2003; California Statutes 2002, chapter 1082.

17   Senate Bill 2140; California Statutes 2000, chapter 1010.

18   Judicial Council, *Leading Justice Into the Future*, p. 9.

19   California Rules of Court, rules 2070–2076.

20   California Rules of Court, rule 861; California Government Code, section 68550.

21   California Code of Civil Procedure, section 215.

22   Judicial Council of California, California Courts Web site, *www.courtinfo.ca.gov /selfhelp*.

23   Judicial Council, *Leading Justice Into the Future*, p. 9.

24   Commission on the Future of the California Courts, *Justice in the Balance*, pp. 35–53.

25   Judicial Council, *Leading Justice Into the Future*, p. 9.

26   *Gideon v. Wainwright*, 372 U.S. 335 (1963).

27   National Conference on the Judiciary, *State Courts: A Blueprint for the Future: Proceedings of the Second Annual Conference on the Judiciary* ([Denver]: National Center for State Courts, 1978), p. 128; John Dombrink and James W. Meeker, "Access to the Civil Courts for Those of Low and Moderate Means" in *2020 Vision: Symposium on the Future of California's Courts: Research Papers* (December 10–11, 1992).

28   Judicial Council, *Leading Justice Into the Future*, p. 9.

29   John K. Hudzik, "Financing and Managing the Finances of the California Court System: Alternative Futures" in *2020 Vision: Symposium on the Future of California's Courts: Research Papers* (December 10–11, 1992), pp. 4–5.

30   Judicial Council, *Leading Justice Into the Future*, p. 9.

31 Larry L. Sipes et al., *Managing to Reduce Delay* (Williamsburg, Va.: National Center for State Courts, 1980).

32 California Constitution, article VI, section 15.

33 California Government Code, section 12011.5(d).

34 Judicial Council, *Leading Justice Into the Future*, p. 9.

35 Ibid.

SELECTED BIBLIOGRAPHY

⁓⊕⌒

Administrative Office of the Courts. *A Guide to AOC People and Programs.* 1999.

——.*People and Programs.* July 2000.

——.Public Information Office. "California Courts Make History, as Last County Unifies Trial Courts Today." Press Release Number 14. February 8, 2001.

American Bar Association, Judicial Administration Division. *Standards Relating to Court Organization.* Standards of Judicial Administration, volume 1. [Chicago]: American Bar Association, 1990.

——.*Standards Relating to Trial Courts.* Standards of Judicial Administration, volume 2. [Chicago]: American Bar Association, 1992.

American Institutes for Research. *Analysis of Trial Court Unification in California—Final Report.* September 28, 2000.

Ames, Alden. "The Origin and Jurisdiction of the Municipal Courts in California." *California Law Review* 21 (1933): 117–28.

Andersen, Cameron Estelle. *The Story of the California Judges Association: The First Sixty Years.* San Francisco: Bancroft-Whitney, 1992.

Arthur Young & Company. *A Report to the Judicial Council on the Language Needs of Non-English Speaking Persons in Relation to the State's Justice System,* Phase I. January 1976.

——.*A Report to the Judicial Council on the Language Needs of Non-English Speaking Persons in Relation to the State's Justice System,* Phase II. May 1976.

——.*A Report to the Judicial Council on the Language Needs of Non-English Speaking Persons in Relation to the State's Justice System,* Phase III. January 1977.

Baldassare, Mark. *California in the New Millennium.* Berkeley: University of California Press, 2000.

Barrett, Robert, Jay Folberg, and Joshua Rosenberg. *Use of ADR in California Courts: Report to the Judicial Council of California Advisory Committee on Dispute Resolution.* San Francisco: University of San Francisco School of Law, December 1991.

Blume, William Wirt. "California Courts in Historical Perspective." *Hastings Law Journal* 22 (1970–1971): 121–95.

Booz, Allen & Hamilton Inc. *California Lower Court Study: Final Report.* September 15, 1971.

———. *Unified Trial Court Feasibility Study: Final Report.* December 3, 1971.

Braun, Richard L. "Federal Government Enters War on Crime." *American Bar Association Journal* 54 (1968): 1163–66.

Bryant, David L. *Judicial Arbitration in California: An Update.* Rand Publication Series N-2909-ICJ. [Santa Monica, Calif.]: Institute for Civil Justice, Rand Corporation, 1989.

California Commission on Judicial Performance. *1976 Annual Report.*

———. *1979 Annual Report.*

———. *1985 Annual Report.*

———. *1987 Annual Report.*

———. *1988 Annual Report.*

———. *1995 Annual Report.*

———. *1997 Annual Report.*

———. *1999 Annual Report.*

———. *In the Matter of Commission Proceedings Concerning the Seven Justices of the Supreme Court of California, Background Report of Special Counsel.* June 11, 1979.

———. *Report of Status and Announcement of Results Regarding Investigation of California Supreme Court Justices.* November 5, 1979.

California Commission on Judicial Qualifications. *1974 Annual Report.*

California Constitution, article VI.

California Constitution Revision Commission. *Proposed Revision of the California Constitution,* part 5. 1971.

California Law Revision Commission. *Recommendation and Study Relating to Arbitration.* December 1960.

——. "Trial Court Unification: Constitutional Revision (SCA 3)." *California Law Revision Commission Reports, Recommendations, and Studies* 24 (1994): 5.

California Legislature. *Joint Hearing on Trial Court Unification Under SCA3.* October 8, 1993.

——. "Partial Report of the Joint Judiciary Committee on Administration of Justice on the California Judiciary." 1959. In *Appendix to the Journal of the Senate* (1959 Regular Session), volume 2, [section 1]: 48.

California Rules of Court (various eds.).

[California] Select Committee on Trial Court Delay. *Report 1.* July 1971.

——. *Report 4.* February 1972.

——. *Report 6.* June 1, 1972.

Church, Thomas, Jr., et al. *Justice Delayed—The Pace of Litigation in Urban Trial Courts.* Williamsburg, Va.: National Center for State Courts, 1958.

Conmy, Peter Thomas. *The Constitutional Beginnings of California.* San Francisco: Native Sons of the Golden West, 1959.

Dahlin, Donald C. "Long-Range Planning in State Courts: Process, Product, and Impact." *Justice System Journal* 17 (1994): 171–92.

Dombrink, John, and James W. Meeker. "Access to the Civil Courts for Those of Low and Moderate Means." In *2020 Vision: Symposium on the Future of California's Courts: Research Papers.* December 10–11, 1992.

Fall, John G., proj. dir. *A Study of the Role of Arbitration in the Judicial Process.* Judicial Council of California, 1972.

Frankel, Jack E. "The Commission on Judicial Qualifications." *Journal of the State Bar of California* 36 (1961): 1008–11.

Friesen, Ernest C., Edward C. Gallas, and Nesta M. Gallas. *Managing the Courts*. Indianapolis: Bobbs-Merrill, 1971.

Geiler v. Commission (1973), 10 Cal.3d 270.

George, Chief Justice Ronald M. State of the Judiciary Address, delivered to a joint session of the California Legislature. March 20, 2001.

Gibson, Chief Justice Phil S. "For Modern Courts." *Journal of the State Bar of California* 32 (1957): 727–37.

———. "Reorganization of Our Inferior Courts." Speech delivered to the Stanislaus County Bar Association. October 28, 1949. Reported in *Journal of the State Bar of California* 24 (1949): 382–93.

Gideon v. Wainwright, 372 U.S. 335 (1963).

Goerdt, John. *Re-examining the Pace of Litigation in 39 Urban Trial Courts*. Williamsburg, Va.: National Center for State Courts, 1991.

Gordon v. Justice Court (1974) 12 Cal.3d 323 [115 Cal.Rptr. 632, 525 P.2d 72].

Grodin, Joseph R., Calvin R. Massey, and Richard B. Cunningham. *The California State Constitution: A Reference Guide*. Reference Guides to the State Constitutions of the United States, no. 11. Westport, Conn.: Greenwood Press, 1993.

Hensler, Deborah R., Albert J. Lipson, and Elizabeth S. Rolph. *Judicial Arbitration in California: The First Year*. Rand Publication Series R-2733-ICJ. [Santa Monica, Calif.]: Institute for Civil Justice, Rand Corporation, 1981.

Hollzer, Judge Harry A. "Report of the Condition of Judicial Business in the Courts of the State of California, together with a Summary of Research Studies of Judicial Systems in other Jurisdictions." In Judicial Council of California. *Second Report of the Judicial Council of California to the Governor and the Legislature*. 1929. Part 2: 11–69.

Hudzik, John K. "Financing and Managing the Finances of the California Court System: Alternative Futures." In *2020 Vision: Symposium on the Future of California's Courts: Research Papers*. December 10–11, 1992.

Hunt, Rockwell Dennis. *The Genesis of California's First Constitution (1846–49)*. Johns Hopkins University Studies in Historical and

Political Science, 13th series, no. 8. Baltimore: Johns Hopkins Press, 1895. [New York: Johnson Reprint, 1973.]

In re Gault (1967), 387 U.S. 1.

In re Winship (1970), 397 U.S. 358.

Institute for the Future. "The California Future Databook." In *2020 Vision: Symposium on the Future of California's Courts: Research Papers.* December 10–11, 1992.

Judicial Council of California. California Courts Web site. *www.courtinfo .ca.gov*

——. *Civil Action Mediation Act: Results of the Pilot Project, Legislative Report.* November 1996.

——. *Court Interpreter Services in the California Trial Courts.* 1995.

——. *Leading Justice Into the Future: Long-Range Strategic Plan.* Updated April 29, 1999.

——. *Leading Justice Into the Future: Strategic Plan.* March 2000.

——. *Report of the Court Technology Task Force.* January 25, 1995.

——. "Report on the Administrative Agencies Survey." *Tenth Biennial Report to the Governor and Legislature.* December 31, 1944. Part 2: 8–46.

——. "Report on Trial Court Unification: Senate Constitutional Amendment No. 3 (Lockyer)." In *Reports and Recommendations.* September 23, 1993. Tab 3.

——. Reports, Biennial Reports, and Annual Reports to the Governor and the Legislature. 1927–2000.

——. "Special Report on Proposed Court of Criminal Appeals." *Sixth Report of the Judicial Council of California.* June 30, 1936. Part 1.

——. *Strategic Plan for Court Technology.* August 14, 1998.

——. *Tactical Plan for Court Technology.* January 26, 2000.

——. "Trial Court Unification: Senate Constitutional Amendment No. 3 (SCA 3)." In *Reports and Recommendations.* May 17, 1994. Tab 5.

——. *Year in Review*. 1996.

——.Access and Fairness Advisory Committee, Gender Fairness Sub-committee. *Gender and Justice: Implementing Gender Fairness in the Courts: Implementation Report*. 1996.

——.Administrative Office of the Courts. *Foundations for a New Century: Annual Report*. 2000.

——.Administrative Office of the Courts. *Invested in Justice: 1999 Annual Report*.

——.Administrative Office of the Courts. *Professional Ethics and the Role of the Court Interpreter*. 1997.

——.Administrative Office of the Courts. *Prompt and Fair Justice in the Trial Courts: Report to the Legislature on Delay Reduction in the Trial Courts*. July 1991.

——.Administrative Office of the Courts. *Report to the Legislature on the Use of Interpreters in the California Courts*. 2001.

——.Administrative Office of the Courts. *Special Report—Proposition 220*. June 12, June 29, and July 16, 1998.

——.Administrative Office of the Courts. *State Court Outlook*. 1995.

——.Administrative Office of the Courts. *Trial Court Funding Resource Manual,* 2d ed. 1998.

——.Advisory Committee on Access and Fairness in the Courts, Access for Persons with Disabilities Subcommittee. *Public Hearings Report: Access for Persons with Disabilities*. (1997).

——.Advisory Committee on Access and Fairness in the Courts, Access for Persons with Disabilities Subcommittee. *Summary of Survey and Public Hearing Reports*. 1997.

——.Advisory Committee on Gender Bias in the Courts. *Achieving Equal Justice for Women and Men in the California Courts*. 1996.

——.Advisory Committee on Racial and Ethnic Bias in the Courts. *1991–92 Public Hearings on Racial and Ethnic Bias in the California State Court System*. 1993.

——.Advisory Committee on Racial and Ethnic Bias in the State Courts. "Report on Fairness in the California Courts: A Survey of the Public, Attorneys, and Court Personnel." Administrative Office of the Courts Report Summary. June 28, 1994. In *Reports and Recommendations.* July 7, 1994. Tab 2.

——.Center for Judicial Education and Research. *Judges Guide to ADR.* 1996.

——.Commission on the Future of the California Courts. *Justice in the Balance, 2020: Report of the Commission on the Future of the California Courts.* 1993.

——.Court Management Committee. *Report and Recommendations Concerning the "El Cajon Experiment."* April 22, 1982.

——.Joint Subcommittee of Trial Court Presiding Judges and Court Administrators Advisory Committees. "Trial Court Unification: Proposed Constitutional Amendments and Commentary." September 11, 1993. In *Reports and Recommendations.* September 23, 1993. Tab 3.

——.Task Force on Appellate Mediation. *Mandatory Mediation in the First Appellate District of the Court of Appeal: Report and Recommendations.* September 2001.

——.Task Force on the Quality of Justice, Subcommittee on Alternative Dispute Resolution and the Judicial System. *Alternative Dispute Resolution in Civil Cases: Report.* August 1999.

——.Task Force on Trial Court Funding. *Final Report to the Judicial Council.* May 3, 1996.

Kempe, C. Henry. "The Battered Child Syndrome." *Journal of the American Medical Association* 181 (1962): 17–24.

Kenyon, Carleton W. *A Guide to Early California Court Organization, Practice Acts and Rules, with the Text of California Supreme Court Rules, 1850–53.* Law Library Paper No. 21. California State Library, August 1968.

Kleps, Ralph N. "Contingency Planning for State Court Systems." *Judicature* 59 (1975): 62–66.

——."Courts, State Court Management and Lawyers." *California State Bar Journal* 50 (1975): 45–49.

——."The Judicial Council and the Administrative Office of the California Courts." *Journal of the State Bar of California* 37 (1962): 329–40.

——.Tribute to Chief Justice Donald R. Wright. *Hastings Constitutional Law Quarterly* 4 (1977): 683–87.

Kloepfer v. Commission on Judicial Performance (1989) 49 Cal.3d 826.

Lucas, Chief Justice Malcolm M. State of the Judiciary Address, delivered to the State Bar Conference of Delegates. August 26, 1990. In Judicial Council of California. *Annual Report to the Governor and the Legislature.* 1991.

Mandela, Nelson. *Long Walk to Freedom.* New York: Little, Brown and Company, 1994, p. 625.

Mason, Paul. "Constitutional History of California." *Constitution of the State of California and of the United States and Other Documents.* California Senate, 1958: 293–323.

McComb v. Commission on Judicial Performance (1977), 19 Cal.3d Special Tribunal Supplement 1.

Mosk v. Superior Court (1979), 25 Cal.3d 474.

National Advisory Commission on Criminal Justice Standards and Goals. *Report on Courts.* Washington, D.C.: Government Printing Office, 1973.

National Conference on the Judiciary. *State Courts: A Blueprint for the Future: Proceedings of the Second Annual Conference on the Judiciary.* [Denver]: National Center for State Courts, 1978.

Nelson, Dorothy W. "Should Los Angeles County Adopt a Single-Trial-Court Plan?" *Southern California Law Review* 33 (1959–1960): 117–62.

Ostrom, Brian J., and Neal B. Kauder, eds. *Examining the Work of State Courts, 1997: A National Perspective from the Court Statistics Project.* Williamsburg, Va.: National Center for State Courts, 1998.

People ex rel. Morgan v. Hayne (1890), 83 Cal. 111.

People ex rel. The Attorney General, ex parte, 1 Cal 85.

Pound, Roscoe. Address delivered to the American Bar Association's National Conference on the Causes of Popular Dissatisfaction with the Administration of Justice. August 29, 1906. St. Paul, Minnesota. Text reported in *The Pound Conference: Perspectives on Justice in the Future.* St. Paul: West Publishing Co., 1979.

Roehl, Janice A., Robert E. Huitt, and Henry Wong. *Private Judging: A Study of Its Volume, Nature, and Impact on State Courts: Final Report.* Pacific Grove, Calif.: Institute for Social Analysis, 1993.

Rogovin, Charles. "The Genesis of the Law Enforcement Assistance Administration: A Personal Account." *Columbia Human Rights Law Review* 5 (1973): 9–25.

Sargent, Noel. "The California Constitutional Convention of 1878–9." *California Law Review* 6 (1917–1918): 1–22.

Sipes, Larry L. "Managing to Reduce Delay." *California State Bar Journal* 56 (1981): 104–7.

———. "Reducing Delay in State Courts—A March Against Folly." *Rutgers Law Review* 37 (1985): 299–317.

Sipes, Larry L., et al. *Managing to Reduce Delay.* Williamsburg, Va.: National Center for State Courts, 1980.

Skoler, Daniel L. "Comprehensive Criminal Justice Planning—A New Challenge." *Crime and Delinquency* 12 (1968): 197–206.

Smith, Malcolm. "The California Method of Selecting Judges." *Stanford Law Review* 3 (1951): 571–600.

Stevens v. Commission (1964), 61 Cal.2d 886.

Stolz, Preble, and Kathleen Gunn. "The California Judicial Council: The Beginnings of an Institutional History." *Pacific Law Journal* 11 (1979–1980): 877–905.

Supreme Court of California. *Supreme Court of California Practices and Procedures.* 1997 revision; June 2000 reprint.

Tigar, Michael E. "2020 Vision: A Bifocal View." In *Alternative Futures for the State Courts of 2020*. State Justice Institute and the American Judicature Society, 1991.

Tobin, Robert W. *Creating the Judicial Branch: The Unfinished Reform*. Williamsburg, Va.: National Center for State Courts, 1999.

Tobin, Robert W., et al. *California Unification Study*. Denver: National Center for State Courts, 1994.

Turner, Kim. *Administrative Implementation of Changes in Intergovernmental Relations Defined in the Lockyer-Isenberg Trial Court Funding Act of 1997: A Summary Report*. March 1999. [San Rafael, Calif.]: Marin County Superior Court, 1999.

U.S. Department of Justice, Bureau of Justice Assistance, National Center for State Courts. *Trial Court Performance Standards and Measurement System Implementation Manual*. Washington, D.C.: Bureau of Justice Assistance, [1997].

Vanderbilt, Arthur T., ed. *Minimum Standards of Judicial Administration: A Survey of the Extent to Which the Standards of the American Bar Association for Improving the Administration of Justice Have Been Accepted throughout the Country*. The Judicial Administration Series. [New York]: Law Center of New York University for the National Conference of Judicial Councils, 1949.

Warren, Earl, U.S. Chief Justice. Speech to opening assembly of the American Bar Association annual meeting. 1958. Quoted in Thomas C. Yager. "Justice Expedited—A Ten-Year Summary." *U.C.L.A. Law Review* 7 (1960): 57–81.

[Wilson, R. A.] "The Alcalde System of California." 1 Cal. 559. San Francisco: Bancroft-Whitney, 1906.

Yankelovich, Skelly and White, Inc. "Highlights of a National Survey of the General Public, Judges, Lawyers, and Community Leaders." In *State Courts: A Blueprint for the Future: Proceedings of the Second Annual Conference on the Judiciary*. National Conference on the Judiciary. [Denver]: National Center for State Courts, 1978.

Yankelovich, Skelly and White/Clancy Shulman, Inc. "Surveying the Future: Californians' Attitudes on the Court System." In *2020 Vision: Symposium on the Future of California's Courts: Research Papers.* December 10–11, 1992.

Ziegler, Dee. "Rose Bird Automates the Supreme Court." *The Recorder* (December 1, 1986): 1, 15.

ABOUT THE AUTHOR

Larry L. Sipes, a member of the California State Bar for forty years, wrote this book as the inaugural scholar-in-residence for the Administrative Office of the Courts, the staff agency for the Judicial Council of California. He brought to bear his perspective as a former president of the National Center for State Courts, which is the principal resource for state courts as they work to improve the administration of justice. He also served as director of the Western Regional Office for the National Center for State Courts and is a president emeritus of that organization.

Mr. Sipes has also served as a special master for the Superior Court of Marin County, the director of the Select Committee on Trial Court Delay, the director of the California Constitution Revision Commission, and an adjunct professor at Hastings College of the Law.

As an advisor on judicial administration, he has consulted in several countries and in the states of California, Oregon, and Washington.

He has been recognized for his contributions to the improved administration of justice by awards from the National Conference of Metropolitan Courts, the National Association of Women Judges, and the National Center for State Courts. He received the Bernard E. Witkin Award from the Judicial Council of California.

Mr. Sipes brought to this book a personal interest that flowed from being acquainted with Chief Justice Ronald M. George and having been acquainted with his five immediate predecessors. He also has known all four Administrative Directors of the Courts. These relationships, past and present, enlivened his efforts, as did his experiences of working in or with the California court system his entire professional life.

INDEX

❦

Bold page references indicate pages with photographs.